AF412679

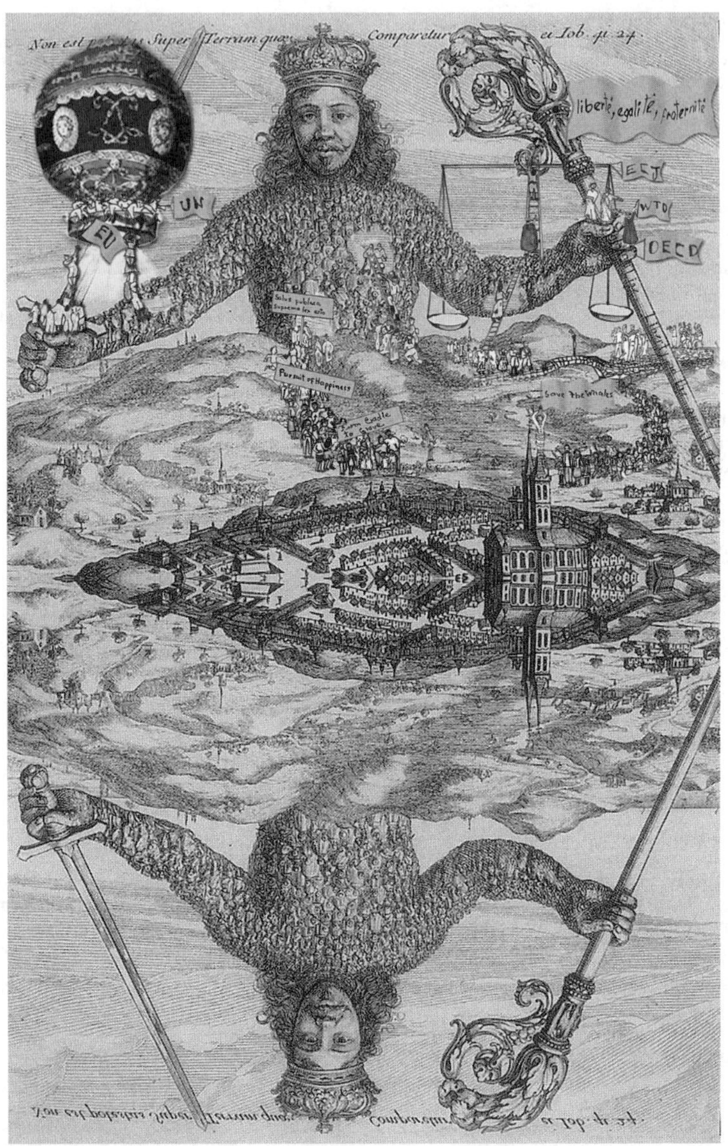

This illustration is taken from the original etching in Thomas Hobbes' *Leviathan* of 1651. Palgrave Macmillan and the editors are grateful to Lucila Muñoz-Sanchez and Monika Sniegs for their help in redesigning the original to illustrate what 'transformations of the state' might mean. The inscription at the top of the original frontispiece reads *'non est potestas Super Terram quae Comparetur ei'* (Job 41.24): 'there is no power on earth which can be compared to him'. In the Bible, this refers to the sea-monster, Leviathan. (Original Leviathan image reprinted courtesy of the British Library.)

Transforming the Golden-Age Nation State

Edited by

Achim Hurrelmann
Assistant Professor of Political Science, Carleton University, Canada

Stephan Leibfried
Professor of Political Science, University of Bremen, Germany

Kerstin Martens
Assistant Professor of International Relations, University of Bremen, Germany

Peter Mayer
Professor of International Relations, University of Bremen, Germany

First published 2007 by
PALGRAVE MACMILLAN
Houndmills, Basingstoke, Hampshire RG21 6XS and
175 Fifth Avenue, New York, N.Y. 10010
Companies and representatives throughout the world

PALGRAVE MACMILLAN is the global academic imprint of the Palgrave Macmillan division of St. Martin's Press, LLC and of Palgrave Macmillan Ltd. Macmillan® is a registered trademark in the United States, United Kingdom and other countries. Palgrave is a registered trademark in the European Union and other countries.

ISBN-13: 978-0-230-52161-2   hardback
ISBN-10: 0-230-52161-4   hardback

This book is printed on paper suitable for recycling and made from fully managed and sustained forest sources. Logging, pulping and manufacturing processes are expected to conform to the environmental regulations of the country of origin.

A catalogue record for this book is available from the British Library.

A catalog record for this book is available from the Library of Congress.

10 9 8 7 6 5 4 3 2 1
16 15 14 13 12 11 10 09 08 07

Printed and bound in Great Britain by
Antony Rowe Ltd, Chippenham and Eastbourne

Contents

List of Tables

Series Preface

When we think about the future of the modern state, we encounter a puzzling variety of scholarly diagnoses and prophecies. Some commentators predict nothing less than the total demise of the state as a useful model for organizing society – its powers eroded by a dynamic global economy and by an increasing transference of political decision-making powers to supranational bodies. Others disagree profoundly and point to the remarkable resilience of the state and its core institutions. Even in the age of global markets and politics, the state remains the ultimate guarantor of security, democracy, welfare and the rule of law. These debates raise complex questions for the social sciences: what is happening to the modern liberal nation-state of the OECD bloc? Is it an outdated model? Is it still useful? Is it in need of modest reform or far-reaching change?

The state is a complex entity, providing many different services and regulating many areas of everyday life. There can be no simple answer to these questions. The Transformations of the State series disaggregates the tasks and functions of the state into four key dimensions:

- the monopolization of the means of force
- the rule of law as prescribed and safeguarded by the constitution
- the guarantee of democratic self-governance
- the provision of welfare and the assurance of social cohesion

In the OECD world of the 1960s and 1970s these four institutional aspects formed the central characteristics of the modern state, creating a synergetic whole. This series is devoted to empirical and theoretical studies that explore changes to this historical model, and the current and future prospects for a traditional conception of the state. Although a political science approach dominates, many books are interdisciplinary in nature and also draw upon law, economics, history and sociology. We hope that taken together these volumes will provide readers with the 'state of the art' on the 'state of the state'.

This book contributes to the work of the Collaborative Research Centre *Transformations of the State* at the University of Bremen (Germany), and is funded by the German Research Foundation (DFG).

The state analyses pursued by the Centre are readily accessible through two overview volumes: Stephan Leibfried and Michael Zürn, (eds), *Transformations of the State?* (2005); and Achim Hurrelmann, Stephan Leibfried, Kerstin Martens and Peter Mayer, (eds), *Transforming the Golden-Age Nation State* (2007), published in the Transformations of the State series. Further information on the Centre can be found at www.state.uni-bremen.de.

Achim Hurrelmann, Stephan Leibfried,
Kerstin Martens and Peter Mayer
Series Editors

Foreword

Until the 1970s, we thought of nation states as self-sufficient 'containers'. Since then, we have become accustomed to stressing their ever-growing interdependence in an age of globalization. While the empirical grounding of this 'paradigm shift' now seems beyond doubt, it is less clear what accelerated globalization does to the state – its territorial control, its arrangements for securing the rule of law, its democratic legitimacy, or its role in the provision of social welfare. What has become of the Western nation state and its interweaving of functions in the decades since the 1970s? Is its fabric worn out, is it unravelling? Will it merely be rewoven and restyled? Or will the fibres of that tightly woven fabric simply separate, each following its individual fate in postmodern fashion, the rule of law moving into the international arena and the nation state clinging to its resources, while the interventionist state comes completely unspun and goes every which way?

The Research Centre 'Transformations of the State', or in short 'TranState', has been set up to study these questions, drawing together expertise from political science, law, sociology, and economics. TranState is a centre of excellence that was founded in January 2003 by three universities in Bremen, Germany: the public University of Bremen, the private Jacobs University Bremen, and the public University of Applied Sciences Bremen. TranState is governed by the University of Bremen; it is funded as a 'Collaborative Research Centre' (*Sonderforschungsbereich*) by the German Research Foundation (*Deutsche Forschungsgemeinschaft*). Working at TranState are some 65 researchers, who welcome and regularly host international visitors interested in state research.

This volume is the sequel and complement of *Transformations of the State?* (Cambridge University Press, 2005) edited by Stephan Leibfried and Michael Zürn. Together with its twin, it provides an introduction to and first synthesis of TranState's research: *Transformations of the State?* has presented one half of TranState's research projects, *Transforming the Golden Age Nation State* offers the other half. These two volumes taken together give a first and complete picture of what TranState's research is all about. In addition, *Transforming the Golden-Age Nation State* introduces our centre's book series 'Transformations of the State' at Palgrave Macmillan.[1] The series now has 11 volumes out or in press. Please consult our website (www.state.uni-bremen.de) for additional material, such as volumes appearing with other publishers, or Working Papers that may be downloaded free of charge.

My co-editors and I thank Philipp Genschel und Bernhard Zangl for their pioneering conceptual and analytical work, intellectual leadership and advice and support of the project during its long gestation. We are grateful to Sophia Ojha, Vicki May, Monika Sniegs, Lukas Jeuck and Henning Wellmann for their technical assistance.

As Director of TranState, I am particularly grateful to my three co-editors, without whom this volume would not have been possible. Achim Hurrelmann, who moved on to Carleton University in Canada, became thoroughly addicted to TranState during his four years in Bremen, and continues the collaboration from overseas. Kerstin Martens committed herself to this volume with the tenacity of Odysseus, resisting the tempting sirens of Humboldt University and tying herself to Bremen and TranState for the duration. Peter Mayer has likewise made an exceptional commitment to this volume and the TranState enterprise. His unusual blend of talents, for both synthesis and scholarly rigour, and his enormous expertise in international relations theory are essential to what is, in large part, an exploration of the changing international-domestic interface of the nation state since its 'golden age'.

Stephan Leibfried, Director, TranState

Note

1 For TranState's current research programme consult Philipp Genschel, Stephan Leibfried and Bernhard Zangl, *Zerfaserung und Selbsttransformation: Das Forschungsprogramm 'Staatlichkeit im Wandel'* (Unravelling and Self-Transformation of the State: The Research Program of 'Transformations of the State'), Working Paper 45/2006, Bremen: TranState. The German version can be downloaded from the Centre's website: www.state.uni-bremen.de. An English translation is in preparation.

List of Abbreviations

Art.	Article
ARC	Accounting Regulatory Committee
ASB	Accounting Standards Board
ASC	Accounting Standards Committee
ATIBT	Association Technique Internationale des Bois Tropicaux (International Technical Tropical Timber Association)
BGB	Bürgerliches Gesetzbuch (German Civil Code)
BIAC	Business and Industry Advisory Committee
BilKoG	Bilanzkontrollgesetz (German Accounting Control Act)
BIS	Bank for International Settlements
CCAB	Consultative Committee of Accounting Bodies
CFSP	Common Foreign and Security Policy
CISG	UN Convention on the International Sale of Goods
CSO	civil society organization
DGRI	Deutsche Gesellschaft für Recht und Informatik (German Association for Law and Informatics)
DIS	Deutsche Institution für Schiedsgerichtsbarkeit (German Institution of Arbitration)
DNS	Domain Name System
DPKO	Department of Peacekeeping Operations
EAG	Education at a Glance
EC	European Community
ECB	European Central Bank
ECJ	European Court of Justice
ECOSOC	UN Economic and Social Council
EEC	European Economic Community
EFRAG	European Financial Reporting Advisory Group
EPC	European Political Cooperation
ESDP	European Security and Defense Policy
EU	European Union
FASB	Financial Accounting Standards Board
FRP	Financial Reporting Council
GAAP	Generally Accepted Accounting Principles
GASB	German Accounting Standards Board
GASC	German Accounting Standards Committee

GD Holz	Gesamtverband Deutscher Holzhandel (German Timber Trade Federation)
GDP	gross domestic product
GHS	Globally Harmonized System of Classification and Labeling of Chemicals
GMO	genetically modified organisms
GTZ	Gesellschaft für technische Zusammenarbeit
HGB	Handelsgesetzbuch (German Commercial Code)
IANA	Internet Assigned Numbers Authority
IAS	International Accounting Standards
IASB	International Accounting Standards Board
IASC	International Accounting Standards Committee
IASCF	International Accounting Standards Committee Foundation
ICAEW	Institute of Chartered Accountants of England and Wales
ICANN	Internet Corporation for Assigned Names and Numbers
ICC	International Chamber of Commerce
ICT	information and communication technology
IdW	Institut der Wirtschaftsprüfer
IFRS	International Financial Reporting Standards
ILO	International Labor Organization
IMF	International Monetary Fund
INES	International Indicators of Educational Systems
IO	international organization
IOSCO	International Organization of Securities Commissions
ITU	International Telecommunication Union
KapAEG	Kapitalaufnahme-Erleichterungsgesetz (German Capital Raising Act)
KonTraG	Gesetz zur Kontrolle und Transparenz im Unternehmensbereich (German Control and Transparency Law)
LDC	least-developed countries
MoU	Memorandum of understanding
NAFTA	North American Free Trade Agreement
NATO	North Atlantic Treaty Organization
NGO	non-governmental organization
NLGA	National Lumber Grades Authority
NPT	Nuclear Non-proliferation Treaty
OECD	Organization for Economic Co-operation and Development

OMC	Open Method of Coordination
OSCE	Organization for Security and Co-operation in Europe
PC	personal computer
PISA	Programme for International Student Assessment
PSC	Political and Security Committee
PTT	postal, telegraph and telephone organization
Q&A	questions and answers
SEC	Securities and Exchange Commission
SME	small and medium sized enterprises
SSR	Security Sector Reform
UK	United Kingdom
UN	United Nations
UNCITRAL	United Nations Commission on International Trade Law
UNCTAD	United Nations Conference on Trade and Development
UNESCO	United Nations Educational, Scientific and Cultural Organization
UNIDROIT	International Institute for the Unification of Private Law
U.S.	United States
USA	United States of America
USAID	United States Agency for International Development
VAT	value added tax
WHO	World Health Organization
WIPO	World Intellectual Property Organization
WSIS	UN World Summit on Information Society
WTO	World Trade Organization
WWW	World-Wide Web

Notes on Contributors

Ralf Bendrath is a Research Fellow (Political Science) at the Collaborative Research Centre 'Transformations of the State', University of Bremen (Bremen, Germany).

Gralf-Peter Calliess is Professor for International and Comparative Business Law, at University of Bremen (Bremen, Germany).

Thomas Dietz is a Research Fellow (Political Science) at the Collaborative Research Centre 'Transformations of the State', University of Bremen (Bremen, Germany).

Martin Herberg is a Research Fellow (Sociology) at the Collaborative Research Centre 'Transformations of the State', University of Bremen (Bremen, Germany).

Jeanette Hofmann is a Senior Researcher (Political Science) at the Social Science Research Centre Berlin (WZB) (Berlin, Germany).

Achim Hurrelmann is Assistant Professor of Political Science at Carleton University (Ottawa, Canada).

Wioletta Konradi is a Research Fellow (Law) at the Collaborative Research Centre 'Transformations of the State', University of Bremen (Bremen, Germany).

Volker Leib is a Research Fellow (Political Science) at the Collaborative Research Centre 'Transformations of the State', University of Bremen (Bremen, Germany).

Stephan Leibfried is Professor of Political Science Director of the Collaborative Research Centre 'Transformations of the State' and Co-Director of the Centre for Social Policy Research, at the University of Bremen (Bremen, Germany).

Kerstin Martens is Assistant Professor of International Relations at the Collaborative Research Centre 'Transformations of the State', University of Bremen (Bremen, Germany).

Peter Mayer is Professor of International Relations at the Institute for Intercultural and International Studies, University of Bremen (Bremen, Germany).

Sebastian Mayer is a Research Fellow (Political Science) at the Collaborative Research Centre 'Transformations of the State', University of Bremen (Bremen, Germany).

Holger Nieswandt is a Research Fellow (Economics) at the Collaborative Research Centre 'Transformations of the State', University of Bremen (Bremen, Germany).

Fabian Sosa is a Solicitor, and was 2002–06 Research Fellow (Law) at the Collaborative Research Centre 'Transformations of the State', University of Bremen (Bremen, Germany).

Jens Steffek is Assistant Professor of Political Science at the Collaborative Research Centre 'Transformations of the State', University of Bremen (Bremen, Germany).

Susanne Uhl is a Research Fellow (Political Science) at the School of Humanities and Social Sciences, Jacobs University Bremen (Bremen, Germany).

Silke Weinlich is an Associate Researcher (Political Science) at the Institute for Intercultural and International Studies, University of Bremen (Bremen, Germany).

Ansgar Weymann is Professor of Sociology at the University of Bremen (Bremen, Germany).

Jochen Zimmermann is Professor of Accounting at the University of Bremen (Bremen, Germany).

Michael Zürn is Professor of Political Science, Dean of the Hertie School of Governance and Director at the Social Science Research Centre Berlin (WZB) (Berlin, Germany).

1
The Golden-Age Nation State and its Transformation: A Framework for Analysis

Achim Hurrelmann, Stephan Leibfried, Kerstin Martens and Peter Mayer[1]

The citizens of the Western world are accustomed to looking to the state as the most important source of political authority. The state is both loved and feared; it is the institution to which demands are addressed and which is blamed if something goes wrong. It exercises enormous powers, but is also charged with considerable responsibilities – guaranteeing the physical security of its citizens, providing them with the institutional means to protect their rights and to make their interests count in the political process, and even taking care of their social welfare.

Faced with all of these tasks in an ever-changing environment, it is clear that state institutions, too, have always been subject to change. Nevertheless, it is often argued that in recent decades, state transformations of an entirely new quality have occurred. According to this argument, not only processes of economic and political globalization, but also domestic changes, such as societal aging, have put established state structures and practices under threat. The state is said to have lost much of its former autonomy vis-à-vis international institutions and societal actors, and is now entangled in a web of multiple and interconnected centres and layers of political authority (Albrow 1996; Strange 1996; Hooghe and Marks 2001; Bache and Flinders 2004; DeBardeleben and Hurrelmann 2007). Some observers go so far as to claim that this loss of autonomy leads to a demise of the nation state as a viable form of political organization (Guéhenno 1995; Ohmae 1995; Appadurai 1996), or at least severely undermines some of its major attributes, such as sovereignty (Camilleri and Falk 1992), the rule of law (Scheuerman 1999; Grimm 2005), democracy (Tully 2002; Crouch 2004), or the provision of welfare (Scharpf 2000). Others vehemently disagree. They point out that the sovereign state has always coexisted with other forms and centres of political authority (Krasner 1999; 2001), that no serious competitor has emerged and only the focus of state activism has shifted (Levy 2006), and that states have proven able to exercise effective control over political decision making even in the most advanced system of multilevel governance, the European Union (Moravcsik 1998).

The state is dead, long live the state. Both groups are right – half right. The challenge for research on 'the state of the state' is to create a detailed map of how state institutions and functions endure and yet, at the same time, change fundamentally. A necessary first step to meet this challenge is to disaggregate the state into various dimensions and then take stock of developments in each of them (Caporaso 2000a, 2000b). Several recent studies of state transformation, each viewing the state from a different disciplinary angle, have taken this approach. From the perspective of political economy, for example, Bob Jessop (2002) analyses economic policy, social policy, the scale of political activities and the means of market regulation to describe how the 'Keynesian welfare national state' of the 1960s and the 1970s is being transformed into a 'Schumpeterian workfare post-national regime'. From the perspective of international relations, Georg Sørensen (2004) focuses on the dimensions of government, nationhood and economy to show how the 'modern state' – characterized by the confinement of democratic government, citizen loyalties and economic interaction to the national scale – is being replaced by a 'postmodern state' in which national boundaries are broken down in all three dimensions.

What these studies have in common is not only that they first disaggregate the state into various dimensions, which they then analyse separately, but also they are quick to identify a new, similarly coherent state (or regime) constellation, which they see as replacing the familiar constellation. By contrast, this volume is more sceptical with respect to the coherence of the 'post-national constellation' that appears to be on the rise. Is it not conceivable, after all, that change affects the different dimensions of the state, its various institutions and functions, in such a way that they no longer effectively complement each other? What if, for example, mechanisms of welfare provision and democratic control emerge on the international sphere at a much slower pace than do mechanisms of economic deregulation? What if the transformation of the state does not lead to a new equilibrium, but takes the form of an *unravelling* of different state functions? Answering these questions demands not only that we distinguish between the state's various dimensions, but also that we develop a common analytical framework that can be applied to all of them, thus making it possible to assess how the respective developments differ and how they relate to each other.

This is what this book sets out to do. It is based on the assumption that there was indeed a time in the 1960s and the early 1970s when the central attributes and functions of Western nation states were in a relatively stable equilibrium. The book assesses how the nation state has changed since this 'golden age', whether its different dimensions, tasks and functions are unravelling, or whether a new equilibrium is emerging. This introductory chapter develops an analytical grid for such an analysis. We define four core functions that characterized the Western state in its golden age and outline major challenges which jeopardize this constellation. We then develop a typology of changes that might occur in reaction to these challenges, concentrating in particular on the internationalization of state functions. We also ask what role state institutions themselves might have played in this transformation, and whether recent changes can adequately be described as a process of 'self-transformation'. The analytical framework developed here is then employed in eight chapters that focus on areas of state activity as diverse as taxation, transnational business law, Internet governance and education policy. Drawing together the results of these chapters in the 'Conclusion', it is then possible to assess whether – and to what extent – the former 'bundle' of different functions of modern statehood is coming apart.

The golden-age nation state

It is clear from the above discussion that there are multiple ways to distinguish dimensions of the modern state. In this book, we follow a conception proposed by Michael Zürn and Stephan Leibfried (2005). It is based on the idea that the state's existence is generally justified in the Western world – both in political theory and public discourse – by pointing to core *normative goods* that state institutions are supposed to secure: (1) peace and physical security, (2) liberty and legal certainty, (3) democratic self-determination and (4) economic growth and social welfare.

These normative goods may be used to define different state functions and different dimensions of state activity. What is remarkable about the 1960s and the 1970s is that, by and large, the modal Western state was not only fairly successful in fulfilling each of these functions, but also virtually held a monopoly with respect to all of them. The nation state of the golden age was a *territorial state* in control of material and institutional resources essential for effective governance and preserving internal and external peace; it was a *constitutional state* with an elaborate legal system institutionalizing personal liberty and the rule of law; it was a *democratic nation state* whose legitimacy was based on the collective self-determination of its citizens; and it was an *interventionist state* using numerous instruments to promote economic growth and to secure the material underpinnings of social stability.

Defining the modern state by these four dimensions has a number of advantages over alternative conceptualizations. First, it can be shown that the normative goods of physical security, legal certainty, democratic self-determination and social welfare are indeed relevant in an empirical sense, since they represent standards by which citizens evaluate the quality of political arrangements (Gilley 2006). No matter whether these goods are adequately secured or not, they are virtually uncontested in the Western world as a yardstick for assessing state institutions and their performance. Second, in a historical perspective, the four normative goods – and the respective dimensions of state activity – can be linked to different phases in the development of the modern state in Western Europe. In a stylized account, which of course cannot do justice to historical peculiarities and regional variation, this development can be portrayed as a process in which the state's responsibility to provide the four normative goods was expanded step by step (Poggi 1990; Gill 2003).

- In a first phase of state development, culminating in the 16th and the 17th centuries, the monopoly of control over key resources was established, providing the basis for the state's constitutive claim, as *territorial state*, to supreme authority within its borders. Of these resources the most critical are the means of force, a functioning bureaucratic apparatus and the ability to raise taxes. In an effort to widen and secure their power base, rulers in the late Middle Ages gradually acquired these resources at the expense of various competitors, thus supplanting feudal arrangements (Giddens 1985; Tilly 1990; Spruyt 1994; Elias 2000). However, in order to mobilize societal resources for war making (eliminating external rivals), state making (eliminating internal rivals) and extraction (acquiring the financial means for carrying out these activities), rulers needed to have something to offer to their subjects in return. Therefore, means of state-controlled force were not only used to expand the ruler's powers, but also to protect the well-being and security of his chief supporters – landlords, armies, churchmen, but increasingly also merchants profiting from the territorial expansion of markets (Tilly 1985).
- The second phase of state development, dominating political struggles in the 17th and the 18th centuries, consisted of the limitation

of state powers by legal means, resulting in the *constitutional state*. Whereas in post-revolutionary France and North America the constitution could be interpreted as the foundation of a new political order (Arendt 1963), constitutionalization in states such as Great Britain and Germany implied that preexisting centres of authority were subjected to the rule of law, thus shaping and limiting the exercise of their power (Castiglione 1996; Möllers 2004). To meet the citizens' demands for liberty and legal certainty, the law was applied to the state itself, and it was increasingly expected that a state's legal rules conform to normative principles such as impartial adjudication and effective enforcement. Nevertheless, one should bear in mind that this process of legalization only resulted in a bifurcated rule of law. Until the end of the 20th century, states were indeed controlled internally by domestic law, but much less so externally by international law.

- The third phase of state development, culminating in the *democratic nation state*, occurred mainly in the 19th and the 20th centuries. Increasingly the idea gained ground that state institutions could only be considered legitimate if they guaranteed the citizens' self-determination by enabling effective participation in decision making on all issues of collective concern. In contrast to the 'first democratic transformation' in the Greek *polis* or medieval city states, this 'second democratic transformation' (Dahl 1994) was complicated by the fact that it involved the application of democratic principles to large-scale entities, so that direct-democratic decision making through citizens' assemblies was no longer feasible. Democracy hence became defined as representative democracy, that is, as a system in which the citizens' self-government primarily consisted in the choice of elected delegates. Both for its normative legitimacy and for its social acceptance, this system depended on the existence of a political community or 'demos' in which some form of collective identity provided a link between the citizens and their representatives. The development of representative democracy was hence closely tied to, and greatly bolstered by, processes of nation building that served to integrate the people living in a certain territory into one political community (Rokkan 1999). Accordingly, the concept of the democratic nation state was grounded on the premise that political and national units could be considered to be more or less congruent (Gellner 1987).

- Finally, the fourth phase, the rise of the *interventionist state*, began in the late 19th century and reached its climax in the 1960s and the 1970s. Attempting to promote economic growth and social justice within its boundaries, Western nation states took on an ever-increasing number of tasks, many of which involved interventions into society that went well beyond those required to provide for the citizens' physical security, legal certainty and self-determination (Flora and Heidenheimer 1981; Flora 1986; Kaufmann 2001). Modern states began to actively regulate individual behaviour, to grant monetary transfers and to provide services in a wide array of social and economic spheres ranging from health care to social security, from labour markets to education, from the regulation of corporate governance to the provision of infrastructure and public services. Various systems of state intervention emerged within this framework, and states came to be classified as belonging to different 'welfare state regimes' (Esping-Andersen 1990; Castles and Obinger 2008) or 'varieties of capitalism' (Hall and Soskice 2001). It was precisely the strong position of the nation state in its golden age – its autonomy in economic and domestic affairs – that made such variance possible, since it enabled the state to choose in relative autonomy among different institutional arrangements (Rothgang *et al.* 2006).

In the golden age of the 1960s and the 1970s, the Western nation state assumed full responsibility for the provision of all these normative goods, and all dimensions of statehood reached maturity. It is important to understand, however, that the golden-age nation state did not just represent an aggregation or compilation of various state functions, but constituted a *synergetic constellation* in which all four dimensions mutually sustained and energized each other. A last advantage of the four-dimensional conceptualization employed here lies in the fact that these synergies can easily be analysed within this framework. To give some examples: The monopolies of force and tax collection were a precondition for the other three dimensions of the state to develop; but at the same time, they would not have been sustainable in the long term without the legitimation that the rule of law, democratic self-determination and social welfare provided for state authority. Similarly, the rule of law and democracy can be portrayed as mutually supporting principles that secure the citizens' liberty (Habermas 1996). The existence of democratic procedures contributed to the expansion of welfare regimes; however, the social security that these regimes provided also had a positive effect on the normative legitimacy and factual acceptance of democratic procedures. In short, the nation state in its golden age clearly represented a coherent political constellation. But, how can this constellation withstand today's threats to nation state authority?

Challenges to the golden-age constellation

There are various reasons why the nation state is under strain today. According to most accounts, the key factor triggering state transformation is economic globalization. In addition, however, other potential sources of pressure on the nation state can be identified, such as migration, new technologies, environmental problems, demographic changes, the spread of new values and the increasing importance of international organizations. In this section, we briefly discuss how these developments challenge the modern state. In particular, we point out that the new challenges the state is faced with regularly involve pressures for an internationalization of state functions, which makes it plausible to ask whether we are witnessing the emergence of a new state constellation at the international level.

The argument that economic globalization poses a risk to the state is well established (Mann 1997; Jessop 2002). While there had been a growth in cross-border economic exchange for some time prior to the end of the cold war, the fall of the Iron Curtain added further momentum to this process. As a result, the relative closure of national economies that characterized the nation state in its golden age has been undermined, as production chains and service provision now increasingly cut across state borders, and trade as well as finance have become transnationalized (Zürn 1998; Hirst and Thompson 1999). The state today operates in a radically new environment – multinational corporations, accountable only to their shareholders, gain bargaining power vis-à-vis the state's democratic institutions by threatening to relocate production. Capital mobility restrains state control over monetary policy. Competitive pressure to lower tax rates undermines the state's resources and has the potential to unleash financial crises that, in turn, trigger cuts in welfare spending. At the same time, it is clear that globalized processes of economic exchange also require political regulation. Is the nation state, with its restricted territorial reach, a viable form of authority to provide this regulation? If not, are we witnessing an internationalization of regulatory competencies? How do these developments affect crucial normative goods such as legal certainty and democratic self-determination?

In addition to economic pressures, several non-economic social trends are consequential for the state. Some are broadly related to globalization. For example, increased migration threatens the control territorial states have traditionally exerted over their borders and undermines the homogeneity of national political communities that used to be taken for granted in democratic theory (Habermas 1998; 2001). Likewise, new environmental problems do not stop at state borders, and often cannot be solved by a single state acting alone (Mann 1997). New technologies, such as the Internet, pose new regulatory challenges and potentially harbour serious threats to security and legal certainty by facilitating various forms of 'cyber crime' or terrorism (Krasner 2001). Other social factors that change the conditions under which state institutions operate are not directly related to globalization. One such example is demographic change (Lynch 2006). Most Western societies are ageing rapidly and putting social security systems under massive strain. How do developments such as these affect the provision of the four normative goods of modern statehood?

A third group of factors that might trigger a transformation of the state are ideational in character. For instance, postmaterialist values have gained ground in Western societies, stressing individual self-determination, inclusion and participation, equal rights and the recognition of difference, and challenging both respect for authorities and the primacy of economic policy (Dalton 2004; Inglehart and Welzel 2005). This means that core ideas underlying the monopoly of force, the legal system, procedures of majoritarian democracy and welfare provision have increasingly come under attack. Similarly, the spread of post-national values across the world, especially the growing importance of human rights, challenges traditional notions of sovereignty and non-intervention (Lapidoth 1992; International Commission on Intervention and State Sovereignty 2001; Biersteker 2002). Can the nation state maintain its character in the face of these radically new expectations? Or are we witnessing a process by which sovereignty becomes meaningless while the rule of law is internationalized through the emergence of robust external constraints on state action?

Finally, threats to the golden-age constellation of the nation state can also originate from the political dynamics triggered by the nation states themselves taking steps towards internationalization – the transfer of political competencies to international or supranational organizations. If the state induces internationalization processes, these can lead to further internationalization by producing 'spill-overs' or 'side-effects' to which the state, in turn, has to react. Such developments are evident, for example, in the case of the European Union and its legal order (Weiler 1999; Alter 2001). The example of the EU shows that a state-sponsored international institution-building project might gradually elude state control. Once they came into existence, these institutions generated pressures for further internationalization. Is the nation state in danger of losing control over these dynamics?

Clearly, these challenges are potentially of tremendous and enduring social and political significance. They affect the modern state in each of its four dimensions, and prompt the question whether an international-ization of state functions is occurring:

- The *territorial state* is threatened from within by a spiralling erosion of resources and classic coercive powers, and from without by the dilu-tion of sovereignty. New threats to the citizens' well-being and physical security – for example environmental problems and international ter-rorism – cannot be effectively regulated at the national level, but it is also doubtful to what extent international institutions can effectively deal with these challenges.
- The *constitutional state* has to cope with new sources of uncertainty, which raises the question whether the rule of law at the national level can be complemented or replaced at a level beyond the nation state, as many relevant legal parameters are now set in international politics.
- The *democratic nation state* may become an empty shell as power shifts to the international level, threatening the citizens' self-determination unless democracy itself can be internationalized and incorporated into international organizations.
- The *interventionist state* may crumble as competitive pressure under-mines state-run social security and public services systems, while the extent to which international institutions are capable of providing for social welfare remains unclear.

Taken together, these challenges endanger not only the provision of the four normative goods of modern statehood, and the state monopoly of their provision, but also the synergetic constellation that characterized the nation state in its golden age. Different state functions are threatened to a greater or lesser degree, and subjected to pressures for international-ization of varying intensity. Is the golden-age nation state unravelling? If it is, how may the ensuing governance arrangements be brought under the rule of law? Are democratic procedures and redistributive policies still conceivable under these conditions? Can the unravelling of the state be brought to a halt; can it be reversed? If there is no return to the *status quo ante*, are there indications that a new constellation is emerging which serves similar purposes, and is as successful as the nation state was in its heyday?

Conceptualizing state transformation

To answer these questions, each of the chapters in this book focuses on one dimension of state activity, asking how the provision of the normative good in question is affected by the challenges discussed above, whether the state has retained its monopoly in securing its provision, or whether it now shares responsibility with institutions at the international level. In doing so, all chapters apply a common analytical grid, which makes it possible to relate the findings to each other and to assess the effects that changes in each dimension have had for the synergetic constellation of modern statehood (Genschel *et al.* 2006). In this section, we introduce and explain this analytical framework, which consists of five key variables:

(1) the level of responsibility for the provision of normative goods that is subject to change;
(2) the type of institution beyond the nation state to which responsibilities are transferred;
(3) the extent to which responsibilities are demonopolized;
(4) the type of state involvement in setting these changes in motion; and
(5) the patterns of reaction across states once the implications of transformative processes become observable, which might lead to the convergence or divergence of various states (corridor effects).

Levels of responsibility for the provision of normative goods

As observed above, the nation state in the golden age exercised a virtual monopoly over the provision of the normative goods of physical security, legal certainty, democratic self-determination and social welfare, meaning that state institutions were responsible for all aspects of making them available to their citizens. Thus, the state was not only obliged – or at least expected – to step in when things went wrong and hitherto unregulated social processes put a normative good in jeopardy, but also it took the crucial legislative decisions on the services needed for the provision of those goods, and even performed these services through its own agencies. In other words, the state was charged with three levels of responsibility at the same time. It bore *outcome responsibility* in the sense that it was the ultimate guarantor of the provision of normative goods; it bore *regulatory responsibility* in the sense that it decided on the processes through which normative goods were to be provided; and it bore *operational responsibility* in the sense that state institutions actually performed the necessary tasks (for a similar distinction, see Schuppert 2000: 400–19).

It is important to note that although all of these types of responsibility once resided with the golden-age nation state, this need not necessarily be the case. Potentially, that is, any of these responsibilities could emerge outside, or disconnect from, the remit of the state. Thus, international law might restrict the state's legislative competencies (i.e., regulatory responsibility) in a certain issue area, or service provision in relation to a normative good (i.e., operational responsibility) might be privatized. As a result, the three levels of responsibility which formerly were in the remit of the state may be unbundled, thus constituting a further aspect of the state's unravelling. All case studies in this volume therefore examine to what extent the state still holds a monopoly on the different levels of responsibility, and what other institutions have appeared on the scene.

Institutions acquiring political responsibility beyond the nation state

Previous studies suggest that the state monopoly for the provision of normative goods is challenged mainly by two types of institutions (Zürn and Leibfried 2005): outcome, regulatory, and operational responsibility may be partially or completely transferred either to *private actors* (the *organizational* aspect of change) or to *international institutions* (the *spatial* aspect of change). This volume focuses on spatial transformation, that is, on change along the national-international axis. Without wishing to deny the importance of privatization processes (overview Zohlnhöfer and Obinger 2005; on welfare states Starke 2007), here we want to put the spotlight on how the relationship between states and international actors is being reconfigured. In this context, however, privatization might well become relevant if it is coupled with internationalization. Transfers of responsibility along the national-international axis, after all, might empower different kinds of actors in the international sphere. The formal or informal institutions beyond the nation state that assume responsibilities for the provision of normative goods may, in Robert Keohane and Joseph Nye's (1972) typology, be either *intergovernmental* (i.e., the members of the collective actor are states), *transgovernmental* (i.e., the members are state bureaucracies), *supranational* (i.e., the members are international public servants or delegates), or *transnational* (i.e., the members are private actors). Clearly, which type of institution profits from transfers of responsibility is of enormous importance for the powers that the state retains, as it is far easier for the state to exercise control over intergovernmental or transgovernmental actors than over supranational or transnational actors. Against this background, the chapters in this volume indicate how the institutions to which state responsibilities are transferred may be characterized in this respect.

Extent of demonopolization

The different types of responsibility for the provision of the normative goods may not only be transferred to different institutions, but also we can distinguish different degrees to which responsibility is transferred, and hence demonopolized. Sometimes the responsibility that institutions beyond the nation state assume detracts from the responsibility of the state, that is, the reallocation of responsibility works according to a zero-sum logic. In these cases, we talk of a *shift* of responsibility. Such a shift may be either *partial* or *complete*, in respect of the relevant level of responsibility. An example for a complete shift of state functions is the transfer of the capacity to set interest rates from national institutions to the European Central Bank. It implied that the member states of the Euro zone relinquished their regulatory responsibility in the field of monetary policy, which clearly reduced their autonomous capacities as interventionist states. However, practices of providing for the normative goods of modern statehood might also emerge beyond the nation state without diminishing state responsibilities. If such a variable-sum logic holds sway, we speak of a *diffusion* of responsibility. For example, if supranational institutions such as the EU reform their decision-making procedures to allow more democratic input, this opens up additional channels for the citizens' self-determination without necessarily fore-closing channels that exist at the nation-state level. Diffusion may come in one of two forms (as may instances of partial shift). The institutions that perform state functions beyond the nation state may be either *disconnected* from states (i.e., operate independently of them) or *interlocked* with states (i.e., cooperate or otherwise interact with them). In the above example, an interlocked form of diffusion would exist if the democratization of the EU further empowered national parliaments; a disconnected form if channels of representation independent of the nation states were strengthened. Using this grid, the contributors to this book assess whether the transfers of responsibilities observed take the form of a (partial or complete) shift or can better be characterized as a (disconnected or interlocked) diffusion of traditional state functions.

Types of state involvement – the self-transformation of the state?

Sometimes the state is depicted as utterly powerless in the face of the challenges outlined above. According to this view, what the state is and what it does – in particular, the role it continues or ceases to play in providing normative goods – is determined by forces beyond its control. But this picture may be inaccurate in several ways, at least in terms of certain dimensions of the state or certain issue-areas in which it operates. When responsibilities for the provision of normative goods are internationalized, we may occasionally find the state in the driver's seat, proactively initiating changes in a move to maintain or retrieve essential and substantial governing capacities by partial and selective retrenchment elsewhere (Milward 1992; Moravcsik 1998). The state, therefore, may act as a direct or immediate *initiator* of its own transformation. Furthermore, even if this is not the case, it may turn out on closer inspection that political decisions made by state actors lie at the root of many of the seemingly 'natural' developments – such as economic globalization, international migration or the spread of new technologies – that the state currently confronts as challenges (Genschel 2004). If this is the case, one can speak of the state acting as an indirect and causally more distant *promoter* of change.

Finally, even if the origin of the pressures challenging its structures is indeed beyond the state's control, it does not necessarily have to 'comply with' external 'imperatives' in a mechanical way. Rather, it might seek to deliberately influence, channel, or shape the changes that are necessitated or promoted by developments in its material and social environment (Swank 2002; Rieger and Leibfried 2003). In this case, the state emerges as an active *manager* of change. All these types of state involvement in its own transformation can be interpreted as instances of the state's *self-transformation*. One core hypothesis pursued in this book is that such instances of self-transformation are actually the rule rather than the exception in the current processes of reconfiguring – or unravellng of – state structures.

Responses to transformative processes, and corridor effects

State-transforming processes that take the form of a shift or diffusion of responsibilities to the international level reverberate back to the state. Even in cases in which they have been triggered by the state itself, the repercussions of such processes may be different from what state actors expected when these were initiated. For example, international institutions might take on additional responsibilities or develop new forms of governance not anticipated when states first approached the international level. This raises the general question of how states react to processes of transformation when their – potentially unintended – implications become apparent.

Do states attempt to regain control over the provision of normative goods at the *international level* by deliberately influencing the shape of international institutions, or by (re)establishing, or reinforcing linkages to them? Do they reform core institutions or policies at the *national level* in order to accommodate processes of internationalization? It is clear that even if transformative processes are triggered by challenges that affect all states in similar ways, states' reaction to these challenges may differ sharply. For example, some states may be more willing or able to oppose a transfer of responsibilities to international institutions, and some may be more active than others when it comes to establishing linkages to them. Ultimately, such reactions might result in either greater or smaller similarities between states, in a broader or narrower *corridor* between individual states (Rothgang *et al.* 2006). In other words, different states might converge or diverge with regard to one or more of the state's constitutive dimensions. With some caution, a blurring of the differences between individual states can be interpreted as indicating that states have suffered losses in autonomy and no longer can afford to maintain idiosyncratic national systems, while an increase or persistence of differences can be considered a sign of the nation state's continual strength. Where applicable, the case studies in this volume also report such 'corridor effects'.

Outline of the volume

Using this analytical framework, the chapters in this book analyse state transformation in specific issue areas, with two chapters focusing on each of the four state dimensions. Chapters 2 and 3 deal with the *territorial state* and its core resources. Despite the centrality and basic character of this dimension of the state, the pillars of the state's monopoly of control – bureaucracies, the military, the police and taxation – hardly figure prominently in current academic debates on the future of the nation state. Given the fundamental importance of these institutions, this neglect is unfortunate. The few studies that have been conducted to date point to surprisingly far-reaching changes, for example in connection with international police cooperation (Jachtenfuchs 2005; Friedrichs 2007). In addition, since the state's control over resources constitutes the prerequisite for the exercise of other state functions, even small changes in control relationships in this dimension could have far-reaching consequences (Genschel 2005; Rixen 2008).

In Chapter 2, *Susanne Uhl* underscores this point by discussing the nation state's power in taxation matters. She shows that contrary to what is often believed, state responsibility in this area has to a large extent shifted to the international sphere, especially within the European Union. The EU tax regime imposes severe restraints on the member states' regulatory and, to a lesser extent, operational responsibilities, leaving only outcome responsibility – that is, the expectation that states are able to intervene in the last resort – substantially intact.

In Chapter 3, *Sebastian Mayer* and *Silke Weinlich* examine another pillar of the territorial state, the military forces. Mayer and Weinlich point out that the increase in the number of military interventions in recent years does not only have implications for the states whose sovereignty is violated, but also for the monopoly of force of the sponsors of such interventions. They go on to examine the question of whether competencies for authorizing and implementing military interventions have been transferred in recent years from states to international or supranational organizations. Focusing on the United Nations and the European Union, they show that structures of multilevel governance are emerging in which regulatory and operational responsibilities are becoming increasingly diffused, that is, they are exercised jointly by nation states and international actors.

Turning to the second dimension of the modern state, chapters 4 and 5 address transformations of the *constitutional state* and the rule of law. Their particular focus is on international legalization, a process that might lead to an internationalization of the emergence, adjudication and enforcement of legal rules. Earlier studies in this research field have detailed remarkable legalization processes in relations between states, such as the increasing importance of international courts or court-like dispute settlement arrangements (Joerges and Godt 2005; Zangl 2005; for a synopsis, see Joerges and Petersmann 2006). The contributions presented in this volume, by contrast, ask whether comparable steps towards an international rule of law can also be found with respect to relations between *private actors*, that is, in the transnational sphere.

In Chapter 4, *Martin Herberg* discusses global informal rule making beyond the state.[2] He argues that such 'soft law', which evolves in reaction to deficiencies of formal law making at the international level, is often remarkably effective, but poses considerable risks for the rule of law. In this situation, as Herberg points out, the nation state and its legal system often serve as an important safety net with the ability to 'domesticate' informal structures. What emerges is a new model of 'interlocked statehood', in which traditional state responsibilities for securing legal certainty are diffused to some extent, but the state, acting as a transmission belt between the transnational and the national sphere, proves its ability to regain some crucial problem-solving capacities.

Gralf-Peter Calliess, Wioletta Konradi, Holger Nieswandt, Thomas Dietz and *Fabian Sosa* make a similar point in Chapter 5. Focusing on economic exchange in cross-border commerce, they show that a variety of private mechanisms have developed in the transnational sphere to guarantee stable business relationships in a situation of 'relative lawlessness'. The authors point out, however, that such private mechanisms always operate 'in the shadow of national commercial law'. Globalized economic exchange, hence, is regulated by an institutional mix of public and private governance mechanisms. Furthermore, the authors observe that nation states increasingly attempt to adapt their legal systems to the new global circumstances, which may eventually enable them to provide legal institutions that can compete more effectively with private structures.

While chapters 4 and 5 come to relatively reassuring conclusions about the rule of law in a globalized setting, the implications of state transformation for democratic self-determination – and by implication for the *democratic nation state* – might be more troublesome. The growing power of unaccountable economic actors and the increasing interconnectedness of national and international governance undeniably challenge the capacity of national 'demoi' to exercise full control over political developments affecting their members. Although these developments do not necessarily lead to an erosion of public support for nation state institutions (Hurrelmann *et al.* 2005), they make it more difficult for the nation state to meet its own standards of democratic legitimacy. The threat this implies for the legitimation of democratic governance, however, could be attenuated if it were possible to democratize political institutions at the international level, thus bringing about what Robert Dahl (1994) calls the 'third democratic transformation'. There is widespread agreement in the literature that this transformation cannot consist of a simple transfer of the institutions of representative democracy from the national to the international sphere (DeBardeleben and Hurrelmann 2007; Dingwerth 2007; Hurrelmann *et al.* 2007). Even in the European Union, which is generally considered to be a particularly promising setting for democratization, many of the societal conditions on which national systems of representative democracy have traditionally relied are not met, as European identities remain weak and transnational public spheres that would allow for pan-European democratic discourses are slow to develop (Peters *et al.* 2005; Peters 2007; Wessler *et al.* 2008). Yet if one moves away from national blueprints of legitimate democratic governance, some avenues for democratization become apparent in the emerging practices and structures of international governance. Chapters 6 and 7 consider whether these are promising routes to democratization beyond the nation state.

In Chapter 6, *Jens Steffek* argues that while the nation state still has – or is perceived to have – outcome responsibility for guaranteeing the democratic quality of governance, the delegation of political authority to international institutions means that it no longer possesses the regulatory or operational competencies necessary to provide this normative good by its own means. Against this background, Steffek analyses the question of whether civil society participation in international organizations might constitute a promising supplementary mechanism to enhance the democratic quality of globalized politics.[3] The empirical evidence he presents on existing forms of civil society involvement, however, is quite sobering. As Steffek points out, international organizations are often insufficiently responsive to arguments brought forward by civil society, and sometimes even actively exclude certain positions. Civil society participation in international organizations therefore seems to have only a limited potential for protecting the normative good of democratic self-determination in globalized political settings.

Ralf Bendrath, Jeanette Hofmann, Volker Leib, Peter Mayer and *Michael Zürn* in Chapter 7 also show how difficult it is to replace the state as guarantor of democratic legitimacy. This chapter focuses on the political regulation of the Internet, in particular the administration of the Domain Name System (DNS), the protection of informational privacy, and the taxation of e-commerce. The authors point out that unsurprisingly, regulatory and operational responsibilities relating to these matters have diffused to transnational actors, although this diffusion was less far-reaching than might have been expected. What is more, they even find indications of a return of the state, with nation states beginning to intervene more vigorously in private self-regulation. Interestingly, this return of the state has been facilitated by the difficulties the new governance arrangements encountered in securing democratic legitimacy. Precisely because international arrangements for Internet regulation were regarded as deficient in a democratic sense, nation states were able to reclaim some regulatory and operational responsibilities.

Finally, chapters 8 and 9 turn to the *interventionist state*. The transformation of the state in this dimension has thus far mainly been analysed with respect to the provision of welfare services, such as healthcare and pensions. Studies in this field of research show that the overall level of state intervention in the Western world has risen rather than fallen in recent years due in part to the catching up of states that are late developers in terms of welfare provision. Furthermore, such studies find that the core of the welfare state has been relatively unyielding despite the pressures of globalization (Obinger *et al.* 2005; Rothgang *et al.* 2005, 2008), even though there are some indications for a convergence of different welfare state regimes (Obinger and Starke 2007). It is important to note, however, that the welfare state is only one component of the inter-ventionist state. Although it is certainly of central importance, a comprehensive assessment of changes effected in the state's interventionist dimension is only possible if other components are taken into account as well. For this reason, the two chapters presented here concentrate on two less eye-catching, but nonetheless important aspects of state intervention – education and the regulation of corporate governance. Education holds the key to the long-term development of 'ageing' Western states, whereas corporate governance might stand for the waning powers of government over private business in an age of global markets.

In Chapter 8, *Kerstin Martens* and *Ansgar Weymann* analyse the education sector, paying particular attention to the growing influence of international organizations vis-à-vis the nation state. They find that responsibility for providing the normative good of social welfare is increasingly diffused, with institutions such as the OECD and the EU assuming central roles.[4] This diffusion is interpreted by Martens and Weymann as an example for the state's self-transformation. In response to dissatisfaction with national governance capabilities, states turned to international organizations to devise internationally applicable solutions. This transfer of responsibilities, however, triggered institutional dynamics which ultimately spiralled out of the states' control and contributed to increased convergence between national education systems.

In Chapter 9, the last case study in this book, an example of regulatory intervention into corporate governance to promote economic growth and social welfare is addressed, namely standard setting in the area of accounting. In this chapter, *Jochen Zimmermann* shows that the two systems of standard setting that coexisted in Europe in the 1960s and the 1970s – state-driven systems in which state institutions bore operational responsibility and market-driven systems in which private bodies served as standard setters – have increasingly converged in response to European integration.[5] Large parts of the regulatory and operational responsibility for setting accounting standards have been shifted to transnational and transgovernmental bodies, while the nation state's responsibility for the effective organization of capital markets – that is, its outcome responsibility – remains intact. Evaluating these new governance arrangements, Zimmermann finds that they are superior in balancing business and public interests compared to the alternative provided by the US system.

On the basis of these case studies, we return in the Conclusion to the hypothesis of an unravelling of the functions and responsibilities that were monopolized by the nation state in its golden age. Drawing together the findings of the individual chapters, we show that the Western state has retained its basic characteristics as territorial state, constitutional state, democratic nation state and interventionist state even after the end of its golden age, but that it now increasingly shares responsibilities for the provision of physical security, legal certainty, democratic self-determination and social welfare with institutions at the international level. While the state itself remains fundamentally intact, this means that the array of functions and guarantees it could once provide to its citizens is indeed unravelling, a development that might threaten the adequate protection of the four normative goods that defined the regime of golden-age statehood.

Notes

1 The ideas presented in this chapter are the product of extensive discussions within the TranState Research Centre. We are particularly indebted to Philipp Genschel and Bernhard Zangl, who, in the process of drafting TranState's research programme for 2007–10 (see Genschel *et al.* 2006), were the first to flesh out many of these systematically. TranState's first attempt to synthesize its approach to state research is spelled out in Leibfried and Zürn (2005).
2 On the same issue, see also the forthcoming volume by Dilling *et al.* (2007).
3 For a more detailed discussion of civil society participation in international governance, see Steffek *et al.* (2007).
4 This topic is discussed in greater depth in Martens *et al.* (2007).
5 The internationalization of accounting practices is discussed in greater detail in Volmer *et al.* (2008).

References

Albrow, Martin (1996) *The Global Age: State and Society Beyond Modernity*, Cambridge: Polity Press.
Alter, Karen (2001) *Establishing the Supremacy of European Law: The Making of an International Rule of Law in Europe*, Oxford: Oxford University Press.
Appadurai, Arjun (1996) *Modernity at Large: Cultural Dimensions of Globalization*, Minneapolis: University of Minnesota Press.
Arendt, Hannah (1963) *On Revolution*, New York: Viking Press.
Bache, Ian and Matthew Flinders, eds (2004) *Multi-level Governance*, Oxford: Oxford University Press.
Biersteker, Thomas J. (2002) 'State, Sovereignty and Territory', in Walter Carlsnaes, Thomas Risse and Beth A. Simmons, eds, *The Handbook of International Relations*, London: Sage, 208–26.
Camilleri, Joseph A. and Jim Falk (1992) *The End of Sovereignty? The Politics of a Shrinking and Fragmenting World*, Aldershot: Edward Elgar.
Caporaso, James A. (2000a) 'Changes in the Westphalian Order: Territory, Public Authority, and Sovereignty', *International Studies Review* 2(2), 1–28.
Caporaso, James A., ed. (2000b) *Continuity and Change in the Westphalian Order*, Malden, MA: Blackwell.

Castiglione, Dario (1996) 'The Political Theory of the Constitution', *Political Studies* 44 (Special Issue), 417–35.

Castles, Francis G. and Herbert Obinger (2008), 'Worlds', *West European Politics* 31 (forthcoming).

Crouch, Colin (2004) *Post-Democracy*, Cambridge: Polity Press.

Dahl, Robert A. (1994) 'A Democratic Dilemma: System Effectiveness versus Citizen Participation', *Political Science Quarterly* 109(1), 23–34.

Dalton, Russell J. (2004) *Democratic Challenges, Democratic Choices: The Erosion of Political Support in Advanced Industrial Democracies*, Oxford: Oxford University Press.

DeBardeleben, Joan and Achim Hurrelmann, eds (2007) *Democratic Dilemmas of Multilevel Governance: Legitimacy, Representation and Accountability in the European Union*, Basingstoke: Palgrave Macmillan.

Dilling, Olaf, Martin Herberg and Gerd Winter, eds (2007) *Responsible Business? Self-Governance in Transnational Economic Transactions*, Oxford: Hart Publishing (forthcoming).

Dingwerth, Klaus (2007) *The New Transnationalism. Private Transnational Governance and its Democratic Legitimacy*, Basingstoke: Palgrave Macmillan (forthcoming).

Elias, Norbert (2000) *The Civilizing Process: Sociogenetic and Psychogenetic Investigations*, Oxford: Blackwell.

Esping-Andersen, Gøsta (1990) *The Three Worlds of Welfare Capitalism*, Cambridge: Cambridge University Press and Princeton: Princeton University Press.

Flora, Peter, ed. (1986) *Growth to Limits: The Western European Welfare States Since World War II*, 3 volumes, Berlin: de Gruyter.

Flora, Peter and Arnold J. Heidenheimer, eds (1981) *The Development of Welfare States in Europe and America*, New Brunswick: Transaction Books.

Friedrichs, Jörg (2007) *Fighting Terrorism and Drugs: Europe and International Police Cooperation*, London: Routledge.

Gellner, Ernest (1987) *Nations and Nationalism*, 2nd edn, Ithaca: Cornell University Press.

Genschel, Philipp (2004) 'Globalization and the Welfare State: A Retrospective', *Journal of European Public Policy* 11(4), 613–36.

Genschel, Philipp (2005) 'Globalization and the Transformation of the Tax State', in Stephan Leibfried and Michael Zürn, eds, *Transformations of the State?* Cambridge: Cambridge University Press, 53–71.

Genschel, Philipp, Stephan Leibfried and Bernhard Zangl (2006) *Zerfaserung und Selbsttransformation: Das Forschungsprogramm 'Staatlichkeit im Wandel'*, TranState Working Paper No. 45, Bremen: TranState Research Centre, available at <www.sfb597.uni-bremen.de/pages/pubApBeschreibung.php? SPRACHE=de&ID=55>

Giddens, Anthony (1985) *The Nation-State and Violence*, Cambridge: Polity Press.

Gill, Graeme (2003) *The Nature and Development of the Modern State*, Basingstoke: Palgrave Macmillan.

Gilley, Bruce (2006) 'The Determinants of State Legitimacy: Results for 72 Countries', *International Political Science Review* 27(1), 47–71.

Grimm, Dieter (2005) 'The Constitution in the Process of Denationalization', *Constellations* 12(4), 449–65.

Guéhenno, Jean-Marie (1995) *The End of the Nation-State*, Minneapolis: University of Minnesota Press.

Habermas, Jürgen (1996) *Between Facts and Norms: Contributions to a Discourse Theory of Law and Democracy*, Cambridge, MA: MIT Press.

Habermas, Jürgen (1998) *The Inclusion of the Other: Studies in Political Theory*, Cambridge, MA: MIT Press.

Habermas, Jürgen (2001) *The Postnational Constellation: Political Essays*, Cambridge, MA: MIT Press.

Hall, Peter A. and David Soskice, eds (2001) *Varieties of Capitalism: The Institutional Foundations of Comparative Advantage*, Oxford: Oxford University Press.

Hirst, Paul Q. and Graham Thompson (1999) *Globalization in Question: The International Economy and the Possibilities of Governance*, 2nd edn, Cambridge: Polity Press.

Hooghe, Liesbet and Gary Marks (2001) *Multi-Level Governance and European Integration*, Lanham: Rowman & Littlefield.

Hurrelmann, Achim, Zuzana Krell-Laluhovà, Roland Lhotta, Frank Nullmeier and Steffen Scheider (2005) 'Is There a Legitimation Crisis of the Nation State?', in Stephan Leibfried and Michael Zürn, eds, *Transformations of the State?*, Cambridge: Cambridge University Press, 119–38.

Hurrelmann, Achim, Steffen Schneider and Jens Steffek, eds (2007) *Legitimacy in an Age of Global Politics*, Basingstoke: Palgrave Macmillan.

Inglehart, Ronald and Chris Welzel (2005) *Modernization, Cultural Change, and Democracy: The Human Development Sequence*, Cambridge: Cambridge University Press.

International Commission on Intervention and State Sovereignty (2001) *The Responsibility to Protect*, Ottawa: International Development Research Centre, available at <http://www.iciss.ca/pdf/Commission-Report.pdf>; last accessed 12 November 2006.

Jachtenfuchs, Markus (2005) 'The Monopoly of Legitimate Force: Denationalization, or Business as Usual?', in Stephan Leibfried and Michael Zürn, eds, *Transformations of the State?*, Cambridge: Cambridge University Press, 37–52.

Jessop, Bob (2002) *The Future of the Capitalist State*, Cambridge: Polity Press.

Joerges, Christian and Christine Godt (2005) 'Free Trade: The Erosion of National, and the Birth of Transnational Governance', in Stephan Leibfried and Michael Zürn, eds, *Transformations of the State?*, Cambridge: Cambridge University Press, 93–117.

Joerges, Christian and Ernst-Ulrich Petersmann, eds (2006) *Constitutionalism, Multi-level Trade Governance and Social Regulation*, Oxford: Hart Publishing.

Kaufmann, Franz-Xaver (2001) 'Towards a Theory of the Welfare State', in Stephan Leibfried, ed., *Welfare State Futures*, Cambridge: Cambridge University Press, 15–36.

Keohane, Robert O. and Joseph S. Nye, eds (1972) *Transnational Relations and World Politics*, Cambridge: Harvard University Press.

Krasner, Stephen D. (1999) *Sovereignty: Organized Hypocrisy*, Princeton: Princeton University Press.

Krasner, Stephen D. (2001) 'Abiding Sovereignty', *International Political Science Review* 22(3), 229–51.

Lapidoth, Ruth (1992) 'Sovereignty in Transition', *Journal of International Affairs* 45(1), 1–25.

Leibfried, Stephan and Michael Zürn, eds (2005) *Transformations of the State?*, Cambridge: Cambridge University Press.

Levy, Jonah D., ed. (2006) *The State after Statism: New State Activities in the Age of Liberalization*, Cambridge, MA: Harvard University Press.

Lynch, Julia (2006) *Age in the Welfare State: The Origins of Social Spending on Pensioners, Workers and Children*, Cambridge: Cambridge University Press.

Mann, Michael (1997) 'Has Globalization Ended the Rise and Rise of the Nation-State?', *Review of International Political Economy* 4(3), 472–96.

Martens, Kerstin, Alessandra Rusconi and Kathrin Leuze, eds (2007) *New Arenas of Education Governance: The Impacts of International Organizations and Markets on Educational Policy Making*, Basingstoke: Palgrave Macmillan.

Milward, Alan S. (1992) *The European Rescue of the Nation-State*, Berkeley: University of California Press.

Möllers, Christoph (2004) 'The Politics of Law and the Law of Politics: Two Constitutional Traditions in Europe', in Erik O. Eriksen, John E. Fossum and Agustín J. Menéndez, eds, *Developing a Constitution for Europe*, London: Routledge, 129–39.

Moravcsik, Andrew (1998) *The Choice for Europe: Social Purpose and State Power from Messina to Maastricht*, Ithaca: Cornell University Press.

Obinger, Herbert, Stephan Leibfried, Claudia Bogedan, Edith Gindulis, Julia Moser and Peter Starke (2005) 'Welfare State Transformation in Small Open Economies', in Stephan Leibfried and Michael Zürn eds, *Transformations of the State?*, Cambridge: Cambridge University Press, 161–85.

Obinger, Herbert and Peter Starke (2007) 'Are Welfare States Converging?', in Irene Dingeldey and Heinz Rothgang, eds, *Governance of Welfare State Reform: A Cross National and Cross Sectoral Comparison of Policy and Politics*, Cheltenham: Edward Elgar (forthcoming).

Ohmae, Kenichi (1995) *The End of the Nation State: The Rise of Regional Economies*, New York: Free Press.

Peters, Bernhard (2007) *Public Deliberation and Public Culture*, edited by Hartmut Wessler, with preface by Jürgen Habermas, Basingstoke: Palgrave Macmillan (forthcoming).

Peters, Bernhard, Stefanie Sifft, Andreas Wimmel, Michael Brüggemann and Katharina Kleinen-von Königslöw (2005) 'National and Transnational Public Spheres: The Case of the EU', in Stephan Leibfried and Michael Zürn, eds, *Transformations of the State?*, Cambridge: Cambridge University Press, 139–60.

Poggi, Gianfranco (1990) *The State: Its Nature, Development and Prospects*, Cambridge: Polity Press.

Rieger, Elmar and Stephan Leibfried (2003) *Limits to Globalization: Welfare States and the World Economy*, Cambridge: Polity Press.

Rixen, Thomas (2008) The Political Economy of International Taxation, Basingstoke: Palgrave Macmillan (forthcoming).

Rokkan, Stein (1999) *State Formation, Nation-Building, and Mass Politics in Europe* (Peter Flora, ed.), Oxford: Oxford University Press.

Rothgang, Heinz, Mirella Cacace, Simone Grimmeisen and Claus Wendt (2005) 'The Changing Role of the State in Healthcare Systems', in Stephan Leibfried and Michael Zürn, eds, *Transformations of the State?*, Cambridge: Cambridge University Press, 187–212.

Rothgang, Heinz, Mirella Cacace, Simone Grimmeisen, Uwe Helmert and Claus Wendt (2008) *The Changing Role of the OECD Health Care Systems: From Heterogeneity to Homogeneity*, Basingstoke: Palgrave Macmillan (forthcoming).

Rothgang, Heinz, Herbert Obinger and Stephan Leibfried (2006) 'The State and its Welfare State: How Do Welfare State Changes Affect the Make-up of the Nation-State?', *Social Policy & Administration* 40(3), 250–66.

Scharpf, Fritz W. (2000) 'The Viability of Advanced Welfare States in the International Economy: Vulnerabilities and Options', *Journal of European Public Policy* 7(2) 190–228.

Scheuerman, William E. (1999) 'Economic Globalization and the Rule of Law', *Constellations* 6(1), 3–25.

Schuppert, Gunnar Folke (2000) *Verwaltungswissenschaft: Verwaltung, Verwaltungsrecht, Verwaltungslehre*, Baden-Baden: Nomos.

Sørensen, Georg (2004) *The Transformation of the State: Beyond the Myth of Retreat*, Basingstoke: Palgrave Macmillan.

Spruyt, Hendrik (1994) *The Sovereign State and its Competitors: An Analysis of Systems Change*, Princeton: Princeton University Press.

Starke, Peter (2007) *Radical Welfare State Retrenchment in Comparative Perspective*, Basingstoke: Palgrave Macmillan (forthcoming).

Steffek, Jens, Claudia Kissling and Patrizia Nanz, eds (2007) *Civil Society Participation in European and Global Governance: A Cure for the Democratic Deficit?*, Basingstoke: Palgrave Macmillan (forthcoming).

Strange, Susan (1996) *The Retreat of the State: The Diffusion of Power in the World Economy*, Cambridge: Cambridge University Press.

Swank, Duane (2002) *Global Capital, Political Institutions, and Policy Change in Developed Welfare States*, Cambridge: Cambridge University Press.

Tilly, Charles (1985) 'War Making and State Making as Organized Crime', in Peter Evans, Dietrich Rueschemeier and Theda Skocpol, eds, *Bringing the State Back In*, Cambridge: Cambridge University Press, 169–91.

Tilly, Charles (1990) *Coercion, Capital, and European States, AD 990–1990*, Cambridge, MA: Basil Blackwell.

Tully, James (2002) 'The Unfreedom of the Moderns in Comparison to their Ideals of Constitutional Democracy', *Modern Law Review* 65(2), 204–28.

Volmer, Philipp B., Jörg Richard Werner and Jochen Zimmermann (2008) *From Nation State Intervention to Global Governance in Accounting*, Basingstoke: Palgrave Macmillan (forthcoming).

Weiler, Joseph H.H. (1999) *The Constitution of Europe: 'Do the New Clothes Have an Emperor?' and Other Essays on European Integration*, Cambridge: Cambridge University Press.

Wessler, Hartmut, Bernhard Peters, Stefanie Sifft, Michael Brüggemann and Katharina Kleinen-von Königslöw (2008) *The Transnationalization of Public Spheres*, Basingstoke: Palgrave Macmillan (forthcoming).

Zangl, Bernhard (2005) 'Is There an Emerging International Rule of Law?', in Stephan Leibfried and Michael Zürn, eds, *Transformations of the State?*, Cambridge: Cambridge University Press, 73–91.

Zohlnhöfer, Reimut and Herbert Obinger (2005) 'Selling Off the "Family Silver": The Politics of Privatization', *World Political Science Review* 2(1), 30–52.

Zürn, Michael (1998) *Regieren jenseits des Nationalstaates: Globalisierung und Denationalisierung als Chance*, Frankfurt a.M.: Suhrkamp.

Zürn, Michael and Stephan Leibfried (2005) 'Reconfiguring the National Constellation', in Stephan Leibfried and Michael Zürn, eds, *Transformations of the State?*, Cambridge: Cambridge University Press, 1–36.

2
Europe, the Nation State and Taxation[1]

Susanne Uhl

In 2005 elections were held in Germany. Angela Merkel – now Chancellor – announced that her party, the conservative CDU, would raise VAT rates by 2 percent if they should win the election. Could the new majority in parliament have passed a motion like this? Yes, they could. Could they have decided autonomously to reduce VAT rates by 2 percent? No, they could not. Could they have acted on Ms Merkel's suggestion to apply zero rates of VAT on children's clothes? No, they could not. Could they have done what Joschka Fischer, former Minister of Foreign Affairs, recommended, and tax luxury goods such as expensive cars at higher rates? Again, no.

This chapter demonstrates that the VAT examples are just the tip of the iceberg of constraints imposed by the European Union on the regulatory responsibility of nation states. Over the years, crucial legislative decision making on relevant matters of taxation has been shifted to the European level. In addition, the European tax regime now imposes significant constraints on the nation state's operational responsibility, namely its ability to exclusively decide on how to collect and administer its taxes even if the agencies to perform those tasks are still the same: national or subnational. Outcome responsibility in tax matters – the normative expectation that the state will be prepared to intervene in the last resort to secure the material underpinnings of the nation's ability to pursue its collective goals – seems up to now invariably attributed to the national level. But in fact, many of the demands concerning taxes expressed by policy makers during the 2005 election campaign in Germany could not have been put into practice by the national parliament through autonomous national decisions, neither in Germany nor in the other EU member states.

Which governance responsibilities in tax matters have the nation states already lost? And what does this transformation mean for today's nation states? These are the leading questions that this chapter tries to answer. Accordingly, the investigation needs a reference point against which transformations of the national tax state can be compared. This reference point is the tax state of the 1960s and the early 1970s, a time when the nation state had the nearly exclusive responsibility to intervene and create new taxes, to take the legislative decisions on tax systems and structures, tax bases and rates (regulatory responsibility), and to collect and administer them autonomously and by its own agencies (operational responsibility).

The tax state that was still in place in the 1960s and the early 1970s was one of the preconditions for the development of the modern Western nation state as such (Leibfried and Zürn 2005). It worked as a link between essential dimensions of the golden-age state: the modern democratic state founded on the rule of law and the welfare state. Indeed, the modern constitutional state is a welfare state essentially because it is a tax state (Forsthoff 1954). In this respect the national tax state is a central pillar to guarantee the normative goods with which this book is dealing: physical security, legal certainty, democratic self-determination and social welfare. The national tax state guaranteed legal certainty by providing the necessary resources for the protection of individual rights, negotiated in a democratic process. And the national tax state applied its tax system to the social function of organizing public redistribution, to ensure social welfare. In this sense, the modern tax state of the 20th century differed from the late medieval state in which taxes or charges were mostly raised as resources to wage war. In those times, the monopoly of control over the key resources – the means of violence and the ability to raise taxes – was important mainly because it provided the basis for the nation state's constitutive claim to final authority over a definitive territory. State functions or principles were confined to matters of internal and external security, that is, military and police issues, and did not yet – as in the golden-age nation state – extend to principles of democracy and social security.

Today, many of the governance responsibilities of the modern national tax state have shifted to the European level. In this chapter, I distinguish between formal and (mere) de facto shifts of governance responsibilities. When the nation state transfers a part of its legal competencies (regulatory or operational responsibilities) to the European level, I call this a formal shift; if it does not make use of legal competencies because of supposed constraints set by the European Union or the other member states, I call this a de facto shift. To develop the argument I investigate the status quo of each of the principal taxes in relation to the question at which level – national or European – the legal decisions concerning the structure of taxes, the bases of assessment and the rates are made (regulatory responsibility), and which level administrates them (operational responsibility). It is shown that there is much more harmonization, due to shifts of regulatory and operational responsibilities, in tax matters than is often claimed – both in the political sphere and in social science literature. I investigate the consequences of this formal and de facto shift for the governance responsibilities of the EU member states. It is shown that the European tax regime has considerable effects and that it was the state itself that has been the initiator of this process of transformation. Finally, I argue that it is necessary to pay more attention to the shift of responsibilities and the ensuing system of multilevel responsibility because of the close connection between the development of the welfare state and the tax state in the 20th century.

The European integration of tax matters and its consequences for the nation state

It is a widely shared opinion that the European integration of tax matters is still in its early stages (Mette 1994; Radaelli 1995; Randzio-Plath 1999; Scharpf 1999; Genschel 2002). For many authors, this lack of progress reflects the wide diversity of national tax systems and rates, combined with the treaty requirement for unanimity on taxation issues in the Council. As Loukas Tsoukalis (2005: 127) states: 'Taxes are an issue on which the Union has spent an inordinate amount of time with rather little to show for it'. Without a doubt, the Union has spent a great amount of time on the issue. But the Union does have quite a lot to show for it.

Value added tax (VAT)

Value added tax (VAT) is a general, broadly based consumer tax, assessed on the value added to goods and services. It applies more or less to all goods and services that are bought and sold for use or consumption. As we have already seen at the beginning of this chapter, there were many demands during the election campaign in Germany which could not have been put into practice by an exclusive German decision. Is this a peculiar German problem? Does not Great Britain, after all, have zero rates of VAT on children's clothes? That is correct, but Britain could not decide this on this matter on its own. It is an exception, granted by all European member states in a unanimous vote, and valid only for a restricted period.

The European integration of VAT

In 1967, the Council decided on the replacement of cumulative multi-stage tax systems, which were in force in the majority of member states, by the common system of value added tax (Directive 67/227/EEC). This was intended to secure competitive neutrality and to guarantee that within each country similar goods bear the same tax burden, whatever the length of the production and distribution chain. First steps towards a harmonization of the bases of assessment were also made in 1967 (Directive 67/228/EEC). However, only the so-called Sixth Directive (77/388/EEC) in 1977 brought a more uniform structure and basis of assessment. The directive defined, for example, which persons are liable to pay tax, clarified the determination of the place where taxable transactions are effected, harmonized the definitions of chargeable events, and drew up a common list of exceptions and deductions.

An old problem concerning VAT came up again with the completion of the single market. As of 1 January 1993, fiscal controls at internal borders were abolished for all transactions between member states. After long debates, the Council, finally acknowledging the demands of the single market, adopted the alignment of VAT rates (Directive 92/77/EEC) and a so-called Transitional VAT System (Directive 91/680/EEC), whereby VAT is charged, as before, at the rate applicable where the buyer resides, that is, in a destination-based system. During a transitional period – which in the meantime has become somewhat permanent – intra-Community transactions were to be taxed in the member state of destination, at the respective member state's rates, and under its conditions. The revenue generated thus went to the country of final consumption.

To minimize the risk of fraud as a consequence of the opening of borders, in 1992 cooperation and mutual assistance measures were agreed upon, and control measures were implemented. The VAT Information Exchange System enabled authorities to monitor and control the flow of intra-Community trade to detect irregularities. In 2003, the regulation was broadened and laid down binding rules for facilitating information exchange and VAT investigations. Though the exact amount of money involved in VAT fraud is difficult to quantify, some member states have estimated their losses at up to 10 percent of net VAT receipts (European Commission 2004, press release IP/04/523).

According to the system in place, the standard VAT rates to be applied are no less than 15 percent and up to 25 percent, with the maximum based on a political commitment. Up to two reduced rates of not less than 5 percent are permitted, but only for certain specified categories of goods and services. The Council may authorize any member state to implement special reduced rates by acting unanimously on a proposal from the Commission.

Constraints on the national governance responsibilities

As it was clear that the harmonization of turnover taxes would lead to substantial changes in member states, there were long and controversial debates in these states concerning the requirements of the directives. In Germany, there was a public dispute that lasted for years. The media coverage was extensive, and several parliamentary hearings were held. In Germany, the dispute quickly revolved around practical problems, while the French newspapers in a fierce debate framed the problem as a loss of national sovereignty. Similar debates took place in the other member states. Most member states – the exception being France – had to change their tax structure in 1967, all of them had to alter their tax base in 1977, and many had to adjust their rates, including Belgium, Greece, Spain, France, Italy and Portugal, which had to abolish their increased rates.

Today, no member state may decide anything on its own concerning VAT apart from the rates within the given range. Exemptions must first be discussed with the Commission, whose explicit position is to minimize member states' reduced rates or zero-rate exceptions, as the new Commissioner Laszlo Kovacs announced (*Frankfurter Allgemeine Zeitung*, 15 February 2005, and 8 November 2005). However, new zero-rate exceptions or increased rates may not be granted to a single member state. To make those exceptions possible, member states, together with the European parliament, must first change European law by acting unanimously on a proposal from the Commission.

To sum up, today, almost no more regulatory responsibility in matters of VAT is left to the nation states. Nearly all regulatory responsibilities have been shifted to the European level by the nation states and, today, the supranational European Commission is setting the regulatory VAT agenda and the intergovernmental Council is unanimously deciding on it. No single nation state can decide anything concerning VAT on its own except for the rate, which, however, must be set within a given range – this leeway may be used by those states that have not yet reached the maximum rate. Operational responsibility in matters concerning VAT is likewise shaped by European law or soft law. The EU's binding guidelines on how to raise taxes and how to collect them in the correct way led to a convergence of the administrative requirements. Former national decisions and requirements are replaced by decisions and requirements set by the Council, the Commission, or teams of experts coming from the national ministries. Although the agencies that put those guidelines into practice are the same as before – in case of VAT, national agencies organized in decentralized units – the staff of different national administrations are by now acting in a similar way, sometimes even using the same forms.

Excise duties

Compared to VAT, the European legal constraints concerning excise duties – indirect taxes on the consumption or the use of certain products, expressed as a monetary amount per quantity of the product – are even more far-reaching, as they affect whole types of taxes. To cite an example, could the German or British parliaments autonomously decide not to tax cigarettes? No? What about creating new taxes? As an isolated, exclusive act, this would likewise not be possible.

European integration of excise duties

The reasons given for the harmonization of excise duties were almost the same as those in the case of VAT: the establishment and functioning of the single market required the free movement of goods, including those subject to excise duties, and this involved the abolition of controls of a fiscal nature at internal borders between member states. European legislation on excise duties was mainly adopted in the context of the establishment of the single market on 1 January 1993. In 1992, a directive (92/12/EEC) prescribed which type of products were subject to the duty, which duties should be repealed, and defined the conditions under which new excise duties could be imposed, namely if they constituted indirect taxes that did not give rise to formalities at the border. Also in 1992, three directives (92/78/EEC; 92/81/EEC; 92/83/EEC) concerning the structure of the taxes (the definition of the product categories), the units on which the excise duty is calculated (e.g.,per hl, per degree alcohol, per 1,000 pieces and so on), and the scope of possible exemptions were applied to three different groups of products: tobacco, mineral oils and alcohol. The minimum rates of the duty were laid down in four additional directives (92/79/EEC; 92/80/EEC; 92/82/EEC; 92/84/EEC). Above those minimum rates, member states were free to set their own rate levels.

To ensure that the tax debt was collected in spite of the opening of the borders in 1992, general arrangements were kept regarding the principle of destination and a so-called system of warehouse keepers (Directive 92/12/EEC) was established. This system of registered warehouses, subject to authorization by the relevant authorities of the member states, replaced the formalities at the borders. The basic principle is that between the warehouses, goods subject to excise duty remain tax-free as long as they are accompanied by a document declaring their movements. In this way, the free movement from the territory of one member state to that of another within the Community should not be impeded by customs checks.

Constraints on national governance responsibilities

The situation concerning excise duties is thus very similar to the VAT. Today there is almost no more national regulatory responsibility in matters of excise duties left. Nearly all regulatory responsibilities have been shifted to the European level by the nation states themselves, apart from the possibilities to decide on tax rates above the minimum rates. And, whole types of taxes cannot be raised any more. Without consulting the supranational Commission, member states are not allowed to introduce new excise duties. Most of the EU member states' operational responsibilities were also shifted to the European level, apart from the fact that taxes are collected by decentralized units of administration.

Member states had similar problems adjusting their national legislation with respect to excise duties as they had with respect to VAT. Even in the 1980s, there was a wide range of about 40 different excise duties within the community – from a tax on bananas in Italy to Germany's tax on salt (Takacs 1998: 447). These variations arose from different national traditions and differences in ecological and health preferences (Clemens and Paulini 1991: 56). National differences in the systems and structures of excise duties were even greater than with turnover taxation. As a consequence of harmonization, member states repealed many of their excise duties.

Indirect taxes that involve border-transit formalities or those similar to European regulated taxes such as VAT, may no longer be raised by the member states. Nevertheless there are smaller excise duties that member states may levy. If, however, a member state wishes to introduce a new excise duty – as Germany did in 2004 with a tax on so-called alco-pops – it has to submit the proposal to the Commission and the other member states, which can veto it if opinions differ on whether the tax will give rise to border-transit formalities or not.

Most of the nation state's former operational responsibilities have also been shifted to the supranational European level. The established system of warehouse keepers implemented by unanimous decisions of the Council, replaced the formalities at the borders and restructured national tax administration in a serious way. Today, all excise duties – regardless of whether they are regulated by European law or not – are raised, administrated and collected in the same way anywhere in Europe, even up to the forms administrative authorities use to calculate taxes. Only the administration units are still formally subordinated to the nation states.

To summarize, no European member state nowadays may make an autonomous decision or act independently in matters concerning existent excise duties or duties they wish to introduce. Most of their regulatory and operational responsibilities have been shifted to the European level. The only scope of action they have retained is, again, to alter tax rates above the minimum rates fixed by Community law – an opportunity which is used by member states to partially redress revenue losses from reduced income tax rates.

Direct taxation on personal and corporate income

Compared to indirect taxes dealt with above, there are less legal constraints on direct taxation, but the consequences of these constraints are increasingly expensive for the member states. Some additional Q&A might help to clarify the problem: would it have been possible for states – for example, the new member states – to have decided *not* to establish an income tax system and nevertheless become members of EU? It is doubtful. But going beyond this level, would it be possible for, say, the German parliament to legally decide to change its global income tax system into a dual tax system, like the Nordic states did,[2] or introduce a flat tax system, like Slovenia? Yes, it would be possible. But could the German parliament vote in an autonomous decision to restrict capital movements by taxing a tax base twice – in the source state as well as in the home state? No, it could not. Could the parliament decide to make capital flight unattractive by improving the status of domestic capital owners *vis-à-vis* foreign capital owners? Again, no. Conversely, could legislators vote to remain or to become a tax haven in order to offer foreign capital better conditions than domestic capital, that is to say maintain a preferential tax regime? Well, yes and no. Yes, because the code of conduct concerning detrimental tax measures is not a legally binding instrument; no, because the European Commission has the opportunity to launch investigations into state aid, as we will see later. Could any parliament in Europe decide to become a tax haven by imposing the lowest tax rates? Yes, this would not be a problem.

European integration of personal and corporate income taxes

In the early days of the European Community, many observers (Schmölders 1953; Vedel 1959; Mersmann 1963) claimed that the national tax structures and fiscal laws of European countries tended to develop in a very similar direction. Wolfgang Mersmann, at the time president of the German

Federal Tax Court (*Bundesfinanzhof*: the German fiscal authority) and participant in the negotiations over the harmonization of the European tax systems, emphasized the positive effects of the discussions at the European level on unilateral income tax reforms in the member states. Today, it is highly questionable whether it would be possible for a state not to introduce taxes on personal and corporate income and still become a member of the Community. In fact, there is no member state in which no income taxes are raised, even if the specific tax structures differ.

Since the founding of the European Communities, company taxation has received particular attention as an important element for the establishment and the completion of the single market, and the Commission has presented several studies (Neumark Report 1962, Tempel Report 1970, Ruding Report 1990), initiatives and proposals. But apart from cooperation in the field of tax collection and mutual assistance between national tax authorities not much happened for several years.

One argument brought forward by the member states to justify this state of affairs was that harmonizing direct taxation was not as urgent as harmonizing indirect taxes on goods and services (Vedel 1959; Hahn 1988; Takacs 1998). It was only the liberalization of the capital market that accompanied the implementation of the single market that has made assets increasingly mobile, and this mobility could be abused to avoid payment of tax. A second reason why the harmonization of direct taxes was not considered as important as the harmonization of indirect taxes was the existence of bilateral double tax treaties, to which member states were obliged by the EC Treaty. The avoidance of double taxation, which is generally defined as 'the imposition of comparable taxes in two or more states on the same taxpayer in respect of the same subject matter and for identical periods' (Vogel 1991: 2) was also seen as an obstacle to the smooth functioning of the common market since the beginning of the Union.

All in all, four factors have nevertheless led to greater harmonization of member states' tax regimes: (1) rules for the avoidance of double taxation were strengthened; (2) the mobility of capital increased as a result of rulings by the European Court of Justice; (3) new measures against harmful tax competition were agreed upon; and (4) new mechanisms of information exchange were introduced. I discuss each issue in turn.

The avoidance of double taxation

While capital controls restricted the international movement of capital up to the 1980s, and as long as transnational tax bases were few in number and fiscally unimportant, the issue of double taxation was not a serious problem, and the number of double tax treaties remained low. By the mid-1950s only about 100 such treaties had been concluded worldwide. Today the total number of treaties is approaching 2000 (Rixen and Rohlfing 2004).

The treaty network began to expand both as a precondition for and a consequence of liberalization. By concluding tax treaties, states agree to restrict their substantive tax law on a reciprocal basis: the contracting states decide which of these shall be bound to withdraw its tax claim, or more illustratively, the states divide tax sources, that is the taxable objects, among them (Vogel 1991: 19).

Beginning with the foundation of the European Communities in the 1960s, the EU member states had an almost complete network of double tax treaties. At the end of 2004, of 300 possible treaties only 32 were not yet signed. Against this background, the European Commission was less concerned with a lack of treaties, but rather with their content. Based on the OECD Model Convention on Income and on Capital, they were – and still are – from the Commission's point of view, not sufficiently far-reaching in relation to the assets of a single market.

With the intention of facing the 'American challenge' (Genschel 2002: 159) posed to the European economy, the Commission planned from the late 1960s to facilitate mergers of companies from different member states. Such mergers should not be hampered by restrictions, disadvantages or distortions arising in particular from the tax provisions of the member states. In order to increase productivity and to improve Europe's competitive strength at the international level, in 1990 the Council adopted the so-called Parent-Subsidiary Directive (90/435/EEC) on the common system of taxation, applicable in the case of parent companies and subsidiaries registered in different member states. The Directive was designed to eliminate tax obstacles to the distribution of profits between groups of companies in the EU by abolishing withholding taxes on payments of dividends and by preventing the double taxation of parent companies on the profits of their subsidiaries. Since 2003, it includes the elimination of double taxation for subsidiaries of subsidiary companies (Directive 2003/123/EC). A further potential for double taxa-tion was also eliminated in 2003 when taxes on interest and royalty payments were abolished in the member state in which they arose in order to ensure that they were subject to tax in one member state only (Directive 2003/49/EC).

Despite these provisions, the Commission is still dissatisfied with the coordination between member states over the avoidance of double tax-ation, and calls for more cooperation concerning cross-border tax problems facing individuals and businesses operating within the single market. In this context, the Commission also refers to rulings by the European Court of Justice (ECJ). Increasingly since the end of the 1990s, different cases have been brought to the Court concerning double tax treaty problems in triangular situations and with regard to third countries.

The European Court of Justice and the Enforcement of the 'Four Freedoms'
Indeed, it is primarily the ECJ which has contributed to the harmonization of the income tax structure since the late 1990s. However, whereas lobby groups of tax consultants celebrate the Court as 'reformer of the year' (Fischer-Zernin 2004: 13), representatives of the fiscal authorities and governments fear that the decisions of the Court will constitute a threat to the member states' tax revenues and national budgets. These two different positions describe at the same time two different consequences of the ECJ case law: the harmonization of member states' income tax structures on the one hand, and their costly effect on national budgets on the other hand, particularly because up to now the judgments are not temporally limited and could be extremely expensive to the nation state in question.

Out of about seventy cases concerning questions of personal and corporate income with potential budgetary consequences for the member states, around sixty date from the past ten years. Although the ECJ consistently held that, in the absence of harmonization, taxes on personal and corporate income fall within the jurisdiction of the member states, it also stated that these must respect the fundamental Treaty principles on the free movement of workers, services, and capital and the freedom of establishment (Articles 39, 43, 49 and 56 of the EC Treaty). In particular, there must not be any direct or indirect discrimination, nor may there be any restrictions to the aforementioned four freedoms.

On the basis of these principles, in most cases the EJC came to the conclusion that national rules stood in opposition to the fundamental freedoms and decided against the member states' national legislation. Although this case law led to a certain harmonization of the member states' tax legislation, it gradually made national measures against capital flight all but impossible.

Measures against harmful tax competition
Of course, the problem of capital flight and tax competition is an older one, but the increasing liberalization of the capital markets, in particular since the mid-1980s, gave rise to a substantial increase in capital flows (Swank 2002: 16). This also triggered a growing public debate about the

negative effects of tax competition and a 'race to the bottom' of tax revenues, thus putting the issue of the detrimental effects of member states' tax practices on other states on the agenda. In 1998, the European Council decided on the establishment of a Code of Conduct for business taxation, to encourage states to roll back the existing tax measures that constituted harmful tax competition and refrain from introducing any such measures in the future. The Code was specifically designed to pinpoint measures that affected the location of business activity in the Community by providing non-residents with a more favourable tax treatment than that which is generally available in the member state concerned, that is with a preferential tax regime. Under the chairmanship of UK Paymaster General Dawn Primarolo, a group of national experts assessed the tax measures that might fall within the scope of the Code. In 1999, the Group named 66 detrimental tax measures: 40 in EU member states, three in Gibraltar and 23 in dependent or associated territories. Apart from Sweden, every member state found itself at least once on the list.

Although the Code is not a legally binding instrument, it can have political force, particularly if the Commission uses its authority to put pressure on the member states by monitoring more intensively their compliance with treaty provisions prohibiting fiscal state aid that 'distorts or threatens to distort competition by favoring certain undertakings' (EC Treaty Art. 87). With reference to these obligations, the Commission decided in 2001 to launch aid investigations under Article 88(2) of the EC Treaty for 11 corporate tax schemes in eight member states. In 2003, the Commission decided that special tax breaks in Belgium, Ireland and the Netherlands constitute state aid and ordered the member states to abolish those tax schemes (European Commission 2001 and 2003, press releases IP/01/982 and IP/03/242).

Nevertheless, when adopting the Code, the Council also acknowledged the positive effects of fair competition. The facilitation of fair and prevention of harmful competition is also the background for current European debates on the harmonization of the corporate tax base. A common consolidated tax base aims to remove tax obstacles that companies face in the single market. The other side of the coin, however, is that a common tax base might increase tax competition among member states.

Information exchange

Another effective method against tax evasion and tax avoidance practices extending across the borders of member states could be mutual assistance, which was made possible in 1977 to complement the existing provisions under bilateral tax treaties concluded between the member states. The directive (77/799/EEC) aimed to improve collaboration between tax authorities within the Community through the exchange of information. But it also gave member states the right to refuse to do so in special cases, for example where this would be in breach of their laws or administrative practices. Meanwhile, the problems associated with the taxation of savings income in the form of interest payments could more or less be solved in 2005: the introduction of a scheme requiring the automatic exchange of information between member states is intended to make effective taxation in the taxpayer's country of residence possible.

Constraints on national governance responsibilities

In the case of direct taxation, there are also by now constraints on national regulatory responsibilities. There are shifts to the European level – both in a formal and de facto sense. The European goal to create a single market and the measures taken in connection with it today structure the member states' direct tax systems. While the national income tax systems still differ, and member states formally have the regulatory responsibility to design their own income tax systems, calls for their convergence are on the increase. National regulatory responsibility is de facto restricted by different aspects of tax competition.

The increasing convergence of European tax systems is driven by competition among member states over mobile capital and investment, which is pushing down corporate tax rates. These cuts not only affect corporate tax revenues, but also, indirectly, personal income tax rates (Ganghof 2006). In any case, the beginnings of a European trend in organizing member states income tax systems are discernable insofar as many European states are considering the levying of a proportional – 'flat' – tax on capital and corporate income, if they have not already introduced such a tax.

In terms of income tax rates, member states still hold their formal regulatory responsibility, but so far they have made only restricted use of their regulatory responsibility by lowering tax rates as a consequence of competition. From a legal point of view, they may also decide to increase tax rates, but in the light of the single market project there is little incentive to do so. During the early 1980s, there was little room for tax competition, as capital was not as mobile. Since the late 1980s, however, member states started to reduce company tax rates, some quite radically. Between 1990 and 2000, the average rate of the ten smallest EU-15 members fell from 41 percent to 33 percent. The large member states' reaction to the new competitive environment was more guarded. The average of the five largest member states fell only slightly from 42 percent in 1990 to

39 percent in 2000 (Ganghof 2006), although this development accelerated in the last five years, for example with regard to Germany.

In fact, concerning tax rates, member states by now acknowledge the alleged positive effects of tax competition which is classified as 'fair'. This reference to fair competition in tax matters is part of the usual phraseology of nearly every European document and Commissioner's speech. This has given rise to a shift in the understanding of 'competition' itself: whereas in the documents until around the 1990s fair competition was understood as the competition among firms or businesses for which the member states ought to establish comparable and favourable terms, today's meaning of competition is related to the member states themselves – they compete with each other for the establishment of businesses or other investment incentives.

With respect to the tax base, there are several formal restrictions on member states' regulatory responsibility. Besides the obligation to conclude bilateral tax treaties, to which the member states responded with an almost complete European network, there were several further measures at the European level. On the one hand, the measures merely redistribute tax revenue among member states, for example by abolishing taxes withheld at source in certain cases. On the other hand, the European member states could not take unilateral measures against the effects of the treaties and the single market, namely tax avoidance and evasion. No single country is allowed to take autonomous measures to preserve its own tax base by, for example, making conditions more favourable for resident taxpayers only.

The improvement of conditions for foreign taxpayers in order to attract foreign mobile capital is legally possible to a certain extent, because the pertinent code of conduct for business taxation is not a binding instrument. The formal restriction on nation states' regulatory responsibility concerning the existent regimes could be made use of by the Commission in furthering the free market project. Beginning with the year 2001, the Commission started to use the Communities' state aid rules to abolish at least some of the preferential regimes.

Since the 1990s, the European Court of Justice has actively restricted the regulatory responsibility of the member states in cases of discrimination and restrictions. Since then citizens and their tax consultants and lawyers have discovered this field in an increasing number of cases for legal action. This lets the European Court of Justice act like a second lawmaker, enforcing the fundamental Treaty principles on the free movement of capital and the freedom of establishment and pressuring national lawmakers to alter national tax law.

One way of preserving national tax revenues in the future would be to extend the practice of automatically exchanging information, which is currently still restricted to interest payments to private individuals. To facilitate the application of this practice, member states to some extent relinquished their national operational responsibility. In all other cases of information exchange, however, existing national rulings – which are de facto applied – for example on confidentiality, may restrict the exchange.

Conclusion

What does all this mean for the transformation of the tax state since its golden age? It means that both links between the tax state and the welfare state of the 1960s and the early 1970s are affected: the social functions within the tax systems and the necessity for tax revenue to guarantee social rights.

First, most European welfare states associated social functions with their tax systems, aiming to organize public redistribution, for example by narrowing income differentials in a more general way through a highly progressive, global income taxation. But today's developments substantially increase income differentials. After all, the European trend to partially redress revenue losses through reduced income tax rates by increasing tax rates on goods, services and excise duties disadvantages people with lower wage incomes and those dependent on social welfare.

Furthermore, tax competition de facto restricts the EU member states' regulatory responsibility on their direct tax system. The tendency to introduce at least a dual income tax system again raises serious equity problems. The higher the tax rate on labour and the lower the tax rate on capital and corporate gains, the more difficult it is to explain why, for example, a worker's income is taxed higher than a rich person's income from speculation on the stock market. Both developments set serious constraints on one basic principle of the tax state of the golden age: they make it almost impossible to find national solutions on how to narrow income differentials through the tax system. This aggravates problems of equity.

Second, the welfare state needs tax revenue to guarantee individual social rights such as a certain minimum income irrespective of the market value of individual aptitudes and abilities, social insurance for those who do not participate in the working society, services in different social welfare areas like health care, universal education and so on (Sandmo 1991). Especially since the 1980s, the demands on the state have grown; slow growth and massive unemployment have put heavy demands on state spending. However, tax revenues have stagnated at best. According to official European data, the total tax take of the average EU state from 1970 up to the year 2002 seemed to hold firm at about 40 percent of the GDP (Genschel 2005: 62). So far there seem to be no signs of a dramatic 'race to the bottom' of member states' tax revenue. But of course those figures remain silent on specific developments in individual member states, where tax revenues may also have declined, such as in Germany as a consequence of various tax reforms over the last few years. In any event, member states' tax revenues today are not sufficient to meet the needs of a welfare state built to guarantee unconditional individual social rights. The question is therefore whether member states may increase their tax revenue by an autonomous act. But this is prevented by the formal and de facto restrictions on the national regulatory responsibility I have outlined in this chapter. In formal terms, states are not permitted to autonomously create new taxes, for instance on capital transactions, jet fuel or tea. And member states are not permitted to reduce or abolish rates for certain goods, which they might wish to do for social reasons, just as they are not permitted to levy increased taxes on luxury goods in order to increase tax revenues.

The de facto restriction, again, results from tax competition. This is, however, not only a problem of a restricted ability, but also a question of volition. The European – or in some cases international – diffusion of neoliberal ideas also in matters of taxation[3] contributes to the problem of insufficient revenue raised from taxes. And there is a causal relationship between the shift in overarching goals that have guided tax policy since the 1980s and the change of methods in harmonizing taxes within the European Union. Since this time, the 'strength of the market' and the competitive powers of the member states were the chosen idea and means of harmonizing tax rates. But this change, in turn, is closely linked to a view of the member states as being sovereign in matters of regulatory and operational responsibilities: only sovereign states in these fields can compete with each other.

The question remains what is to be done about the problem that states have lost much national control over taxation, while the responsibilities for the provision of the normative good of social welfare largely remain nationally organized. It would be a first step to recognize that European member states have to a large extent lost their regulatory and operational responsibilities in tax matters, but that this must not constitute a disaster. The lost responsibilities are shifted to the European level. Things would get worse, however, if national policy makers and citizens still take for granted the national responsibilities and opportunities to decide and act in tax matters and member states continued to compete against each other in tax matters. This would curtail the options for a welfare state reform and make it impossible to further develop the achievements of the golden-age welfare state in striving for greater liberty to participate within civil society and for the guarantee of unconditional individual social rights. Therefore, as European citizens – people of different nationalities, religions, customs, habits and so on and scattered over an immense territory – we should give up on the notion of still having national outcome responsibility. Thinking, and acting as Europeans would be a good start!

Notes

1   I am grateful to Vicki May, Philipp Genschel, Thomas Rixen, Ingo Rohlfing, Dieter Wolf and, of course, the editors of this book, for their comments to earlier drafts of this chapter.
2   In contrast to a global income tax system, in which a single tax is applied to 'global income', to be precise the sum of taxpayers' incomes from all sources, the Nordic Dual Income Taxation system combines a separate proportional – so-called 'flat' – tax rate on income from capital (e.g., interest, dividends, taxable capital gains) and corporate gains, with a progressive tax applied to the taxpayers' total income from other sources (e.g., labour income, private and public pensions).
3   National structures of taxation have not been immune to neoliberalism, as Duane Swank (2003: 2) has shown. Beginning in the early 1980s, policy makers throughout the OECD world have significantly altered the content of tax policies. The relative priority accorded to equity and growth targets, the use of investment and behavioral incentives and the level of tax rates have all changed notably: marginal income and corporate profits tax rates were scaled down, the number of brackets were cut and inflation indexed and so on.

References

Clemens, Reinhard and Monika Paulini (1991) *Harmonisierung der indirekten Steuern im europäischen Binnenmarkt*, Stuttgart: Poeschel.
Fischer-Zernin, Justus (2004) 'Der Europäische Gerichtshof wird Motor der deutschen Steuergesetzgebung', *Frankfurter Allgemeine Zeitung*, 28 December, 13.
Forsthoff, Ernst (1954) 'Begriff und Wesen des sozialen Rechtsstaates', *Veröffentlichungen der Vereinigung der Deutschen Staatsrechtslehrer (VVDStRL)*, 12(8), 30–8.
Ganghof, Steffen (2006) *The Politics of Income Taxation: A Comparative Analysis*, Colchester: ECPR Press.
Genschel, Philipp (2002) *Steuerharmonisierung und Steuerwettbewerb in der Europäischen Union*, Frankfurt a.M.: Campus.
Genschel, Philipp (2005) 'Globalisation and the Transformation of the "Tax State"', *European Review* 13(1), 53–71.

Hahn, Walter (1988) *Steuerpolitische Willensbildungsprozesse in der Europäischen Gemeinschaft: Das Beispiel der Umsatzsteuerharmonisierung*, Frankfurt a.M.: Peter Lang.

Leibfried, Stephan and Michael Zürn, eds (2005) *Transformations of the State?*, Cambridge: Cambridge University Press.

Mersmann, Wolfgang (1963) Das künftige EWG-Steuerrecht, *Deutsche Steuer-Zeitung* 51(18), 293–6.

Mette, Stefan (1994) *Europäischer Binnenmarkt und Mehrwertsteuerharmonisierung: Entscheidungsprozesse in der Europäischen Gemeinschaft*, Baden-Baden: Nomos.

Radaelli, Claudio M. (1995) 'Corporate Direct Taxation in the European Union: Explaining the Policy Process', *Journal of Public Policy* 15(2), 153–81.

Randzio-Plath, Christa (1999) Steuerpolitik in der Union: Keine Reklame für den Binnenmarkt, *Wirtschaftsdienst* 79(11), 665–70.

Rixen, Thomas and Ingo Rohlfing (2004) 'Bilateralism and Multilateralism: Institutional Choice in International Cooperation', paper presented at 'American Political Science Association Meeting', Chicago, 3–7 September.

Sandmo, Agnar (1991) 'Economists and the Welfare State', *European Economic Review* 35(4), 213–39.

Scharpf, Fritz W. (1999) *Governing in Europe: Effective and Democratic?*, Oxford: Oxford University Press.

Schmölders, Günter (1953) 'Die Angleichung der Europäischen Steuersysteme', *Public Finance* 8(2), 243–54.

Swank, Duane (2002) *Global Capital, Political Institutions, and Policy Change in Developed Welfare States*, Cambridge: Cambridge University Press.

Swank, Duane (2003) 'Tax Policy in an Era of Internationalization: An Assessment of a Conditional Diffusion Model of the Spread of Neoliberalism', paper presented at the Conference 'International Diffusion of Political and Economic Liberalization', Harvard University, 3–4 October.

Takacs, Peter (1998) *Das Steuerrecht der Europäischen Union unter besonderer Berücksichtigung der Regelungen Österreichs und Deutschlands*, Wien: Ueberreuter.

Tsoukalis, Loukas (2005) *What Kind of Europe?*, Oxford: Oxford University Press.

Vedel, George (1959) 'Die steuerlichen Gesichtspunkte des Gemeinsamen Marktes', *Steuer und Wirtschaft* 36(1), 530–44.

Vogel, Klaus (1991) *On Double Taxation Conventions: A Commentary to the OECD-, UN- and US Model Conventions for the Avoidance of Double Taxation of Income and Capital*, Deventer: Kluwer Law and Taxation Publishers.

3
Internationalization of Intervention? UN and EU Security Politics and the Modern State

Sebastian Mayer and Silke Weinlich

Since the early 1990s, international security organizations such as the United Nations (UN), the North Atlantic Treaty Organization (NATO) and, more recently, the European Union (EU), have undertaken numerous military operations in order to protect human rights, to prevent civil wars or the collapse of states, to end domestic conflicts or to prevent their re-emergence. Prominent examples include international involvement in Bosnia, Kosovo and Afghanistan. Often these operations were paralleled with or followed by civilian efforts such as the provision of humanitarian aid or socioeconomic and political assistance in order to (re-)establish state structures.

Scholars have analysed the consequences of these interventions for target states, often aiming to explore the conditions for their success and failure (Cousens and Kumar 2001; Sriram and Wermester 2003; Schneckener 2005). Other authors have been interested in the erosive effects of interventions on the norm of sovereignty as well as the normative implications of humanitarian interventions (Holzgrefe and Keohane 2003; Mayer 2005). But, so far, the consequences of multilateral interventions for the interveners themselves have been neglected. In this chapter, we explore some of these effects by paying attention to how the preparation, decision making and implementation of interventions at the international level affects the provision of the normative good of security in Western countries and thus may effect change in the resource dimension of the modern state.

Historically, the genesis of modern statehood was closely interwoven with the emergence of a state monopoly of force that has since become a constitutive principle of the Westphalian state (Tilly 1985; Elias 2000). In the golden age of modern statehood, the state was in sole possession of the legitimate right to use force. Internally, represented by its executive agencies such as police and judiciary, it governed the relations among citizens as well as between citizens and the state while the citizens in turn refrained from the individual use of violence. Externally, the state commanded a national army and possessed the legitimate power, lightly fenced in by international law, to use physical force against other states. It is through the establishment of the monopoly of the legitimate use of physical force that more complex forms of social interactions became possible (Jachtenfuchs 2005). The link between the legitimacy and authority of a state and the production of security for its citizens can be considered fundamental to the modern nation state. Any significant changes in this link – for example an internationalization of (dimensions of) security politics – are thus bound to have severe consequences concerning the nature of modern statehood.

Since the end of the cold war, *interventions*, understood here as military and non-military measures taken with the intention to interfere with the internal affairs of a country for the explicit purpose of preventing, resolving and managing conflict, have become an important component of national security politics. Most have taken place within the framework of international organizations. Does this mean that international organizations have taken over state-like responsibilities concerning intervention politics? Has there been a partial or even complete shift of statehood to the international level? Or do developments at the international level go hand in hand with developments at the national level indicating a mere diffusion of statehood? In the following section, we specify what we mean by 'internationalization of intervention policies' and develop analytical tools that permit us to assess the scope and the consequences of these transformations on the resources dimension of the state. Then, the evolution of two specific security organizations with regard to interventions are scrutinized. The focus is on the UN and the EU, as both have become particularly active in a wide range of operations. Furthermore, looking at organizations that vary at a number of levels – membership, structure, competences, financial resources – might reveal a more general trend with regard to the scope and shape of an ongoing internationalization of intervention politics and its consequences for the modern state.

Internationalization of intervention politics

Although military interventions are by no means a novel phenomenon, their scope, aims and strategies as well as the number of actors involved have changed profoundly since the early 1990s (Czempiel 1994; Crocker 2001).

Traditionally, states, by and large, had undertaken interventions to preserve their vital interests, to widen their national spheres of influence and to expand their territory. While material or geo-strategic considerations still play a role, Western interveners nowadays in addition perceive their non-military security to be threatened by external conflicts, and they respond to morally motivated demands to prevent human suffering abroad. Geographical distance no longer provides adequate protection against new threats emerging from transnational terrorism, collapsed states, or organized crime (Zangl and Zürn 2003). Intensified by the 9/11 terrorist attacks, a stated objective of Western security politics lies in the strengthening of democratic state structures, the pacification of global trouble spots and if necessary, the (re)construction of fragile, conflict-torn states. To cope with the multidimensional challenges of such ambitious peacebuilding objectives, the toolbox interveners draw on exceeds military means and requires cooperation with a multitude of actors.

Strikingly, interventions have been increasingly conducted within the framework of international organizations. While there is surely no comprehensive trend towards a supranationalization of security politics that would lead towards the establishment of a world monopoly of force (Senghaas 2007), we find indications of an increase in responsibilities at the international level. Different aspects of intervention politics – planning, decision-making procedures, resources, decision-making authority and implementation – are either deliberately transferred from the national level to the international level or simply taken over by international organizations, a phenomenon we refer to as 'internationalization', with 'Europeanization' as a special case. Similar processes have been identified in a multitude of policy fields, but for a long time, security politics seemed to be the last bulwark of the Westphalian state: the production of the normative good of security constitutes the core of state sovereignty, and states have traditionally been reluctant to formally grant international organizations any powers in this respect (Reinalda and Verbeek 2004). However, a range of scholars describe transformations in the field of security such as emerging fragmented and multilayered governance structures (Rosenau and Czempiel 1992; Webber *et al.* 2004), or point out the strengthening of international norms governing interventions (Zangl and Zürn 2003; Jachtenfuchs 2005).

How can we assess the scope and the consequences of the alleged internationalization of intervention politics? Neither all forms of internationalization nor all changes in, or expansions of, the functions and capacities of international organizations automatically affect the nation state and its role in the provision of security. As spelled out in the introductory chapter of this volume, it is analytically helpful to distinguish between different dimensions of state responsibility for the provision of normative goods. In its golden age, the modern nation state came close to bearing all three dimensions of responsibility. In the realm of security politics, this means that its operational responsibility was ensured by having national agencies such as police and the armed forces taking care of national security. The decision when, where and how to intervene by force was taken in national decision-making arenas and guided by the national interest, taking place mostly insulated from international considerations or pressure, thus granting the state regulatory responsibility. The overall outcome responsibility for guaranteeing the security of its citizens and for the success or failure of military operations clearly lay with the nation state.

We use these different dimensions of responsibilities in order to get an adequate and sufficiently fine-grained picture of the internationalization of intervention politics. To pin down changes with regard to operational responsibility we use two indicators. First, we analyse whether international organizations have taken over *new tasks* that were formerly accomplished by state actors or did not exist. Second, we examine whether international organizations have obtained *new resources*, such as money, personnel or administrative capacities, over which they exert at least some discretionary power. With regard to regulatory responsibility, we analyse whether international organizations have acquired greater *legal competences* concerning the preparation and/or decision making of interventions. Second, we explore whether international organizations have gained *informal competences*, especially by being more involved in agenda-setting processes or decision-making procedures using informal means of influence – such as persuasion, peer pressure, or shaming – regardless of formal changes in their mandates. We focus on these two levels of responsibility, because there are no signs that international organizations are about to take over (outcome) responsibility for guaranteeing the provision of security for Western societies.

Furthermore, in order to get a more precise picture of any shift or diffusion of responsibilities, we distinguish between the intergovernmental and supranational elements of an international organization. Following Moravcsik (1998: 67), we understand supranational bodies characteristically to be 'permitted to take certain autonomous decisions, without an intervening interstate vote or unilateral veto'; moreover, they are mostly composed of international civil servants. In contrast, intergovernmental bodies are those elements of an international organization that are mostly made up of government officials, having unanimity as voting procedure. Arguably, an increase in the responsibilities of supranational bodies (such as the Secretary-General and the UN Secretariat and the European Commission) indicates a more extensive internationalization process than a sole increase in the responsibilities of intergovernmental bodies (such as the UN Security Council, the General Assembly, or the European Council). Because supranational bodies are more remote from direct control of states and develop organizational dynamics, interests and influence of their own (Barnett and Finnemore 2004; Liese and Weinlich 2006), the expected consequences for states would be more substantial.

Intervention politics of the United Nations

The United Nations possesses a broad and unique mandate for all forms of intervention (Ziring *et al.* 2005). Taken together with its specialized agencies, funds and programmes, the UN also has a worldwide presence and possesses some of the operational capacities that are conducive to the implementation of multidimensional interventions combining civil and military aspects. At the same time, the questions if, when and how to intervene have been highly controversial within the organization. Some members of the non-aligned movement remain critical if not opposed. They fear that interventions – whether military or civilian – present a new form of Western colonialism camouflaged by humanitarian language, and they are apprehensive of any expansion of the UN's security agenda which they perceive to occur at the expense of its economic and social tasks (Thakur 2004). Western states, in contrast, have actively but selectively promoted UN interventions, although they are anxious to keep costs low and avoid contributing troops at a bigger scale. Especially, the permanent five members of the Security Council remain cautious not to establish an intervention automatism. Yet disagreement seems to have decreased over time: in the world summit's final declaration in 2005, all member states acknowledged their collective obligation to prevent or stop wide-spread human suffering where a state does not live up to its responsibility to protect its population.

The most important intergovernmental bodies dealing with military intervention policies are the 15-member Security Council and, mostly because of its budgeting authority, the General Assembly. Due to the veto power of the five permanent members and its anachronistic regional composition, Western interests strongly influence Security Council decision making. In the General Assembly, by contrast, each of the presently 192 member states has one vote, granting the majority of countries from the developing world a greater say. Yet most decisions, including budgetary decisions, are customarily taken by consensus, thus giving major donor countries a de facto veto (Peterson 2006). The supranational body of the organization – the UN Secretariat and its executive head, the Secretary-General – implement decisions taken by the intergovernmental bodies, or act upon the request of member states. The supranational body also possesses a proper, albeit vague, mandate for autonomous activities concerning questions of peace and security (Gordenker 2005). The various Secretaries-General have used this room of maneuver with different degrees of assertiveness (Newman 1998). Wary of a too independent Secretariat, member states have always sought to set limits to the expansion of the Secretary-General's political role (James 1993).

Notwithstanding the Charter's provisions for coercive interventions, the UN's intervention record – military and other – during the cold war was not very substantial. Security problems from 1945 to 1990 differed fundamentally from the challenges of the post-cold war world. Apart from decolonization struggles, the majority of conflicts took place *between* states, and the foremost aim of all UN intervention efforts was to avoid an escalation of any conflict into a nuclear war between the two superpowers. Moreover, the superpower antagonism mostly paralysed the Security Council, and the norm of non-intervention provided protection from unsolicited interference. Military interventions were explicitly authorized only twice, in Korea and, on a more limited scale, in Congo. On the whole, the system of collective security as envisaged in the Charter did not work; the more so as provisions for a military staff committee to advise the Security Council as well as for permanently available forces were never turned into reality. To come to terms with the system's malfunctioning, the instrument of peacekeeping was invented and repeatedly employed, mostly for monitoring borders or compliance with ceasefires.[1] Between 1945 and 1988, the intergovernmental bodies sent no more than 14 operations to various conflict areas.

With the thawing of the cold war at the end of the 1980s, and paralleled by a relative rise in the frequency and brutality of conflicts within states, the UN quickly became a key intervention actor. The organization was entrusted with a multitude of new tasks that went well beyond its cold war activities in a quantitative as well as qualitative manner. Peacekeeping operations were tried out as remedy for all sorts of internal conflicts but soon proved to be no panacea, especially when underfinanced, understaffed, and lacking in political support from major players. While all UN military action is authorized by the Security Council, interventions differ with regard to the implementing actor and the scope of the mandate. Enforcement operations and robust peace operations are mandated under Chapter VII UN Charter, while more traditional peace operations are based on Chapter VI mandates that limit the use of force – at least in theory – to self-defence. Between 1989 and 2006, the Security Council authorized roughly 20 times other actors, namely states, coalitions, or regional organizations, to use force – some only *ex post facto*.[2] Since the end of the 1990s, hybrid missions become more common and in which UN troops serve before, alongside, or after state coalitions or regional actors that often are prepared to use force on a bigger scale (Jones 2003; Pugh and Sidhu 2003).

Altogether on 14 occasions since 1989, the Security Council mandated UN peace operations under Chapter VII, enabling the missions to fulfil (parts of) their mandate by force, if necessary.[3] Only twice, in Somalia and in Bosnia-Herzegovina, peace operations under UN command engaged in peace enforcement activities. Most of the other Chapter VII missions are thus robust operations, their mandate paying tribute to difficult circumstances arising from fragile ceasefires, continuing violence, or the collapse of state institutions.[4] Between 1989 and October 2006, 33 peace operations were authorized under Chapter VI, making it a total of 61 peace operations under UN command since the organization's founding. Some of them experienced mission creep or were later 'upgraded' to Chapter VII missions, and nearly all of the newer missions also engaged in peace building activities (Sens 2004). Despite the periodically resurfacing debate about the UN's irrelevance, its activities in the realm of peacekeeping and peace building remain in great demand. In autumn 2006, they have reached yet another peak with regards to the number of parallel missions and the personnel serving under UN command.

Beginning in 1988, the Security Council and the General Assembly, as well as the Secretary-General and the UN Secretariat have clearly been more active with regards to military interventions than ever before. In consequence, the related resources have skyrocketed in the 1990s. The financial resources spent on peacekeeping continue to make up the biggest part of the organization's financial expenses and have been exceeding its regular budget. Between 1991 and 2006, peacekeeping expenditures amounted to roughly US $35,556 billion, which is about eight times as much as the expenditures spent in the first 44 years of the organization, where the total came to about. US $4640 billion.[5] A similar increase can be observed for UN staff dealing with peace operations. During the cold war, a mere handful of people close to the Secretary-General were in charge of peacekeeping and peacemaking activities (Goulding 2003). Today, more than 550 officials in the Department of Peacekeeping

Operations (DPKO) in UN Headquarters are responsible for 72,561 uniformed personnel – troops, police and military observers – and 15,394 civilians deployed or working in 16 peacekeeping operations worldwide.[6] The increase in peacekeeping personnel is even more significant when compared to the overall decline in the number of UN headquarter staff (Ziring *et al.* 2005: 70). DPKO also professionalized in terms of personnel and organizational structure that now comprises a 24/7 Situation Room, a Best Practices Unit, a Mine Action Service and a Police Division. While during 1992–97, many officials had been seconded by member states, it is now mostly staffed by UN Officials (Durch *et al.* 2003).

Particularly the Security Council and the supranational actors – Secretary-General and Secretariat – have gained competences in the area of military intervention, thus taking over responsibilities that formerly resided in the nation state. The Security Council has autonomously enlarged its competences without a formal UN Charter revision, interpreting its legal foundations to include the responsibility for non-military threats and intra-state war (Wallensteen and Johansson 2004). When the Council authorizes state coalitions or regional organizations to implement military interventions, the UN itself has no operational role and does not bear any financial burden, although the intervening actors are obliged to report to the Council on the action taken. Given the growth in such non-UN missions, the Security Council has gained here some weak form of regulatory responsibility, but no operational or outcome responsibility. With regards to UN missions, the Security Council has attained more substantial responsibilities: on the basis of recommendations by the Secretariat, the Council sets the parameters for the UN's involvement, determining the level of troops, police and other personnel, outlining the goals of an intervention, possibly defining time lines and specific tasks. In addition, it is responsible for the political guidance of an operation. It thus holds regulatory responsibility that might not fundamentally differ from the one the Council had over earlier missions, but that nevertheless has reached a new quality because of the frequency and the depth of the post-cold war interventions. However, the Council's responsibilities are constrained because it neither has funds nor troops at its disposal; it relies on the General Assembly and voluntary troop contributors. The General Assembly's fifth committee is responsible for the release of funding on the basis of a budget plan prepared by the Secretariat. Although the General Assembly cannot completely withhold the financing of an operation, it can and has introduced financial cuts with sometimes severe consequences – UN peace operations have generally not been generously or even adequately equipped for their often highly ambitious mandates. To further add to the complexity, many member states – most notably the USA – do not pay their obligatory annual contributions to the regular budget or the peacekeeping support account unconditionally, on time, and to the full amount (Hüfner 2003). Troops and other personnel are supplied by member states on a case-by-case basis. To facilitate force generation, a system of stand-by troops has been introduced in the mid-1990s, but each contributor still has a final say whether to contribute at all, on which scale, and with which components. Since the mid-1990s, the top troops contributing countries are in the South (Centre on International Cooperation 2006).

The Secretary-General and Secretariat have gained new competences because the Security Council, on a case-by-case basis, has entrusted them with the planning, preparation, launching and management of multi-dimensional UN Operations, including the generation of troops and other personnel necessary for an intervention (Durch 1993a; Shimura 2001). With the exception of the operation in Congo in the 1960s, the Secretariat's peacekeeping activities prior to 1988 were similar, but far less comprehensive: they were less intrusive, less missions were managed in parallel, there were less personnel in the field. Yet, the UN Charter still does not mention peacekeeping, and the Secretariat has still not obtained a more general mandate for peace operations. But the supranational body has won substantial operational responsibility that no one would have ever foreseen at the founding of the organization, above all in East Timor and Kosovo, where the UN de facto took over government functions (Chesterman 2004). Peace enforcement under UN command remains an exception and has not been repeated after the failures of the mid-1990s. Despite these substantial gains, crucial limitations to the Secretariat's operational responsibility persist: in the field, the total dependency for finances and troops, the reliance on political support by key states, the general shortage of resources, as well as command and control problems over participating troops have presented severe impediments (United Nations 2000).[7] Moreover, in UN headquarters, scarcest (human) resources, high time pressure and a severe lack of planning and analysis capabilities, originating, *inter alia*, in member states' aversion against too strong a secretariat, hamper the supranational actor's capacity to meet its operational responsibility (Findley 2002: 342–5; Durch *et al.* 2003). Further limits to the responsibility of the supranational actor are set by tight administrative control, rules and procedures that, despite some improvements, are still based on the conception of peacekeeping as a temporary emergency phenomenon, detailed scrutiny by the intergovernmental organs, and last but not least, political inference by states (Salomons and Dijkzeul 2001).

In sum, after the end of the cold war, there has been a significant expansion of the tasks and related resources with regards to military interventions undertaken by the UN. Despite failures and repeated criticisms of the organization, the Security Council has developed into the primary global framework for decision making on international peace-keeping and military action. This does not preclude that several military interventions take place outside the UN Framework. The Council has gained a weak form of regulatory responsibility over military interventions by states, coalitions of the willing or regional organizations, and more substantial responsibilities concerning UN operations. Although there is no single state worldwide in possession of regulatory responsibilities comparable to those of the Security Council, the Council's responsibilities, due to lack of provision with troops and adequate financial resources, remain fragmented and dependent on UN member states. In a similar way, the UN Secretariat, having gained wide-ranging operational responsibility in a high number of peace operations worldwide, bears constraints on its autonomy that in turn limit the scope of its responsibilities. Taken together, there is no evidence for a shift of responsibilities to the United Nations Organization, whereby the UN would have become responsible for providing citizens of Western countries with security. Instead, there are indications for a diffusion of responsibilities: supranational and intergovernmental bodies share responsibilities with state actors and other international organizations.

Intervention politics of the European Union

Efforts by a number of EC members in the 1950s to establish a European Defence Community – a joint European army – eventually failed due to a veto of the French *Assemblée Nationale*. In 1970, EC members concluded an agreement on European Political Cooperation (EPC), which implied increased coordination, yet within strictly intergovernmental confines outside the EC procedures. The result was closer cooperation among governments in vital foreign policy issues, which permitted the adoption of common positions towards Africa, the Arab–Israeli conflict and at the negotiations within the Conference for Security and Cooperation in Europe. Yet, security and defence had been entirely excluded from the EPC. Duchêne (1972) therefore depicted the EC polity, with its powerful institutional provisions in trade and economics but comparatively weak political and non-existing security structures, as a 'civilian power' in international relations. Among scholars of European integration, the notion was widespread that 'high politics' – foreign affairs, security and defence – was virtually immune from integrative impulses (Hoffmann 1966).

Against the background of the alleged erosion of American global economic hegemony since the early 1970s, the renewal of cold war hostilities in the late 1970s and suspicions about the credibility of the American security guarantee for Western Europe, the German and Italian Foreign Ministers in 1981 unsuccessfully tried to extend the EPC by introducing a security component and integrating the reformed mechanism into the EC Treaty. Even after receiving a formal institutional basis in 1987 within the Single European Act, the EPC rules remained vague and cooperation was confined to the issuance of political statements without binding commitments. Security and defence coordination was still entirely excluded from the EC.

Only in the 1990s did a Common Foreign and Security Policy (CFSP) and a European Security and Defence Policy (ESDP) materialize, which incorporated these policy fields into the European integration process. This institutionalization was prompted by the member states' confrontation with the problem of violent conflicts and crises at their periphery, and against the background of an American disengagement in Europe. After the CFSP had been established in November 1993 by the entry into force of the Maastricht Treaty, conflict prevention increasingly became an established item on the EU agenda. Later, the Amsterdam Treaty in 1999 introduced the ESDP within the CFSP framework and integrated the 'Petersberg Tasks' into the EU's scope of functions.[8] Since 2003 the Union has carried out several military as well as civilian operations, among others in Macedonia, Congo and Bosnia. In general, their purpose is to prevent the escalation of tensions and to contribute to a safe and secure environment in the area of deployment. In total, by the end of 2006, the EU has completed or is still conducting four military and 13 civilian ESDP missions.

A number of permanent military and political bodies have been established to conduct the operations, some of them with a hybrid intergovernmental/supranational character. The EU Military Committee, staffed with national military personnel, advises the Political and Security Committee (PSC), de facto the highest ranking intergovernmental CFSP decision-making body.[9] It also directs the work of the EU Military Staff, a permanent integrated military structure which provides military expertise and support to the ESDP, including the planning of EU-led military operations. The Military Staff implements decisions as directed by the Military Committee and thus performs important tasks for the provision of security. Although no troops are subordinated to it, the Military Staff earmarks European national and multinational forces and develops suitable strategies, whereas the national governments have to agree on the ultimate deployment of their forces. In order to meet its obligations, the Military Staff had been provided with several vital resources, such as an early warning unit, a logistics division, a civil-military cell, or an intelligence unit, which member states are expected to feed with information from their national services. Despite reporting to and standing under the military direction of the intergovernmental Military Committee, the Military Staff has the status of a General Directorate within the Council General Secretariat, provides the High Representative for the CFSP with military expertise and stands directly under his ambit on a day-to-day basis. Accordingly, in addition to a modest form of internationalization through the creation of intergovernmental bodies at the EU level, there are more extensive internationalization tendencies through the instigation of permanent military and defense related structures within the Council Secretariat General.

The High Representative (currently Javier Solana) contributes to the formulation, preparation and implementation of decisions agreed upon at the Council level, and acts on behalf of the Council in conducting political dialogues with third parties. Yet, he and his political cabinet are not easily assigned to either the intergovernmental or to the supranational level of decision making within the EU. On the one hand, they formally assist the Council and Council Presidency. On the other hand, the competences of the High Representative and the resources which he directly controls are significant. Indeed, they have increased since Solana's appointment in 1999 and make for a considerable degree of autonomy of the incumbent from direct Council control. Accordingly, Lewis (2003: 1005) refers to an 'independent, supranational influence of the Secretary-General's office'.

The High Representative participates in Council meetings on a regular basis and even chairs the PSC when it meets with the NATO Council. Also, he is able to informally pre-structure the Council mandates given to his Special or Personal Representatives. Their number increased from two in 1996[10] to 12 in 2006. Hence, the Council General Secretariat has been expanded and meanwhile split into an 'old Secretariat', responsible for rather legalistic and rule-centred tasks, and a 'new Secretariat' which conducts diplomatic activities and disposes of some degree of autonomy from the intergovernmental committees, such as the PSC or the Military Committee (Christiansen 2001: 756–8). For the latter, the units in the 'new Secretariat' have become indispensable information and implementation resources. Again, these units are not supranational, but neither do they follow a strictly intergovernmental logic.

There are a number of functions building the basis for modest and merely informal Commission competences. Although the Commission has been 'fully associated' with the work of the PSC since the Treaty of Amsterdam, legal decisions on the formulation of the military operations are taken entirely by the member states or the intergovernmental committees, backed by the Council General Secretariat's resources. The Commission may send its representatives to the PSC and similar bodies, but it does not have a vote there. It may, however, refer questions and submit proposals to the Council relating to CFSP issues, ask the Council Presidency to convene extraordinary Council meetings, or make suggestions to the Policy Planning and Early Warning Unit, the Council General Secretariat's strategic forward planning division. These functions indicate a sharing of regulatory responsibility, which aggravated fears of a 'supranational contamination' on the part of the Council (Stewart 2003: 24).

This concern also arises from the Council's shortage in implementation resources and from functional linkages between the EC and EU treaty. Whereas the Council may single-handedly adopt regulations for Joint Actions,[11] a critical CFSP tool, their implementation heavily relies on the supranational Commission, as the latter is responsible for their budgetary execution and implementation (Müller-Brandeck-Bocquet 2002: 19).[12] For that reason, Joint Actions are frequently dependent on resources and policy instruments from the first pillar, whereas crucial decisions are often taken in the intergovernmental CFSP structure (Winn and Lord 2001: 176). This leads to what has been referred to as 'cross-pillarization': an emerging setting that connects the first and the second pillar of the EU treaty due to pressures stemming from functional indivisibilities (Gourlay 2004; Stetter 2004). As a consequence, intergovernmental and supranational decision making become increasingly intersected. While the intergovernmental bodies largely retain their regulatory responsibility, first pillar structures assure their proper implementation and thereby take over important operational responsibilities.

It is important to note, however, that only civilian operations can be funded from the EC budget, whereas out of legal necessity, member states are directly charged with the costs of operations with military or defence implications.[13] The common costs of the latter, such as for an EU headquarters, infrastructure, or medical support, are covered by ATHENA, a time-saving, permanent financial mechanism working on behalf of the participating states, which calculates their expected contributions on a GDP-based key. The mechanism works outside the Community budget and thus circumvents the rigid Commission procedures. ATHENA is also not subject to direct parliamentary control. For the basic support of their own forces in the field, participants pay individually according to the 'costs lie where they fall' principle (Henry L. Stimson Centre 2004). The ATHENA scheme as well as national funding assure that the financing of military operations does not become 'infected' with Community procedures, and prevents a subsequent increase in operational or even regulatory competences by the EU's supranational actors.

Notwithstanding the limits to Community influence in military and defence, there is an increasing integration and coordination of military and civilian dimensions of operations due to the multidimensionality of challenges, the abundance of instruments and the multiplicity of responsibilities. This gives the Commission an indirect influence on military operations. A large number of tools have been created, following multiple logics which are not always well matched. In consequence, Crisis Response Coordination teams have been established, composed of Commission and Council General Secretariat representatives. They are supposed to enhance coherence between military and civilian tasks of both bodies. The teams, which convene only in crisis situations, are charged with drawing up Crisis Management Concepts,[14] ultimately to be approved by the Council. Hence, the teams have some operational responsibilities. Also, Security Sector Reform (SSR), covering a wide range of topics, including small arms, armed non-state actors or civilian–military relations, and an avowed major EU objective within the ESDP, encompasses competencies of both the Commission and Council. Therefore, the underlying strategic concepts for SSR have been developed in close consultation between the two institutions (Nowak 2006: 32).

There are several signs for an interlocking of operational responsibilities. The European Council set the goal of establishing a military Rapid Reaction Force for crisis management, comprising 60,000 troops, ready for deployment within 30 days and sustainable for one year. The forces do not represent a standing army, but a database of national force contributions. An additional Headline Goal focuses on the establishment of 'battle groups',[15] working in a similar fashion. These and other capabilities are managed by the EU itself, particularly the Military Staff, as well as by its member states. In addition, the EU is in the process of establishing a 'European Defence Agency' for the development of defence capabilities, research, acquisition and armaments.

Taken together, substantial resources in the area of military action have been established from scratch, and there has been a substantial increase in intervention tasks assigned to the EU from the late 1990s onwards. CFSP and ESDP received functional bodies performing a number of state-like responsibilities. Within military and defence politics, regulatory responsibilities – formal decision-making structures – remain entirely within the intergovernmental realm of the EU, and therefore point only to a small degree of internationalization. However, the preparation of legislative proposals, and particularly their implementation depends – fully or partially – on EU structures of either a supranational (Commission) or a hybrid character (Council General Secretariat), which implies a higher degree of internationalization. It also indicates a diffusion of 'statehood' particularly on the operational level of responsibility. This is due to formal linkages as well as to the multidimensionality of the security challenges, which require both civilian and military strategies.

Conclusions

Taking the UN and the EU as case studies, the aim of this chapter was to ascertain the scope of the internationalization of intervention politics and to assess its consequences for the modern state. Despite fundamental differences of the analysed international organizations in terms of membership, structure, competences and finances, we found a number of striking similarities that suggest a general trend towards an internationalization of intervention politics.

Both the UN and the EU have undergone significant changes after the end of the cold war in order to accommodate the emergence of multilateral intervention politics. They have gained significant additional resources for their new tasks, although especially in the case of the United Nations, many times the financial and other means did not come forward timely and did not match the ambitious objectives of interventions. Also, the resources typically were not at the free disposal of the organization but subject to tight intergovernmental control, including the possibility to withhold them altogether. Moreover, neither organization has been provided with standby troops or a general intervention budget, but instead ultimately rely on member states. The intergovernmental bodies of both the UN and the EU clearly have gained competences with regard to military interventions and acquired regulatory responsibilities that they exercise jointly with member states and the supranational actors. The UN Security Council has availed itself with the responsibility for non-military and non-state threats to peace, and, despite certain setbacks, has strengthened its unique authority to legitimize military action, which it increasingly uses also for authorizing state coalitions or regional organizations. Likewise, the European Council has begun to claim responsibility for interventions and has created functional bodies staffed with military and civilian experts able to provide guidance to EU operations.

In a similar manner, the supranational bodies of both organizations now are better equipped for interventions and possess more responsibilities than before 1989, mostly in the operational dimension.

We also observed differences that, among other things, are especially revealing concerning an emerging international configuration: the legal and institutional development of the EU in the realm of defence and intervention policy has taken place at an impressive speed and accelerated considerably at the beginning of the 21st century when the military developments within the UN had been stagnating for some years. While the EU started conducting military interventions no sooner than at the end of the 1990s after legal and institutional changes, the UN had begun to intensify its military activities a decade earlier. Building on former peacekeeping experiences, elementary institutional structures within the Secretariat, and the UN Charter as legal basis, the UN pioneered multidimensional peacekeeping, peace enforcement and peace building efforts. In the mid-1990s it became clear that the UN was ill-suited for peace enforcement activities. From then, the use of force in operations under UN command has been limited. Although the EU so far has not carried out any 'real' war fighting intervention, in some of its operations it displays a greater military muscle than what states typically make available to the UN. The EU, moreover, becomes engaged in areas that are close to its border or are otherwise important to national security perceptions of member states, whereas the UN's centre of activity lies in Africa where, until now, Western interests have been less articulate.

Interestingly, there are reasons to suspect that the informal influence of the supranational body in the UN might here be higher than that of the EU. The supranational EU Commission, so powerful in other issue areas, has mostly gained informal influence, much of it due to the interconnectedness of civil and military means of intervention. So far, it bears no proper regulatory or operational responsibility concerning military interventions. The UN Secretariat however is very active with regard to peace operations. Moreover, despite the detailed supervision and scrutiny from the UN intergovernmental bodies concerning secretariat activities, national military expertise is not present to the same extent in New York as it is in Brussels. At the same time, the UN secretariat is subject to bigger constraints than the EU General Secretariat. They stem from the heterogeneous membership of the organization, the institutionalized preponderance of some of its members, especially the United States, and a general unwillingness to equip the organization with meaningful resources and to entrust it with more autonomously exerted responsibility.

Not surprisingly, there are clear limits to the internationalization of intervention politics. In both organizations, Western states on the one hand have acted as initiators of the internationalization, delegating new tasks to the respective organization. On the other hand, national resistance against losing regulatory responsibility, and to a more limited degree operational responsibility, remains strong. This can be observed on a larger scale in the UN case, where most Western countries even have discontinued contributing troops to peace operations under UN command. But it is also obvious in the EU case, in which, despite a stronger commitment to the organization on the part of the member states, the troops and financial means necessary for an intervention are generated outside of community structures.

While we cannot observe any tendencies towards a shift of responsibilities for the provision of national security to the international level, the changes observed do constitute a significant transformation, which is best described as an interlocked diffusion of responsibilities: intergovernmental bodies take decisions that do not substitute for national decision making on national security, but merely supplement them, and supranational bodies gain some operational responsibility that they can only execute with the support of national governments. At the same time, the responsibilities emerging at the international level have gained a new quality. First, there is no single state – with the possible exception of the USA – that could shoulder any of them alone. Second, one might even argue that the international level is in the process of acquiring a weak form of outcome responsibility for providing those citizens in the non-OECD world with physical security whose states do not live up to their duties. While there is ample evidence that international organizations do not act on this responsibility when Western national security interests are not in favour, it is nevertheless an important development that also affects the relation between the modern state and the provision of security in the OECD world.

Notes

1 Traditional peacekeeping operations famously fall under 'chapter 6½' of the Charter: they can neither be categorized as fully peaceful because they involve the deployment of military observers and armed personnel, nor do they consist of 'real' coercive activities because these soldiers are stationed with the consent of the parties involved and follow the principles of impartiality and minimal use of force. For overviews of the evolution of peacekeeping, see Bellamy *et al.* (2004) and Durch (1993b, 1996).
2 Single state and coalition interventions by force include Iraq/Kuwait 1990, Somalia 1992, Rwanda 1994, Haiti 1994, Albania 1997, East Timor 1999, Sierra

Leone 2000. Regional organizations undertook military operations with differing degrees of assertiveness in Haiti 1993, Bosnia and Herzegovina 1995 and 1996, Central African Republic 1997, Sierra Leone 1997, Macedonia 1998, Kosovo 1999, Afghanistan 2001, Côte D'Ivoire (2002), Liberia 1991 and 2003, Democratic Republic of Congo 2003 and 2006 and Sudan 2005; see Jones (2003), Malone (2004: Appendix 2); Roberts (2004).

3 See Malone (2004: Appendix 1) (updated with data from the UN homepage).

4 Especially since the Panel on UN Peace Operations (the 'Brahimi Commission') issued its assessment and recommendations in 2000, the Security Council has authorized operations with robust mandates (Findley 2002).

5 Data compiled by the Global Policy Forum, available at <http://www.globalpolicy.org/finance/tables/pko/expend.htm>, last accessed 8 August 2006.

6 See Centre on International Cooperation (2006) for the number of DPKO staff in 2005; for number of personnel deployed in operations see UN Background Note 31 August 2006.

7 At the World Summit in 2005, however, member states endorsed the creation of a small standing police capacity, the first standing capacity the UN has at its disposal.

8 The 'Petersberg Tasks' were originally set out in the Petersberg Declaration, adopted at the Ministerial Council of the Western European Union in June 1992. They include humanitarian and rescue tasks, peacekeeping and tasks of combat forces in crisis management, including peacemaking.

9 Formally, the Committee of the Permanent Representatives, made up of the heads or deputy heads of EU missions, is the highest decision-making authority below the Council and therefore acts as a *filtre unique*. Yet, it has rather a legal function and is often not fully acquainted with security and defence affairs.

10 They then were labelled *Special Envoys*.

11 Examples are the appointment of a Special Representative or the setting up of a monitoring mission.

12 Within this implementation procedure, the Commission adopts a financing decision, sets up a contract between the Commission and the implementing body (such as a Special Representative or an international organization), and may at any moment conduct on-site controls or order an audit to verify whether implementation proceeds according to the terms of the contract.

13 Art. 28 Treaty on European Union, Amsterdam.

14 Crisis Management Concepts specify the EU's objectives in a given crisis and identify several appropriate instruments.

15 These are battalions of 1,500 well-equipped troops, including support, deployable within ten days.

References

Barnett, Michael and Martha Finnemore (2004) *Rules for the World: International Organizations in Global Politics*, Ithaca: Cornell University Press.

Bellamy, Alex J., Paul Williams and Stuart Griffin (2004) *Understanding Peacekeeping*, Cambridge: Polity Press.

Centre on International Cooperation (2006) *Annual Review of Global Peace Operations 2006*, Boulder, CO: Lynne Rienner.

Chesterman, Simon (2004) *You, the People: The United Nations, Transitional Administration and State-Building*, Oxford: Oxford University Press.

Christiansen, Thomas (2001) 'Intra-Institutional Politics and Inter-Institutional Relations in the EU: Towards Coherent Governance?', *Journal of European Public Policy* 8(5), 747–69.

Cousens, Elizabeth M. and Chetan Kumar, eds (2001) *Peacebuilding as Politics: Cultivating Peace in Fragile Societies*, Boulder, CO: Lynne Rienner.

Crocker, Chester A. (2001) 'Intervention: Toward Best Practices and a Holistic View', in Chester A. Crocker, Fen Osler Hampson and Pamela Aall, eds, *Turbulent Peace: The Challenges of Managing International Conflict*, Washington, DC: United States Institute of Peace, 229–43.

Czempiel, Ernst-Otto (1994) 'Die Intervention: Politische Notwendigkeit und strategische Möglichkeiten', *Politische Vierteljahresschrift* 35(3), 402–22.

Duchêne, François (1972) 'Europe's Role in World Peace', in Richard Mayne, ed., *Europe Tomorrow: Sixteen Europeans Look Ahead*, London: Fontana, 32–47.

Durch, William J. (1993a) 'Running the Show: Planning and Implementation', in William J. Durch, ed., *The Evolution of UN Peacekeeping: Case Studies and Comparative Analysis*, New York: St Martin's Press, 59–75.

Durch, William J., ed. (1993b) *The Evolution of UN Peacekeeping: Case Studies and Comparative Analysis*, New York: St Martin's Press.

Durch, William J., ed. (1996) *UN Peacekeeping, American Politics, and the Uncivil Wars of the 1990s*, New York: St Martin's Press.

Durch, William J., Victoria K. Holt, Caroline R. Earle and Moira K. Shanahan (2003) *The Brahimi Report and the Future of UN Peace Operations*, Washington, DC: Henry L. Stimson Centre.

Elias, Norbert (2000) *The Civilizing Process: Sociogenetic and Psychogenetic Investigations*, Oxford: Blackwell.

Findley, Trevor (2002) *The Use of Force in UN Peace Operations*, Oxford: Oxford University Press.

Gordenker, Leon (2005) *The UN Secretary-General and Secretariat*, London: Routledge.

Goulding, Marrack (2003) *Peacemonger*, Baltimore: Johns Hopkins University Press.

Gourlay, Catriona (2004) *Feasibility Study on the European Civil Peace Corps*, Brussels: ISIS Europe.

Henry L. Stimson Centre (2004) *Funding for Post-Conflict Operations: NATO and the EU*, Washington, DC: Henry L. Stimson Centre.

Hoffmann, Stanley (1966) 'Obstinate or Obsolete? The Fate of the Nation-State and the Case of Western Europe', *Daedalus* 95(3), 862–916.

Holzgrefe, Jeff L. and Robert O. Keohane, eds (2003) *Humanitarian Intervention: Ethical, Legal and Political Dilemmas*, Cambridge: Cambridge University Press.

Hüfner, Klaus (2003) 'Financing the United Nations: The Role of the United States', in Dennis Dijkzeul and Yves Beigbeder, eds, *Rethinking International Organizations: Pathology and Promise*, New York: Berghahn Books, 27–53.

Jachtenfuchs, Markus (2005) 'The Monopoly of Legitimate Force: Denationalization, or Business as Usual?', *European Review* 13(1), 37–52.

James, Alan (1993) 'The Secretary-General as an Independent Political Actor', in Benjamin Rivlin and Leon Gordenker, eds, *The Challenging Role of the UN*

Secretary-General: Making 'the Most Impossible Job in the World' Possible, Westport: Praeger Publishers, 22–42.

Jones, Bruce (2003) *Evolving Models of Peacekeeping: Policy Implications and Responses*, External Study, New York: UN Peacekeeping Best Practices.

Lewis, Jeffrey (2003) 'Informal Integration and the Supranational Construction of the Council', *Journal of European Public Policy* 10(6), 996–1019.

Liese, Andrea and Silke Weinlich (2006) 'Verwaltungsstäbe internationaler Organisationen: Lücken und Tücken eines (neuen) Forschungsgebiets', in Jörg Bogumil, Werner Jann and Frank Nullmeier, eds, *Politik und Verwaltung (Politische Vierteljahresschrift Sonderheft No. 37)*, Wiesbaden: VS Verlag für Sozialwissenschaften, 491–524.

Malone, David M., ed. (2004) *The UN Security Council: From the Cold War to the 21st Century*, Boulder, CO: Lynne Rienner.

Mayer, Peter (2005) 'Die Lehre vom gerechten Krieg – obsolet oder unverzichtbar?', in Egbert Jahn, Sabine Fischer and Astrid Sahm, eds, *Die Zukunft des Friedens, Band 2: Die Friedens- und Konfliktforschung aus der Perspektive der jüngeren Generationen*, Wiesbaden: VS Verlag für Sozialwissenschaften, 381–407.

Moravcsik, Andrew (1998) *The Choice for Europe: Social Purpose and State Power from Messina to Maastricht*, Ithaca: Cornell University Press.

Müller-Brandeck-Bocquet, Gisela (2002) 'The New CFSP and ESDP Decision-Making System of the European Union', *European Foreign Affairs Review* 7(3), 1–26.

Newman, Edward (1998) *The UN Secretary-General from the Cold War to the New Era: A Global Peace and Security Mandate?*, New York: St Martins Press.

Nowak, Agnieszka (2006) 'Civilian Crisis Management within ESDP', in Agnieszka Nowak, ed., *Civilian Crisis Management: The EU Way*, Paris: Institute for Security Studies, 15–37.

Peterson, M. J. (2006) *The UN General Assembly*, New York: Routledge.

Pugh, Michael and Waheguru P.S. Sidhu, eds (2003) *The United Nations and Regional Security: Europe and Beyond*, Boulder, CO: Lynne Rienner.

Reinalda, Bob and Bertjan Verbeek (2004) 'Patterns of Decision Making Within International Organizations', in Bob Reinalda and Bertjan Verbeek, eds, *Decision Making Within International Organizations*, London: Routledge, 231–46.

Roberts, Adam (2004) 'The Use of Force', in David M. Malone, ed., *The UN Security Council: From the Cold War to the 21st Century*, Boulder, CO: Lynne Rienner, 133–52.

Rosenau, James N. and Ernst-Otto Czempiel, eds, (1992) *Governance without Government: Order and Change in World Politics*, Cambridge: Cambridge University Press.

Salomons, Dirk and Dennis Dijkzeul (2001) *The Conjurers' Hat: Financing United Nations Peace-Building in Operations Directed by Special Representatives of the Secretary-General*, Oslo: Fafo Institute of Applied Social Science.

Schneckener, Ulrich (2005) 'Post-Westfalia trifft Prä-Westfalia: Die Herausforderung der Gleichzeitigkeit dreier Welten', in Egbert Jahn, Sabine Fischer and Astrid Sahm, eds, *Die Zukunft des Friedens, Band 2: Die Friedens- und Konfliktforschung aus der Perspektive der jüngeren Generationen*, Wiesbaden: VS Verlag für Sozialwissenschaften, 189–212.

Senghaas, Dieter (2007) *On Perpetual Peace: A Timely Assessment*, Oxford: Berghahn Books.

Sens, Allen G. (2004) 'From Peace-Keeping to Peace-Building: The United Nations and the Challenge of Intrastate War', in Richard M. Price and Mark W. Zacher, eds, *The United Nations and Global Security*, New York: Palgrave Macmillan, 141–60.

Shimura, Hisako (2001) 'The Role of the Secretariat in Organizing Peacekeeping' in Albrecht Schnabel and Ramesh Thakur, eds, *United Nations Peacekeeping Operations: Ad Hoc Missions, Permanent Engagements*, Tokyo: United Nations University Press, 46–56.

Sriram, Chandra L. and Karin Wermester, eds, (2003) *From Promise to Practice: Strengthening UN Capacities for the Prevention of Violent Conflict*, Boulder, CO: Lynne Rienner.

Stetter, Stephan (2004) 'Cross-pillar Politics: Functional Unity and Institutional Fragmentation of EU Foreign Policies', *Journal of European Public Policy*, 11(4), 720–39.

Stewart, Emma (2003) *The EU's Conflict Prevention Policy: A Unique Contribution to a Global Problem?*, Loughborough: University of Loughborough.

Thakur, Ramesh (2004) 'Developing Countries and the Intervention-Sovereignty Debate', in Richard M. Price and Mark W. Zacher, eds, *The United Nations and Global Security*, New York: Palgrave Macmillan, 193–208.

Tilly, Charles (1985) 'War Making and State Making as Organized Crime', in Peter Evans, Dietrich Rueschemeyer and Theda Skocpol, eds, *Bringing the State Back In*, Cambridge: Cambridge University Press, 169–91.

United Nations (2000) *Report of the Panel on United Nations Peace Operations* (A/55/305, S/2000/809), New York: United Nations.

Wallensteen, Peter and Patrick Johansson (2004) 'Security Council Decisions in Perspective', in David M. Malone, ed., *The UN Security Council: From the Cold War to the 21st Century*, Boulder, CO: Lynne Rienner, 17–33.

Webber, Mark, Stuart Croft, Jolyon Howorth, Terry Terrif and Elke Krahmann (2004) 'The Governance of European Security', *Review of International Studies* 30(3), 3–26.

Winn, Neill and Christopher Lord (2001) *EU Foreign Policy Beyond the Nation-State: Joint Actions and Institutional Analysis of the Common Foreign and Security Policy*, Basingstoke: Palgrave Macmillan.

Zangl, Bernhard and Michael Zürn (2003) *Frieden und Krieg: Sicherheit in der nationalen und postnationalen Konstellation*, Frankfurt a.M.: Suhrkamp.

Ziring, Lawrence, Robert E. Riggs and Jack C. Plano (2005) *The United Nations: International Organizations and World Politics*, Belmont: Thomson Wadsworth.

4
From Diffusion to Interplay: Rethinking the Constitutional State in the Age of Global Legal Pluralism[1]

Martin Herberg

This chapter addresses the dynamics of global informal rule making and the emergence of new modes of governance beyond the state. The focus is on the subtle and sometimes even hidden processes of norm evolution in different policy sectors, primarily in the fields of social and environmental regulation. The emerging norms and rules, often referred to as 'soft law' (Shelton 2000), indicate a diffusion of governance from the constitutional state to various actors of the transnational sphere. Partly, the retreat of the state on the level of its operational responsibility seems to be compensated by several efforts to bring the emerging legalities under the rule of law, and thereby, the state is taking the role of a manager of change and a switch-man of the current transitions.

The unity of law revisited: Globalization and global law-making beyond the state

Basically, the participation of various private actors, expert groups and standards bodies in all phases of the policy process is a well-known phe-nomenon, which characterizes the architecture of modern statehood in general. From the 1970s, the sovereign state has intensified the delegation of tasks to other bodies, which was often accompanied by a move from operational task fulfilling towards rather supervisory functions and more indirect forms of regulation (Ayres and Braithwaite 1992; Rhodes 1997). Still, these mixed arrangements were not invalidating the state's monopoly of law making, since the various forms of governance remained embedded into an overall constitutional framework. As many authors have noticed, governance in the EU is pointing to the same direction (Kohler-Koch 2004). Due to its limited standard-setting capacity, the European Commission has delegated many of its competencies to various technical committees and non-state actors. In addition, negotiating the common issues on an official level has always been a rather sluggish process, whereas the formulation of standards by technical committees and transgovernmental networks proves to be a relatively elegant and flexible mechanism.

However, compared to these various forms of interlocked governance on the national and the European level, the emergence of global legal pluralism challenges our understanding of law making in a more radical way. While in the first two cases the multiple sources of law are still integrated into an intact institutional framework, the various phenomena of informal rule making on the global level are characterized by an astonishing degree of autonomy. On the national level, the state's capability to switch back, at least in cases of doubt, into a rather single-handed and hierarchical mode, is an important driving force for private initiatives, often labelled as the 'shadow of law', and the same is true for governance in the EU. Often, the state keeps the various standards bodies under its influence by creating mechanisms of proceduralization, that is, by defining criteria of procedural fairness, participation and transparency.

In contrast, the emerging norms of the transnational sphere not only bypass the state's monopoly of law making, they seriously challenge the state's constitutional prerogatives, including its operational responsibilities for social and environmental regulation. Transnational actors often adopt the envisaged regulatory tasks without any mandate from the official institutions. Instead of applying for an authorization from 'above', they seem to authorize themselves to fulfil the relevant tasks. Accordingly, although the emerging governance mechanisms often abstain from traditional juridical mechanisms such as contract or treaty, they are based on their own sources of bindingness and validity. Some of the standards under research present themselves as mere recommendations, while, in effect, by asserting the state of the art in the field of concern, they bear their own power of persuasion. Partly, informal rule making is accompanied by explicit self-obligations, which certainly marks one of the most elementary means to establish normativity beyond the realm of formal law.[2]

Given their problem orientation and their paralegal status, the emerging governance mechanisms nevertheless cause a number of problems in the dimension of democracy and the rule of law. From a rather minimalist perspective, one could perceive their legitimacy simply in the fact that they exceed the legal requirements in the different countries of concern. Yet, if one takes into account that the involved agencies de facto work as global norm makers, more ambitious standards of legitimacy come into the picture, for instance, the request for an increased level of transparency, aspects of improved third-party access and a fair procedure of dispute resolution in cases of norm violation. If one considers the modern nation state as the provider of these normative goods, the diffusion of the various governance functions to different transnational actors in the gaps and interstices of the institutional architecture compels us to redefine the nation state's role under the new conditions.

For many authors, the new constellation is putting the – already weakened – nation state out of action: 'Where states were once the masters of markets, now it is the markets which, on many crucial issues, are the masters over the governments of states' (Strange 1996: 4). Processes of global rule making by several unidentified actors and the prevailing lack of transparency indicate the danger of an evolving 'nobody's rule' (Beck 2002: 13). From this view, state law and informal law making are continuously drifting apart, leaving the constitutional institutions as an empty shell, with their influence on political affairs ever more restricted.

Of course, the asserted erosion of the constitutional state leaves us dissatisfied in a normative sense, but also under empirical aspects this diagnosis seems to be insufficient. Rather, we are facing a variety of regulatory interactions and a patchwork of interconnections, from which a new intermediate zone between the national and the transnational spheres originates. This perspective – as opposed to the view of an ever-more restricted reach of formal state law – has been discussed under the catchword of 'interlegality' by several authors (Santos 1995: 473; Günther and Randeria 2002; Piciotto 2007), although the empirical application still represents an outstanding task. Doing research on interlegality requires an empirical excavation of the emerging transnational norm structures, as a basis for the study of relevant readjustments in the sphere of formal state law. Against this background, the changing role of the constitutional state can be delineated, even if this transition often takes place in a rather implicit and incremental manner.

Varieties of law: surveying the field of global legal pluralism

At present, a comprehensive theory of transnational norm evolution does not exist; yet, there are numerous concepts and methodological principles that are commonly employed by research in the field. First, the challenge is to portray the new governance mechanisms not in a deficient mode, but to define them in their inherent rationality and their productive potential: due to their informality, notwithstanding the juridical and institutional problems caused by them, the emerging norms of the transnational sphere bear a considerable problem-solving capacity in several policy fields. They come into play, where the conventional legal mechanisms prove to be too inflexible, and where possible solutions are pulverized between the national interests of sovereign states.

In addition, research into the global emergence of norms requires a bottom-up approach – an approach that focuses on processes of self-organization and self-authorization that cut across the political geography of sovereign nation states (Ladeur 2004). As stated by Rosenau, approaching the sphere of transnational norm generation means moving into a highly fragmented, if not chaotic and amorphous playing ground: 'Global governance is the sum of a myriad – literally millions of – control mechanisms driven by different histories, goals, structures, and processes' (Rosenau 1995: 9). However, it should be possible to detach some of the most elementary patterns, classifying the various norm structures on the basis of the characteristic actor constellations behind them. Globalization and global governance is by no means a synonym for the disappearance of clear-cut borders – even though the old borders are partly replaced by new borders. Likewise, the emergence of transnational networks and cross-border interactions by no means signals the disappearance of identifiable responsibilities, even though these competencies tend to be located where most people would not expect them.

In what follows, three constellations are portrayed which form important reference points for transnational norm evolution. First, initiatives of self-regulation within the corporate world have to be addressed. While states generally cannot extend their law to other continents, multi-national corporations can very well define binding rules concerning their various subsidiaries in foreign countries. Another important source of informal norm making is transgovernmental networks of specialized state agencies. Here, the cooperation between various administrative units of different countries leads to the evolution of binding norms and standards, which often gain notable regulatory effects, even without any incorporation into formal law. A third root of transnational norm generation lies in the activities of legal counsellors, transferring legal norms from one country to another, combining them in their own, creative way and often completing them on the basis of their own legal concepts and practical experiences.

In all three cases, we are facing occurrences of a particular informal and 'decoupled' law, which rests upon transboundary processes of self-organization and self-authorization. Often, private actors or trans-governmental networks step into the 'power vacuum left by a weak state' (Hall and Biersteker 2002: 16), providing public goods that the state and also international institutions have failed to provide so far. The norms under research are bypassing the classical procedures of formal law making, and often, they heavily rest upon stocks of tacit knowledge and implicit concepts of governance and justice. The following exposition aims to capture the broad contours of the emerging norm structures, and in doing so, it clings to a rather programmatic style, since empirical evidence is still rather selective in this field of concern.

Private authority: Multinational enterprises as actors of global governance

Multinational enterprises are often perceived as global troublemakers – their potency and power can lead to the result that existing regulatory gaps will be exploited in an unscrupulous manner. Theoretically, the legal construction of the independently managed foreign subsidiary can be strategically employed to immunize the parent enterprise against the legal consequences of damages. The quest for generally binding standards becomes manifest in the political discourse as well as on the level of international law: in a series of documents, international institutions have been defining what they regard as responsible conduct on the part of multinationals; but, as international law still represents a rather decentralized order, these guidelines never turned out to be more than recommendations and non-binding expectations (Horn 1980).

The fears of unethical multinationals are stoked by the vision of the 'footloose' company. From this view, the companies are in a steady motion, only interested in quick profits, while overarching rules or an organizational structure in the classical sense are lacking (Kahn-Freund 1971). However, in a more differentiated perspective, decentralized production networks of this kind, although they may exist in several sectors, should not be taken for the normal case. That is to say, in many industries multinational enterprises are interested in long-term investments, and often, instead of exploiting the prevailing legal gaps to the full extent, they undertake considerable efforts to create and implement their own social and environmental standards.

Partly, this has to do with public pressure: On the part of civil society, multinational corporations are often expected to exceed the existing legal standards on a voluntary basis, according to their above-average financial power and their access to modern technology. Additional driving forces for norm generation are processes of intra-organizational learning on the basis of new experiences and occurrences of failure. For example, in the chemical industry, the Bhopal catastrophe of 1984 and several other malpractices made it even more evident that headquarters, in order to maintain a minimum of normality at their subsidiaries, have to integrate them into a tight net of internal controls (Jasanoff 1994).

Often, these processes of organizational learning result in the evolution of dynamic, multilevel systems of norms and rules. For example, many companies, among them the eight largest corporations of the German chemical industry, have seized the opportunity to define detailed operational standards concerning the safe storage of chemicals, waste water treatment and many other issues for their foreign subsidiaries (Herberg 2006). To implement these norms, special organs were installed as an element of the internal corporate governance structure, which are controlling the implementation of these standards on a regular, three- or four-year basis. The internal auditors have developed a broad range of methods and strategies to detect occurring breaches and deficiencies and, they intervene in cases of violations, addressing their instructions and directives towards the local management. While the publicly available codes and guidelines comprise only a rather vague description of these systems, the relevant norms and practices are of a well-established character inside the companies.[3]

Another type of private governance is the emergence of multilateral standard-setting between independent firms from different countries, and often even between firms from different industries. Sometimes, these processes take place on an equal footing, but often, some of the bigger – and often, more experienced – firms take the role of the 'lead firm' (Gereffi and Korzeniewicz 1994), addressing obligatory norms and standards towards their business partners, which again is often combined with specific control structures and forms of monitoring. An example is the evolution of transnational private sector regimes concerning the safe use and labelling of chemicals. Some of these regulations are linking industrial actors from different industries, especially: from the automobile and the chemical sectors (Dilling 2007; Lindenthal 2007). Thus, network-like arrangements such as these by no means lead to the disappearance of order, power and identifiable agencies, but, on the contrary, serve to define the various actors' roles, duties and competencies as precisely as possible.

To sum up, in many cases, multinational companies create their own rules governing conduct, and often, these regulations significantly exceed the sphere of the individual enterprise, as well as single industrial sectors. The norm structures under examination do not simply represent an incoherent pool of social norms, recommendations and principles, instead, they represent a kind of 'living law' of commerce and industry: a 'global law without a state' (Teubner 1997). At the same time, the emergent regulatory systems are precarious under legal aspects, because of their limited transparency and their often underdeveloped possibilities for third party participation (Kocher 2002; Glinski 2007). As stated by many authors, the 'attribution of public functions to private actors directly challenges democratic and liberal theories of governance and law' (Cutler 2002: 33). This peculiar double-edged character of private norm setting raises the question whether the states' formal law could contribute to the configuration of the new legalities, providing them with a new degree of transparency and accessibility.

Standard-setting by transgovernmental networks

From a traditional international relations view, state executives have little motivation to transcend their own country's national goals and interests as officially defined by the domestic government. However, on a level below international diplomacy, various forms of cross-border coordination between mid-level state officials can be observed, leading to the intensification of 'transgovernmental relations' (Keohane and Nye 1974) and 'global governance networks' (Slaughter 2005), which are not – or at least not completely – controlled by the foreign policy organs of national governments. In these arrangements, national state officials have a twofold loyalty, a loyalty to their national employers and also to the need to solve problems of a transboundary scope. In many cases, the activities of these networks significantly exceed the pure production of knowledge or expertise – in fact, they are a mechanism of transnational law making themselves.

Thus, here again, the nation state's law-making monopoly is crisscrossed by various processes of transnational network building and governance, which fundamentally challenge the state's role as the provider of procedural justice and transparency. The global government networks under research are basically characterized by their informality, because many of them neither enjoy legal personality, nor have special headquarters or stationery (Slaughter 2005: 127). Often, international institutions, especially those of the United Nations, are used as a source of material and logistic provisions, but even if the activities of the particular network are explicitly located under the umbrella of an international organization, the connection is rather loose.

Sometimes, the mandate for transnational networking is derived from an existing international agreement or resolution – for example, from Agenda 2000, which serves as an important point of reference for many practitioners in environmental policy sectors – but often it is primarily the officials themselves, who draw on the relevant goals and principles, using them as a normative resource for their activities. Processes of self-authorization also shape the situation on the national level, since transnational activities often take place without a formal directive from above. Today, many of the classical regulatory tasks of state agencies imply an intense communication with their counterparts in other countries, and often, the transition to joint action goes unnoticed by the superior authorities. Once created, such networks of specialized state agencies gain a life of their own. Internally, a commonly shared basis of perspectives, goals and interests evolves, which are to some degree decoupled from the home countries' national goals and interests.

While the agreed-upon norms and standards of transnational bureaucracy networks often lack legal bindingness in the classical sense, they nonetheless function as law should – they are authoritative and effectively binding. Under normative aspects, the bindingness often results from the expertise of the involved practitioners, blurring the clear-cut distinction between 'norms' and 'facts' in classical legal thought. Many elements of the emerging transnational law are addressed to private actors, and often, it is the internationally shared knowledge on industrial risks and dangers, which drives the generation of standards in transgovernmental networks, proving to be an essential basis to distinguish between acceptable and unacceptable practices. Thus, transgovernmental networks are a mechanism of what has been called 'bottom-up transnational lawmaking' (Koven 2005), confronting us with the evolution of law beyond the classical forms, especially beyond the forms of international treaties based on the voluntary commitment of sovereign states.

An instructive example for this mode of standard-setting is the Globally Harmonized System of Classification and Labelling of Chemicals (GHS). The standards include criteria for the classification of chemicals by types of hazard as well as harmonized labels and safety data sheets (Warning 2005). Over the years, the initiative has been formally assigned to the United Nations Sub-Committee of Experts on the Transport of Dangerous Goods, but still, it connects various administrative actors from different agencies in many different countries. Although the GHS standards are not legally binding, the existence of a unified framework on the global level exerts considerable pressure on all relevant actors to adapt to the system. Among the reasons for this are the various disadvantages that non-compliant actors, especially non-compliant private actors, are facing: adherence to the old standards – as they exist in most of the developed countries, yet in many different versions – would force them to switch back and forth from one classification system to another and to bear the costs accruing with the labelling and re-labelling of their products.

In the case of the GHS, like in many other cases of transnational standard setting, the emerging governance mechanisms significantly exceed what might be called the lowest common denominator harmonization of existing standards. In fact, the involved agencies try to build on the innovative elements of the different national systems, and they also integrate current issues and additional aspects into their work, which have not been addressed so far on the national level. Of course, despite their considerable degree of autonomy, state officials working in transnational networks can not ignore the national interest of their home countries, but at the same time, the standard setting often takes place in sectors where clear-cut national goals and ambitions have not yet evolved, and where a cautious design of the relevant governance mechanisms helps to reduce risks and damages in a cost-effective way.

Thus, just like the emerging forms of private governance, informal law making by global government networks often bears an enormous problem solving capacity, but again, under aspects of legitimacy, the new modes of governance are not trouble-free. In many cases, transnational standard setting emanates from a rather small number of countries, and other countries are not integrated until the major decisions are already made, which considerably weakens their position. Furthermore, despite their often fairly progressive goals with regard to aspects of environmental protection and social regulation, global government networks do not always reach consent in all relevant points, and sometimes, second-best solutions will be accepted as the price for quick completion. Accordingly, saving the flexibility of transnational networks, while minimizing their adverse effects, can be denominated as one of the most challenging tasks of contemporary law making on the national as well as on the international level.

Legal counselling: knitting a transnational legal patchwork

Throughout the golden age of the nation state, there were manifold interactions between national legislations – among them various forms of legal borrowing, legal adaptation and processes of mutual learning (Watson 1974). However, under the conditions of globalization, these processes have obtained additional significance. Intensifying the interplay between national legislations, globalization makes the 'nomadic' character of legal norms and concepts ever more visible (Legrand 1997: 112), with an increasing number of norms travelling across jurisdictions, being displaced, and transplanted. Only partly, this amalgamation of different legal elements is accomplished by actors from inside the recipient legislation. In fact, above the different nation states and across their borders, a new superstructure of legal practices has emerged, with legions of law professors and legal practitioners acting as carriers and bearers of norms and rules.

Thus, here again, one is facing a diffusion of formerly state-centric functions to other actors.

Only loosely coupled with the political discourse in the respective countries, these transnational actors develop model codes and legal blueprints for various fields of law. The legal systems of different countries are studied for innovations, with a view to adopting these into new instruments and solutions. The vivid culture of the emerging transnational juridical community becomes manifest in the huge number of international conferences on specific legal problems of any type and size, as well as in the huge amount of money – more than US$ 100 million – spent on legal counselling per annum (Gaul 2001: 103). International and national organizations such as the World Bank, the European Bank for Reconstruction and Development, the United States Agency for International Development (USAID) and the German *Gesellschaft für technische Zusammenarbeit* (GTZ) are important sponsors, especially when legal counselling is conducted in the developing countries of Africa, Asia, Latin America and Eastern Europe.

Thus, transnational lawyering represents another type of global law making, emerging in the interstices of the state-centric world, and furthermore, it serves as a mechanism of global governance, helping to overcome the legal gaps and deficiencies of national legislations. Under today's conditions, where the hierarchical imposition of binding standards by international institutions serves as an exception, decentralized strategies such as the horizontal transfer of norms and rules can be seen as an important governance device. Often, transnational legal counselling takes place in sectors in which the decision-making process in the recipient countries is still in its early stages, giving room for persuasion and raising awareness of activities. Here again, the creation of intelligent solutions can help achieve considerable progress towards environmental and social regulation at low cost – provided that the legal practitioners are sufficiently flexible to anticipate the specific administrative and socioeconomic conditions of the recipient country.

Due to their status as Western experts, the counsellors often enjoy enormous authority and room for maneouvre. Formally, they are only draftsmen of preliminary statutes, which subsequently are assessed and adopted by the national parliaments or other legislative bodies, but, in reality, this constellation often involves an implicit delegation of legislative functions towards the consultant. In a way, legal counselling tends to perforate the recipient state's sovereignty from below, with the legitimate organs merely ratifying the norms and rules that were imported from outside. In part, the counsellors' authority stems from their knowledge of the whole range of existing legal constructions in different countries, partly it flows from their connection with powerful donor organizations, and partly it is the combination with other instruments of aid and assistance which makes their proposals hard to refuse.

As a matter of fact, there is little research on the transnational legal community and its numerous experts engaging in legal reforms all over the world. Probably, there are different subgroups and various 'local dialects' (Friedman 1996: 77), with their own conceptions of what is wrong and what is right, and with their own ideas of good governance and justice. Undoubtedly, socialization in different regional cultures still plays an important role, but, at the same time, distinct milieus crystallize around different policy sectors and agendas. In particular, politically charged fields such as labour law and environmental law seem to promote the formation of transboundary networks among lawyers, the exchange of experiences and the emergence of commonly shared standards.[4]

In accordance with the other types of informal law making discussed above, the practice of transnational lawyering implies its own rationality as well as considerable potential to remedy the prevailing legal gaps and deficiencies at the national level. At the same time, their legitimacy in terms of democracy and procedural justice is at stake. Often, supervision by donor organizations is rather superficial, and in most cases, codified standards for the evaluation of law reform projects are missing. Here and there, the generation of guiding principles is observed – for example the demand of a preferably participative proceeding, or the demand to combine the drafted statute with an elaborate report and justification. However, the legal status of these principles is unclear, which makes it rather unlikely that legal consultants could be held accountable for their activities.

Re-embedding the disembedded – legal pluralism, interlegality and the rule of law

The previous delineation of three emerging governance mechanisms – standard setting by multinational corporations, global government networks and transnational legal counsellors – confirms the pluralist perspective on legislation and law under today's conditions: 'Law as an instrument of normative ordering becomes more diffuse and is now derived from multiple sources not necessarily limited to the machinery of constitutional lawmaking and exerts validity far beyond the territorial borders of political systems' (Schepel 2005: 11). The fundamental principles of modern legal thought – as represented by Kelsen and his various successors – especially the concepts of the unity of law and of the state's law making monopoly, become more and more questionable in a situation of global legal pluralism.

As pointed out, many decisive norms and rules are created by self-authorized actors beyond the state, leading to a continuous growth of informal governance mechanisms in the interstices and lacunas of state law. As a result, the legal practitioners inside the state find it increasingly difficult to differentiate between legally relevant and irrelevant norms, and to determine the precise demarcation between admissible and inadmissible practices. Just like state law, many of the emerging norms and rules are of a long-lasting and binding character. They establish obligation, shape and reshape the rights and liabilities of the different parties, and often, the involved actors in the various contexts have a strong confidence in their partners' norm-compliance. But, at the same time, the emerging norms and rules abstain from any use of the conventional juridical forms, such as contracts or treaties, and sometimes, they even explicitly emphasize their non-binding character, which causes several irritations and an increasing degree of legal uncertainty.

The severe nature of these problems becomes evident if one takes into account the current restrictions of formal law making. For example, if one takes the case of private standard setting by corporate actors, it must be said that the so-called 'shadow' of state law, and its potential to advance private self-regulation, seems to be rather underdeveloped in the transnational sphere. Since, in the foreseeable future, no overarching regulatory framework is expected on the international level, it is primarily the private actors' own conceptions of right and wrong which shape their self-made steering mechanisms. Of course, one important trigger for private governance is the pressure from civil society, but still, it is the companies themselves that interpret these demands and put them to action. Another driving force is processes of organizational learning against the background of previous errors and failures, but here again, it is the firms that evaluate their behaviour, and there are no guarantees that every firm within the industry adopts the new structures, or that falling back to the old routines does not occur.

The research gaps regarding the details of transnational norm generation and the forces behind it only allow for some preliminary conjectures. Surely, one important factor for norm evolution is the increased demand of harmonized standards, which permit stabilized expectations in cross-border interactions. But, as soon as the quest for harmonized standards is on the table, the problem of their substantial content is thematic, too. Often, ecologically or socially engaged actors in key positions can push the process in a progressive direction, so that the standards significantly exceed the least common denominator between former regulations. Despite the cross-boundary character of the involved organizations and networks, one should not forget that most of them still have some footage in their countries of origin, and accordingly carry many of the achievements of Western culture, which exert some influence on the processes in the transnational realm.

Notwithstanding their problem-solving capacity in many policy sectors, the emerging governance mechanisms nevertheless cause several legal and institutional problems, especially in terms of procedural justice, democracy and the rule of law. First, and foremost, we are facing the danger of an increasing predominance of particularistic interests, even if the emerging elite of rule makers orient themselves toward the common good. Many decisions are made behind closed doors, and although some form of third party participation is often admitted, it is of rather sporadic character. The lack of public deliberation is all the more problematic, since the relevant norms often not only define minimum standards, but also imply upper limits of the reasonable effort to be taken. Thus, measured against the classical principles of equal access to the decision-making process and the protection of minorities, many of the paralegal systems clearly fall back behind the provisions of the modern constitutional state.

The same is true regarding questions of transparency and the problem of enforceability in cases of violations. From a rule of law perspective, law must first be published to be obligatory, because nobody can comply with laws the existence of which is concealed, and because access to basic legal information can be seen as an indispensable prerequisite of civil rights (Sward 2004: 402). For example, regarding the case of corporate governance, often just a brief abstract of the existing norms and standards is published – normally in the form of corporate codes and guidelines – while the more concrete standards are circulating as internal instructions, leading to considerable information gaps on the part of the stakeholder vis-à-vis the organization.

Similar problems are raised by two other principles of modern law, namely the right of access to the courts and the right to be heard before a court, which are generally recognized as inherent in the concept of the rule of law. Although the different types of transnational law often bear significant problem-solving capacity, for example preventing environmental damage by controlling foreign subsidiaries, breaches and deviations can occur, but mechanisms of dispute settlement and possibilities of third-party enforcement are rather scarce. It is against this background that the notion of a particular 'decoupled' law shows its full severity. Indeed, we are faced with the emergence of law-making processes beyond the state, or, put differently, a diffusion of formerly state-centric competencies to transnational actors, the activities of which are not bound to the same criteria of democracy and procedural justice as state-defined legislation. The paralegal systems of world society are supplementing or substituting the existing national legislations with additional – and often, more ambitious – norms and rules, but, at the same time, they heavily challenge the essential principles of constitutional law.

In a rather pessimistic view, global legal pluralism leads to a continuous marginalization of formal law as an instrument of normative ordering: 'Following the de-centreing of politics, there is no authority in sight in a position to undertake the coordination of societal fragments' (Fischer-Lescano and Teubner 2004: 117). But, in a more differentiated view, one might argue that, notwithstanding the lack of an overarching legal framework, a variety of interactions between the different normative structures are on the way, as indicated by the above-mentioned concept of 'inter-legality' (Santos 1995: 473). Step by step, the legal institutions of the constitutional state can very well integrate the paralegal systems into their scope, and on a case-by-case basis, they surely exert authority, for example, when breaches against self-made standards by individual actors are taken as a reference point for liability according to tort law.

From this point of view, the trend towards informalization is criss-crossed by several dynamics towards re-embedding and reshaping the emerging structures. Surely, a clear-cut mechanism, governing the transition from the transnational to the national sphere, is not to be found, instead, on all levels of the *Rechtsstaat*, we are facing a variety of actors struggling for an adequate readjustment of the existing institutions. If the classical positivist model of law as a systematic and cohesive apparatus is on the end of its rope, then the adjacent picture of the legal practitioner as an expert specialized on written laws and statutes has to be revised, too. Instead of applying the norms of the one and only, unitary and codified law, the judge today is in the business of negotiating between different normativities, trying to gain substantiated insights into the extra-legal norms and rules that form the broader context of the matters in dispute.

It is important to see that the dynamics towards the juridification of the emerging legalities are not just a result of individual actors' efforts, since modern law as such is predisposed to integrate societal norms and facts into its scope. On the surface, this has to do with the various blanket clauses and normative references in the design of modern laws; just think of the 'reasonable man' in classical tort law, but on a closer look, modern law in general is of a dynamic character, due to several elements of substantive and pragmatic rationality that drive the legal system to stay in close contact with the emerging normative society. Concerning the quality of legal decisions, formal criteria and aspects of legal certainty are only one dimension – equally important are aspects of more substantive character (Weber 1972: 397); among them the need for a realistic definition of cases under examination, as well as questions of problem adequacy. The unity of the law is neither a pre-established harmony, nor is it an illusion, but instead it is a practical accomplishment on all levels and in all stages of the law-making process.

An outstanding example for such a mechanism generating new and creative solutions in the interplay between formalistic and substantial concerns, is the protection of trust. The principle of trust and confidence plays a constitutive role in every sector of social life, both public and private. It serves as an indispensable prerequisite of law's rationality and, in some ways, it represents a 'natural law element' in modern law (Köndgen 1981: 5). Historically, this principle has always played a vivid role in overcoming too formalistic elements of juridical practice, be it in administrative law or in contract law. The key idea is the protection of legitimate expectations, which the trusting party derives from the promises of their interaction partners, to some extent also from their advertisement and self-presentation, as well as from the customs and professional standards in the relevant field of practice. In all of those cases, the exclusion of informal obligations from the realm of formal law would surely lead to distorted or paradoxical legal results, and for this reason, the principle of confidence and trust has triggered a broad range of innovative legal concepts, among them the litigation for promises in certain contexts, and the successive juridification of professional standards.

Accordingly, the principle of trust and confidence also serves as an important platform for the institutional re-embedding of global legal pluralism. For instance, in present-day jurisprudence, there is an intense debate concerning the enforceability of corporate guidelines and codes of conduct in cases where breaches have caused damages on the part of employees, consumers or residents – undoubtedly an important tool to provide the informal norms with a higher degree of reliability.[5] The same applies to the standards set by transgovernmental networks. To the extent that the standards, apart from their existence on paper, are observed by a significant number of firms all over the world, national courts will use them as an important reference point – even if the standards have not been formally adopted by the legal system of the country concerned.

How this is carried out in practice is an empirical question, but generally, the successive juridification of the emerging norms gives room for new ways of regulation, which otherwise, in a hierarchical command-and-control style, would not have been possible. Above all, in the course of their juridification, the informal norms strip off many of the deficiencies. For example, by demanding information on the relevant norms and standards, the legal authorities foster their publication, and by picking up cases of violations, they re-establish civil rights.

Concluding remarks: The constitutional state in the age of global legal pluralism

Under the conditions of globalization, with many processes exceeding the national territory, the modern nation state's problem-solving capacity is at stake. In addition, governance in terms of international diplomacy is also restricted in many ways, because sovereign states and their representatives often have little motivation to take action beyond the limit of their national interests. At the same time, on an informal level, various forms of law making are taking place from below, filling the zones where national and international policy have not succeeded thus far. At first glance, this could lead to a situation where the concerned policy sectors are permanently blocked off from action on the part of the state. According to this view, we would face various processes of informal law making on the one hand, and a successive marginalization of the constitutional state on the other hand.

Indeed, the danger of erosion of the legal achievements of modern statehood is not mere rhetoric or fantasy. Although the emerging norms and rules of the transnational sphere represent a fruitful supplement to the more conventional governance devices, there is little reason to consider them as an institutional equivalent to state law. That is to say, their efficacy comes with considerable deficiencies under aspects of democracy and procedural justice. Thus, instead of a harmonic coexistence, the emerging legalities heavily conflict with the law. Especially, the nation state's constitutional law, which ought to provide the blueprint for the entire legal order, is confronted with new challenges under these conditions, since the more that rules are created beyond the state, the less constitutional law can fulfil its function as a generally binding framework for the entire legal order.

However, the modern nation state's legal system serves as an important safety net, apt to domesticate emerging structures. As indicated by the concept of interlegality, the decoupling between state law and informal rule making is paralleled by various processes towards the converse direction: due to the great practical relevance of the informal mechanisms, there are numerous interactions with existing state-defined law. Often, the emerging governance mechanisms lack fair procedures for dispute resolution, and that is why in cases of breaches, the judicial institutions of the state remain an important platform. The law sees itself confronted with new normativities from many directions, and thereby, it is starting to change its own identity.

In these processes, a transition in some ways can be observed from a nation state tied to a territory, towards the nation state as a transmission belt – or, more precisely, as a plurality of transmission belts – between the transnational and the national sphere. The authorities and courts of the different countries become successively interwoven into the various normativities of the transnational sphere, and they develop a certain creativity to gain a new balance. In the long run, the manifold interconnections might very well sum up to a new model of interlocked governance and statehood, with the state regaining its operational responsibility as well as its regulatory competence inside and, to some extent, also outside of the national territory.

Thus, the emergence of lawmaking competencies beyond the nation state that are exercised by transnational actors should not be perceived as a zero-sum game. Moreover, by interlocking its action with the informal governance mechanisms of the transnational sphere, the state not only provides the informal norms and rules with a higher degree of reliability, transparency and legitimacy, but also it increases its own problem-solving capacity. Where the state acts as a manager of (self-)transformation, adequately adapting its institutions to the new challenges, it remains a relevant actor in the global steering process. By creating transmission belts between the national and the transnational sphere, the nation state helps to increase the reliability of the emergent governance mechanisms, and in many cases, it represents an important clearing house for claims that emerge whenever the informal governance mechanisms fail.

Here too, in principle, it is true what is being said about the different forms of indirect and 'reflexive' regulation within the national sphere. In its search for useful steering mechanisms, the nation state intensively has to make use of the intelligence and practical knowledge of societal actors (Mayntz and Scharpf 1995). An indispensable prerequisite for this is an as differentiated as realistic perspective on the process called globalization, taking the emerging appearances of global law making seriously in their own right, but at the same time taking care not to abandon the institutional achievements of modern statehood in a rush. While forcing us to modify many of the old, unitary and hierarchical notions of order, globalization does not per se lead to a situation of anomy or amorphousness.

Notes

1   The chapter presents results of a research project on 'Transnational Governance and Interlegality' conducted by the author in collaboration with Professor Gerd Winter, ass. jur. Olaf Dilling and Dipl. Pol. Alexandra Lindenthal. The author is indebted to Hannes Künemund and Michael Warning for helpful comments on an earlier version of this chapter.
2   Of course, not every single norm or rule from the social world shows this para-legal character. To be part of the 'living law' of society, the relevant norms have to sum up to larger norm structures with some degree of internal differ-entiation, a minimum of durability, some orientation towards issues of common concern, and some degree of bindingness in the relevant field of practice (for further discussion, see Herberg 2007: 18–28).
3   Ironically, many of the governance mechanisms as employed on the oper-ational level have not found their way into any official documents, while many of the highly visible and formalistic regimes such as that provided by the ISO 14000 standard 'Environmental Management and Auditing' are of a rather restricted, if not even counterproductive effect under practical aspects (Herberg 2006).
4   The concept of transnational 'communities of practice' by no means excludes competition between the various practitioners, nor does it presuppose any institutional association between them. Rather, it is the occurrence of a com-monly shared field of experience and the similarity of their daily problems and routines which constitutes these communities and subgroups.
5   An important example for the juridification of private governance under the rule of common law is the so-called 'Good Samaritan' principle, stating that parent companies whose conduct – either in their self-presentations, or in their internal management systems – shows a certain degree of responsibility concerning the state of affairs at the foreign subsidiaries should also compen-sate for occurring liabilities and damages (Schepel 2005: 389).

References

Ayres, Ian and John Braithwaite (1992) *Responsive Regulation: Transcending the Deregulation Debate*, Oxford: Oxford University Press.
Beck, Ulrich (2002) *Macht und Gegenmacht im globalen Zeitalter: Neue weltpolitische Ökonomie*, Frankfurt a.M: Suhrkamp.
Cutler, Claire (2002) 'Private International Regimes and Interfirm Cooperation', in Rodney Hall and Thomas Biersteker, eds, *The Emergence of Private Authority in Global Governance*, Cambridge: Cambridge University Press, 23–40.
Dilling, Olaf (2007) 'Risky Uses for Safe Technologies: Towards a Legal Reconstruction of the User Perspective', in Haakan Haakanson and Alexandra Waluszewski, eds, *Using Technologies*, London: Routledge (forthcoming).
Fischer-Lescano, Andreas and Gunther Teubner (2004) 'Regime-Collisions: The Vain Search for Legal Unity in the Fragmentation of Global Law', *Michigan Journal of International Law* 25(4), 999–1046.
Friedman, Lawrence M. (1996) 'Borders: On the Emerging Sociology of Transnational Law', *Stanford Journal of International Law* 32(1), 65–90.

Gaul, Wolfgang (2001) 'Sinn und Unsinn internationaler Rechtsberatung', in Christian Boulanger, ed., *Recht in der Transformation: Rechts- und Verfassungswandel in Mittel- und Osteuropa*, Berlin: Berliner Debatte Wissenschaftsverlag, 102–268.

Gereffi, Gary and Miguel Korzeniewicz, eds (1994) *Commodity Chains and Global Capitalism*, Westport: Praeger.

Glinski, Carola (2007) 'Legal Effects of Corporate Codes of Transnational Environmental Conduct', in Olaf Dilling, Martin Herberg and Gerd Winter, eds, *Responsible Business? Self-Governance and the Law in Transnational Economic Transactions*, Oxford: Hart (forthcoming).

Günther, Klaus and Shalini Randeria (2002) 'Recht, Kultur und Gesellschaft im Prozess der Globalisierung', *Arbeitspapiere der Werner Reimers Stiftung*, H. 4, Bad Homburg.

Hall, Rodney and Thomas Biersteker, eds (2002) *The Emergence of Private Authority in Global Governance*, Cambridge: Cambridge University Press.

Herberg, Martin (2006) 'Private Authority, Global Governance, and the Law', in Gerd Winter, ed., *Multilevel Governance of Global Environmental Change*, Cambridge: Cambridge University Press, 149–78.

Herberg, Martin (2007) *Globalisierung und private Selbstregulierung: Umweltschutz in multinationalen Unternehmen*, Frankfurt a.M.: Campus.

Horn, Norbert (1980) *Legal Problems of Codes of Conduct for Multinational Enterprises*, Deventer: Kluwer.

Jasanoff, Sheila (1994) 'Introduction: Learning from Disaster', in Sheila Jasanoff, ed., *Learning from Disaster: Risk Management After Bhopal*, Philadelphia: University of Pennsylvania Press, 1–21.

Kahn-Freund, Otto (1971) 'A Lawyer's Reflections on Multinational Corporations', *Industrial Relations Journal* 14(4), 332–44.

Keohane, Robert and Joseph Nye (1974) 'Transgovernmental Relations and International Organizations', *World Politics* 27(1), 39–62.

Kocher, Eva (2002) 'Private Standards between Soft Law and Hard Law: The German Case', *International Journal of Comparative Labour Law and Industrial Relations* 18(3), 265–80.

Kohler-Koch, Beate (2004) 'Interdependent European Governance', in Beate Kohler-Koch, ed., *Linking EU and National Governance*, Oxford: Oxford University Press, 10–23.

Köndgen, Johannes (1981) *Selbstbindung ohne Vertrag: Zur Haftung aus geschäftsbezogenem Handeln*, Tübingen: Mohr Siebeck.

Koven, Janet (2005) 'A Bottom-Up Approach to International Lawmaking: The Tale of Three Trade Finance Instruments', *Yale Journal of International Law* 30(1), 125–210.

Ladeur, Karl-Heinz (2004) 'Globalization and Public Governance – A Contradiction?', in Karl-Heinz Ladeur, ed., *Public Governance in the Age of Globalization*, Aldershot Ashgate, 1–24.

Legrand, Pierre (1997) 'The Impossibility of Legal Transplants', *Maastricht Journal of European and Comparative Law* 1(4), 111–24.

Lindenthal, Alexandra (2007) 'Transnational Management of Hazardous Chemicals by Interfirm Cooperation and Associations', in Olaf Dilling, Martin Herberg and Gerd Winter, eds, *Responsible Business? Self-Governance and the Law in Transnational Economic Transactions*, Oxford: Hart (forthcoming).

Mayntz, Renate and Fritz Scharpf (1995) *Gesellschaftliche Selbstregulierung und politische Steuerung*, Frankfurt a.M.: Suhrkamp.

Piciotto, Sol (2007) 'Regulatory Networks and Multi-Level Global Governance', in Olaf Dilling, Martin Herberg and Gerd Winter, eds, *Responsible Business? Self-Governance and the Law in Transnational Economic Transactions*, Oxford: Hart (forthcoming).

Rhodes, Rod W., ed. (1997) *Understanding Governance: Policy Networks, Governance, Reflexivity, Accountability*, Milton Keynes: Open University Press.

Rosenau, James (1995) 'Governance, Order and Change in World Politics', in James Rosenau and Ernst-Otto Czempiel, eds, *Governance without Government: Order and Change in World Politics*, Cambridge: Cambridge University Press, 3–17.

Santos, Boaventura de Sousa (1995) *Toward a New Common Sense: Law, Science and Politics in the Paradigmatic Transition*, London: Routledge.

Schepel, Harm (2005) *The Constitution of Private Governance: Product Standards in the Regulation of Integrating Markets*, Oxford: Hart Publishing.

Shelton, Dinah (2000) 'Law, Non-law and the Problem of "Soft Law"', in Dinah Shelton, ed., *Commitment and Compliance: The Role of Non-binding Norms in the International System*, Oxford: Oxford University Press, 4–10.

Slaughter, Anne-Marie (2005) 'Global Government Networks, Global Information Agencies, and Disaggregated Democracy', in Karl-Heinz Ladeur, ed., *Public Governance in the Age of Globalization*, Aldershot: Ashgate, 121–56.

Strange, Susan (1996) *The Retreat of the State: The Diffusion of Power in the World Economy*, Cambridge: Cambridge University Press.

Sward, Ellen E. (2004) 'Justification and Doctrinal Evolution', *Connecticut Law Review* 37(2), 389–493.

Teubner, Gunther, ed. (1997) *Global Law without a State*, Aldershot: Dartmouth.

Warning, Michael (2005) 'Die Legitimierung transnationalen Rechts am Beispiel der transnationalen Chemikalienregulierung', TranState Working Paper No. 11, Bremen: TranState Research Centre.

Watson, Alan (1974) *Legal Transplants: An Approach to Comparative Law*, Athens: University of Georgia Press.

Weber, Max (1972) *Wirtschaft und Gesellschaft: Grundriss der verstehenden Soziologie*, Tübingen: Mohr.

5

Transformations of Commercial Law: New Forms of Legal Certainty for Globalized Exchange Processes?

Gralf-Peter Calliess, Thomas Dietz, Wioletta Konradi, Holger Nieswandt and Fabian Sosa

Commerce, defined as the marketing of goods and services, is dependent on a tremendously complex set of institutions. According to the New Institutional Economics (Furubotn and Richter 2005; Menard and Shirley 2005), such institutions roughly divide into two groups. On the one hand, *property rights*, that is, rights in moveables and immoveables as well as in intellectual property, have to be *defined and protected*, the latter including the protection from non-voluntary transfers (e.g., theft and fraud). On the other hand, *contractual commitments* as a means for the voluntary exchange of property rights have to be *enforced* (Hadfield 2005). Such *transactions* are organized by *alternative modes of governance* (Williamson 2005), principally spot markets (classical contracting), hybrids (relational contracting) and hierarchies (firms, understood as a nexus of contracts).

The 'economic institutions of capitalism' (Williamson 1985) do not only cover substantial parts of what is known as private law in legal terms, such as property, trademark, copyright, tort, contract and company law. They extend to public law as well, as for instance to criminal, regulatory, or competition law. The term 'institution' refers not only to the substantive 'rules of the economic game', but also more broadly to the procedural set of arrangements for their implementation and enforcement (Hadfield 2005). Apart from the protection of property rights and the enforcement of contracts, commerce also relies on various non-legal institutions such as stable currency, a well-educated labour force and all kinds of infrastructure for communication, and transport (Gessner 2008). Finally, economic institutions are embedded in cultural settings, which is highlighted by the difficulties that transformation states face on their way to market economies and which – more generally – limits the possibilities of institutional reform (Eggertson 2005; North 2005).

In order to deal with the complexity of the topic of economic institutions and their evolution as described above, this chapter focuses on the institutions of *contract enforcement* as a core prerequisite for commercial activity and in particular on commercial law in a narrow sense. Since both the welfare of modern societies and the capacity of the nation state to intervene with society are based on economic growth, there is a public interest in fostering commerce by providing efficient institutions for contract enforcement. In other words, *legal certainty* for commercial transactions is a *normative good*, at least in the market economies of OECD countries. However, this does not necessarily imply that the state takes over sole responsibility for the provision of legal certainty in all three dimensions (*outcome, regulatory, operational*).

Institutions that support contractual commitments may also be provided without the state by means of *private ordering* (Ellickson 1991; Dixit 2004; Williamson 2005). Different private governance mechanisms, namely social norms, alternative dispute resolution and social sanctions may eventually be bundled into effective private regimes (Bernstein 1992, 2001; Hadfield 2001; Teubner 2004). This is well established for the spontaneous evolution of the law merchant or the *lex mercatoria*, which came about with the commercial expansion in late medieval Europe (Benson 1989; Milgrom *et al.* 1990; Greif 2006). Substantial parts of modern commercial law, be it the validity of informal contracts, securities law, insurance and transport law, or company law, originate from trade customs that developed in the practice of commerce. These customs were increasingly formalized in the adjudication of merchant courts, institutionalized at the important sea ports and trade fairs, and enforced through social sanctions administered by merchant guilds (Goldschmitt 1892; Burdick 1902).

This ancient law merchant coexisted for centuries as a common European mercantile law with canon, royal (imperial) and local laws, thus creating the medieval legal pluralism which was constitutive for the western legal tradition (Berman 1983).[1] However, in the late 18th and the 19th century, the rising sovereign nation states modernized their judicial systems and the law merchant was integrated into and absorbed by national private and commercial laws (Cutler 2003: 141–79; Oldham 2004: 79–98). Some relics of the ancient law merchant survived, such as the participation of merchants as lay judges in commercial cases or the reference to trade usages in modern codifications of commercial law. The nation states also continued to recognize the right of private parties to submit a dispute to arbitration by private judges instead of using the state judicial system. Notwithstanding this exception with regard to the operational responsibility, in principle, nation states took over the regulatory and operational responsibility for the provision of the normative good of legal certainty by enacting codifications of substantive commercial law and procedural law as well as by providing dispute resolution services through a public court system and enforcing the resulting judgments through public agents.

However, from the very beginning of this process, one important caveat applied: the nation state's jurisdiction to prescribe (regulatory responsibility) as well as its jurisdiction to adjudicate and enforce (operational responsibility) was limited to its territory. While formalizing and rationalizing commercial law for the *domestic market* through the production of legal unity in the substantive dimension and through the provision of reliable legal services in the procedural dimension, the once uniform European law merchant was nationalized. Thus, commercial law became more predictable, but territorially fragmented (Bar and Mankowski 2003). Although this did not result in a complete denial of justice for international commerce, in a *cross-border situation* additional uncertainties arose with regard to the questions of which court has jurisdiction, which national law this court shall apply, and whether a resulting judgment could be enforced in another nation state. These three issues are resolved by the conflict rules of private international law, but contrary to the prima facie meaning of the word there are no uniform rules on the international level, each nation state has its own conflict rules.

In order to prevent cross-border trade from suffering, the idea arose to create a 'world private law' by means of international treaty harmonization as early as in the late 19th century, in the so-called first phase of economic globalization (Zitelmann 1888; Berger 2001). This endeavour, however, turned out to be more difficult than expected. More than one hundred years of work within different public international organizations like the Hague Conference on Private International Law (since 1893), the International Institute for the Unification of Private Law (UNIDROIT, since 1926) and the United Nations Commission on International Trade Law (UNCITRAL, since 1966) have resulted in little but fragments (Bar and Mankowski 2003), for example the 1980 UN Convention on the International Sale of Goods (CISG) (Ferrari 2005). The post-Second World War ideological division into the West, the East and the South was, of course, not particularly favourable, but even after the fall of the Iron Curtain, matters did not improve. The negotiations on a worldwide convention on the recognition and enforcement of foreign judgments in civil and commercial matters, initiated in the early 1990s in The Hague (Zekoll 1998; Black 2000; Traynor 2000), recently failed for reasons of a purported transatlantic *Justizkonflikt*, suggesting that even OECD member states are unable or unwilling to join a common constitution of world trade (Baumgartner 2003; Calliess 2004).[2] After all, the hopes for a world private law based on multilateral treaties have been deflated (Drobnig 2001; Kronke 2001, 2003, 2005).

To sum up, during the 18th and 19th centuries the nation state took over the full-fledged responsibility for the provision of the normative good of legal certainty for commercial transactions. Due to its territorially limited jurisdiction, however, the state fulfilled this promise with regard to domestic commerce only, while the endeavour to create efficacious public institutions for the enforcement of cross-border commercial transactions by means of international cooperation between states failed.

Globalization and the institutional organization of commerce

Oliver Williamson's (2005: 2) 'economics of governance' revealed that a need for private ordering arises even where the state has created and enforces efficacious rules of commercial law. While legal certainty provided by national commercial law may suffice for one-shot transactions on spot markets, in long-term business relationships (hybrids), where transactions occur frequently and parties make relation-specific investments, additional uncertainties arise. Here, even despite an effective public legal system, parties employ different bilateral (e.g., the – metaphorical – exchange of hostages) or trilateral (e.g., arbitration) private governance mechanisms in an effort to induce additional order to their relationship (*private ordering in the shadow of law*). When asset specificity and frequency are very high, transactions may even be taken out of the market by means of vertical integration into the hierarchy of a firm (*unified governance*).

However, circumstances where the state law is very costly, slow, unreliable, corrupt, weak, or simply absent (*lawlessness*) pose additional private ordering challenges (Williamson 2005: 14). Given the absence of state support, for example in developing countries or transformation states, parties simply have no choice but to do their best to create their own bilateral or trilateral mechanisms to support otherwise problematic exchange (Dixit 2004). Again, the ancient law merchant may serve as a historical example (Greif 2006), but empirical research suggests that private ordering or even private legal systems play an important role in the contemporary institutional organization of commerce as well (for an overview, see Konradi and Fix-Fierro 2005).

It follows that public and private governance mechanisms in the institutional organization of commerce play a role as *functional equivalents* that supplement and, to a certain extent, substitute each other. This insight is particularly relevant in the context of globalization, since the public institutions that support cross-border commerce are – as explained above – quite weak. Against this background, our hypotheses on the transformation of the state with regard to the institutional organization of international commerce are the following:

Hypothesis 1: Since the golden age of the nation state, the extent to which commerce is conducted across borders has risen substantially. Economic globalization thus has led to a *shift in the demand structure* for institutions that support commerce. Over the past forty years the need for institutions adapted to international commerce has increased. In other words, a trend emerged towards the internationalization of the state function to provide for the normative good of legal certainty for commerce.

Hypothesis 2: Since the nation states' attempts to shift the regulatory responsibility for the institutional organization of cross-border commerce to public international organizations and to exercise the operational responsibility by means of judicial cooperation in commercial matters according to the thus created international treaties have had little success, the *normative vacuum* left by nation states was filled by all kinds of private governance mechanisms and private legal services for international commerce. As a result, private or hybrid actors took over not only operational, but also regulatory responsibility.

Hypothesis 3: These trends towards the internationalization and privatization of responsibility for the provision of legal certainty combine to what we call the *transnationalization of commercial law*. While the state continues to take responsibility for domestic commerce, economic globalization leads to a decrease in the relative weight of public institutions and to a corresponding increase in the overall importance of private ordering with regard to the provision of the normative good of legal certainty for commerce.

In Table 5.1, we give an overview of public and private governance mechanisms employed in commercial transactions, categorized by the three classical state powers of legislation, adjudication and enforcement. The upshot is that there is a top-down shift from public governance to trilateral and bilateral private governance. In addition, many cross-border transactions are subject to unified governance. Recent estimates suggest that transnational corporations account for one-third of world exports (UNCTAD 2002: 1).

Table 5.1:   Public and private governance mechanisms in international commerce

	Dimension		
Regulator	**Legislation**	**Adjudication**	**Enforcement**
Public	Parliamentary act	Courts	Legal sanctions
Private trilateral	Social norms	Arbitration	Social sanctions
Private bilateral	Relational norms	Negotiation	Exit/hostages
Private unified	Corporate norms	Board decision	Hierarchy

In order to test our hypotheses on the transnationalization of commercial law, it was necessary to learn more about how cross-border commerce *in fact* is institutionally organized. Therefore, we conducted field studies based on interviews with involved merchants and lawyers as well as a participant observation and file analysis in a law firm. In the following we present results of three studies, one on *relational contracting* in the field of international outsourcing of software development, another on the *lex mercatoria* in the field of international timber trade, and a third on the role of *law firms* in the organization of cross-border commerce.

International outsourcing of software development

The software industry, as a relatively young and knowledge-based industry with high use of new information and communication technologies, is a good example of modern globalized commerce. The case of international software development outsourcing can be taken as exemplary for complex and globally distributed exchange relationships. Our study examined international business relations between client companies based in Germany and software suppliers situated in Bulgaria, India and Romania, which came into fashion during the 1990s mainly for reasons of differences in labour costs (Dietz and Nieswandt 2008).

Cooperation for the development of tailor-made software solutions is extremely complex. Software development projects often last for many months or even years. They usually consist of a *planning period*, where a system proposal is designed by the supplier in accordance with the targeted performance criteria of the user and the related technical specifications are negotiated and recorded in a comprehensive duty book; a *construction period*, where the software is developed, implemented and tested step by step according to agreed-upon milestones, and training of the client's staff is provided; and a *warranty period*, in which the software supplier – after a final test of the system – guarantees that the system will stay in operation and that he will provide maintenance services. In each period, the contract parties have to cooperate and are dependent on each other in the proactive creation of solutions, including amendments to the initially agreed-upon product specifications as well as related renegotiations of payment. Software development contracts, therefore, contain less strict and definitive substantive arrangements than classical contracts for the purchase of goods. Instead, detailed procedures for the management of the project with regard to iterative refinements or unforeseen changes are stipulated, such as duties to cooperate, steering committees with equal representation of supplier and user, and subsequently the involvement of third-party expert advice, mediation, or arbitration as well (Schneider 2003; Ullrich and Lejeune 2006).

Research in the field of relational contracting stresses the importance of relational norms in long-term business relationships with a focus on the enforcement of such norms through sanctions administered by the immediate parties to an exchange, mainly termination and future refusal to deal (Macaulay 1963, 2000; Macneil 1980, 1985, 2005).

> As against simple market exchange, private governance is predominantly concerned with ongoing contractual relations for which *continuity of the relationship is a source of value*. Given that incomplete contracts need to be adapted to disturbances for which contractual provision was not made or was incorrectly made at the outset, continuity can and will benefit from a spirit of cooperation. But therein lies the rub: continuity can be put in jeopardy by defecting from the spirit of cooperation and reverting to the letter [of the formal contract]. (Williamson 2005: 2)

In other words, there is a clash between relational norms, which by encouraging flexibility and solidarity aim at enabling future cooperation, and public contract law, which by providing for specific performance and damages is intended to retrospectively cope with past default.

In general, relational norms are considered to be self-enforcing where the value of a continuing business relationship for each party is higher than the potential gain from defection in a single transaction (*repeated game*) (Posner 2000: 15). To a large extent, such bilateral dependency is a function of asset specificity. If one party to a transaction makes durable investments in assets (physical or human) that can be redeployed to alternative uses and users only at a loss of productive value (sunk costs), the probability of opportunistic behaviour is low. Often, however, there is an imbalance between the parties with regard to the value of the relationship, which, in addition, is subject to variation over time. Where a client initially may have the choice between several suppliers, who in a bidding process have to make specific investments initially, once the choice is made the costs of switching the provider may become prohibitive for the client. The basic idea of relational contracting, thus, is to balance the mutual dependency of both parties by creating *credible commitments* (Williamson 1983). On the one hand, if one party according to the nature of the transaction has to make specific investments, the other party may offer hostages in exchange by voluntarily exposing assets to the other party, for example through entrance fees, deposits, advance payments, excess penalty clauses for early termination and other kinds of bonds (*bilateral governance*). On the other hand, private third-party services such as escrow, evaluation, mediation and arbitration may be employed *ex ante* in order to ensure that both parties live up to the cooperative spirit of the agreement *ex post* (*trilateral governance*).

Our analysis of cross-border business relationships in the field of software development confirms the relevance of relational contracting for the stabilization of expectations. However, traditional relational norms, which build on embedding exchanges in so-called F-connections (family, friends and firms) (Ben-Porath 1980) and which enable long-term business relationships even in the absence of formally drafted contracts are of little importance. Instead, agreements for software development are recorded in a very formalized and contractual manner, leaving little space for social norms of behaviour. Bilateral contract enforcement, however, is largely advantaged by modern information and communication technologies. Intense communicative interconnection between the business partners creates transparency and virtually provides the cooperation partners with *real-time control mechanism*. Any deviance from contractual agreements can be detected immediately before it escalates into severe conflict. By subdividing the project into an *iterative process* of achieving *milestones* with consecutive payment obligations, the parties limit their mutual exposure. In addition, procedural stipulations (e.g., steering committees) allow for the necessary flexibility with regard to contractual refinements. As a result, problems arising in the cooperation process can be managed effectively within the business relationship, mostly without the help of a third party (Dietz and Nieswandt 2008).

Still, such bilateral mechanisms do not suffice for the stabilization of expectations in the analysed business relationships. The trilateral *reputation mechanism*, which involves the social sanction of third party refusal to deal, is also of crucial importance. Before entering into an agreement for software development, clients usually engage in a due diligence exercise in which the track record of potential software suppliers is screened. On the one hand, references of former cooperation partners are required. Since the number of qualified players in the software industry is relatively small, such references are considered a reliable source of information. German-based clients usually trust either former business partners that they know in person or they rely on the judgement of large companies, which are known for their in-depth evaluation of cooperation partners. On the other hand, suppliers of software are certified by third parties. The most important examples of such certificates are the 'Capability Maturity Model Integration' (CMMI) as well as ISO 9001 and ISO 15504. Providers of standardized software tools that are tailored to customers by third parties such as SAP, in addition, issue specific certificates confirming the competencies of a software firm with regard to the products and processes of the issuing company.

Moreover, bilateral and trilateral governance mechanisms may be combined in a way that the latter builds on and thus reinforces the former. As mentioned above, contracts frequently stipulate that conflicts on necessary refinements of the product and resulting adaptations of remuneration that arise in the *construction period*, shall be solved by a *steering committee* in which both parties are equally represented. Building on this bilateral mechanism, contracts often contain a clause for third-party *conciliation or arbitration*, thereby integrating a trilateral mechanism which the parties may invoke if problems persist. In Germany, for instance, such services are offered by a professional association for information technology (IT) law.[3]

Another problem is pertinent to the *warranty period*. Since the source code and the technical documentation of the software product remains intellectual property of the supplier unless the contract provides otherwise, the client will unable to maintain and further adapt the licensed software if the supplier ceases business. Therefore, the source code in these cases usually is deposited at an *escrow service* provider, which under standardized contract terms will release the code to the client in the case of bankruptcy of the supplier.[4]

The above-described bilateral and trilateral private governance mechanisms are also employed in domestic transactions. However, they work differently in the shadow of national commercial law. Although going to court in software development is generally a redress mechanism of last resort, German standard form contracts for software development usually contain a choice of forum clause for a state court (Schneider 2003: 1605). In fact, in Germany there is a considerable amount of case law published in a variety of specialist IT law journals, indicating that going to court is a not so rare choice. Some district courts, such as that in Munich, have even acquired a reputation for building up expert knowledge in special chambers and, thus, are referenced more frequently by choice of forum clauses.

In international outsourcing of software development, in contrast, recourse to the state legal system is possible only to a very limited extent. Three reasons are pertinent. First, uncertainty prevails on the side of German clients with regard to the enforceability of German judgments in countries such as India and Romania.[5] Second, going to court in Germany is associated with unreasonable costs for many foreign software suppliers. Third, the capability of state courts to relate to the technical complexities of software development and to render a predictable judgment is limited. However, state law remains important as a last resort for the enforcement of certain crucial framework agreements such as the non-solicitation clause that forbids the parties to recruit each other's employees (Dietz and Nieswandt 2008). International contracts, therefore, often contain an arbitration clause under the auspices of the International Chamber of Commerce (Schneider 2003: 1608). Resulting arbitral awards may be enforceable under the 1958 New York Convention on the Recognition and Enforcement of Foreign Arbitral Awards, but are implemented by contracting parties predominantly for reasons of reputation in the industry (Dietz and Nieswandt 2008).

To sum up, the case study on international outsourcing in the software industry revealed that the responsibility for the enforcement of contracts, which traditionally was borne by the state through the provision of commercial law, is taken over by private governance mechanisms. This holds true for the operational responsibility, where the parties to software development agreements rely predominantly on various mechanisms of self-help (relational contracting, reputation) or private judges (arbitration), instead of relying on public courts and enforcement institutions. To a large extent, even the regulatory responsibility is taken away from the state, where parties try to substitute the rigour of formal contract law by relational norms aiming at the preservation of the cooperative spirit of the business relationship, while the autonomous implementation of such norms is safeguarded by procedural arrangements such as internal steering committees or external conciliation and arbitration procedures. Still, the state retains some responsibility in providing mandatory legal rules that parties must respect when drafting and enforcing contracts, and when strongly aggrieved players use the state as a final resort to enforce certain crucial stipulations of a contract.

The international timber trade

The international timber trade was chosen as an example for a highly organized industry with a long-standing tradition of self-regulation. The empirical findings of this study are based on expert interviews with managers of German companies involved in international timber trade as well as with representatives of timber trade associations and intra-industry arbitrators (Konradi 2008). The timber industry is characterized by its network-like structure. It is composed of family-owned, mid-sized companies that have been operating in the business for generations. Most businesses are aligned by their membership in different domestic and international industry associations, which facilitate trade by releasing technical standards on product quality, by drafting model contract forms, and by organizing intra-industry arbitration.

Timber is not a standardized commodity. Despite the existence of technical standards, the quality inspection of timber products often takes place at a meeting of the business partners, which renders the business a personal matter. Due to the fact that dealing with a natural product makes it necessary to put some energy into learning to handle it and to find appropriate suppliers, exchanges predominantly take place within long-term business relationships. To quote a company representative:

> You can only be successful in this industry if you are able to build business relationships that have a strong personal character. The term *business friendship* really means friendship: the connections to the plurality of our suppliers and with most of our clients are intense friendships which we strive to keep. A friendship is a value you do not easily deceive whereas it is easy to break up a business relationship if there are no personal bonds. Hence, we try to build personal relations to create an atmosphere which guarantees that problems in everyday situations can be solved in a way that both parties feel comfortable with. This is vital to make sure the business relationship does not break up. Buy once and never again: this is not our practice; this is not an option in our company. No doctoral degree, no studies, no computer, nothing, only fostering the relations with our clients and suppliers is the key to our success. (quoted in Konradi 2008)

This indicates that relational norms in the traditional, non-legal sense (Macaulay 1963, 2000; Macneil 1980, 1985, 2005) as well as the above-quoted F-Connections (Ben-Porath 1980) are constitutive even in cross-border exchanges that are common to the timber trade. Formal contract law seems to be less important. To quote another company representative:

> You may in principle avoid a lot of eventualities and hide behind regulations specified by the contract, but in real life the business turns out to be incompatible with strict regulations: a contract – this is not much more than a piece of paper, when it comes to practice. In practice a lot of things are handled completely differently (quoted in Konradi 2008).

Nevertheless, model contracts are of great importance to the industry, the most popular being 'Germania 1998'. This contract form was developed by German and Scandinavian industry organizations to govern the import of sawn wood from Finland, Sweden and Norway to Germany, but also it became widely used in other international transactions. 'Germania 1998' contains detailed stipulations regarding all aspects of the trade. The endeavour to render any reference to national private law dispensable in its application is highlighted by the fact that the form contains no choice of law clause. While state courts do not recognize a *contrat sans loi*, private arbitrators are much more likely to respect the will of the parties not to subject a cross-border transaction to any national private law (Berger 2006). In fact, 'Germania 1998' stipulates that all disputes arising from the contract shall be settled by means of final and binding industry arbitration, thus creating a self-regulatory regime.

In addition to such model contract forms, the timber industry developed technical standards such as uniform grading rules and quality standards, for instance the 'NLGA (National Lumber Grades Authority) Standard Grading Rules for Canadian Lumber' or the 'Standard Grading Rules for Southern Pine Lumber', which have been produced by branch organizations and are applied in the practice of international trade. Moreover, trade associations have engaged in the codification of trade usages and customs. For example, the *Tegernseer Handelsbräuche*, originally developed for domestic trade by the German trade association *Gesamtverband Deutscher Holzhandel* (*GD Holz*), obtained relevance also in international transactions.

The timber industry has also established a system of intra-industry arbitration. While arbitration is only considered where an amicable agreement cannot be found, and the parties to an exchange in principle are free to choose any private arbitrator ad hoc, trade organizations such as *GD Holz* and the International Technical Timber Association (ATIBT) in Paris offer institutional arbitration proceedings according to industry-specific rules such as the *Bremer Freundschaftliche Arbitrage*. Under these rules, conflicts are not disputed in lengthy formal proceedings between lawyers, but settled by acknowledged and experienced intra-industry experts within two weeks. The resulting arbitral awards are not executed under state law, but rather accepted by the conflict parties as a matter of retaining intra-industry reputation, where some trade associations maintain black-lists of non-cooperative traders (Konradi and Fix-Fierro 2005). Interestingly, the number of industry arbitrations has declined recently. During the past five years, for instance, only three arbitrations were initiated under the 'Germania 1998' contract form. An interviewed arbiter, who used to carry out about 20–40 arbitrations per year, stated that he hardly got any requests in recent years. He assumed that it became more common to reach an amicable agreement these days (Konradi 2008).

To sum up, the international timber trade is institutionally organized by private bilateral and trilateral governance mechanisms, which to a large extent operate independently of the state. This result correlates to the findings of empirical studies of the diamond industry (Bernstein 1992) and the cotton trade (Bernstein 2001), in which trade clubs, exchanges, or comparable industry associations were successful in bundling various private governance mechanisms into effective *private legal systems*. To be sure, the private regime of the timber industry is not a direct result of the post-Second World War internationalization of commerce. Instead, the timber trade has been governed privately long before. However, economic globalization was tackled by the industry mainly through an extension of originally domestic or regional private rules and networks to also include other countries and market participants. Thus, one can say that the private regime of the timber industry increasingly became transnational by industry cooperation within the OECD and by its unilateral extension beyond.

The role of law firms

The role of law firms in the institutional organization of cross-border commerce became an important subject of research during recent decades. Obviously the significance of lawyers increases where the existing legal structures are weak (Friedman 1989). In international commerce, a situation of relative lawlessness, lawyers have to act as 'managers of uncertainty' (Flood 1991), 'legal entrepreneurs', or 'legal engineers' (McBarnet 1994), they have to engage in 'creative lawyering' (Powell 1993; Gardner 2003). Correspondingly, the dominance of Anglo-American mega law firms in the global legal field was explained by the fact that common lawyers are more used to work within an incomplete legal framework than their continental colleagues (Shapiro 1993; Trubek *et al.* 1994; Silver 2000). In contrast to the nation states, mega law firms were able to adapt to the globalization of commerce by going global themselves. Having successfully established a worldwide reputation, it is the mega law firm which sanctifies a global transaction. Without the imprimatur granted in their documentation, business dealings will always appear somewhat profane and suspect. However, the services of mega law firms are not the optimal solution to each and every type of international transaction. Mid-sized law firms have also specialized in the provision of legal services to international commerce (Sosa 2007).

Since the role of smaller law firms is less well researched, we conducted a one-year participant observation in the international department of a German law firm employing approximately 90 lawyers as opposed to mega law firms with an average of 1,000 professionals (Sosa 2008). The clients by and large were small and mid-sized companies that carry out national as well as international activities. We conducted 40 case file studies, supplemented by the analysis of contracts, participation in the daily work of the law firm, participation in negotiations, interviews with lawyers and so forth. The international work of the law firm had a strong focus on German-Spanish commerce, but it was also related to other countries, for example the United States, France, the United Arab Emirates and Mauritania. In this chapter, we use international commercial arbitration as an example to illustrate the role of law firms in what we call *recombinant governance,* namely a functional and instrumental approach to the use of public as well as private governance mechanisms in the creation of workable arrangements for international commercial transactions on an individual case-by-case basis.

Mid-sized law firms are not involved in the extremely high value arbitration cases often referred to by the literature on the new law merchant (Dezalay and Garth 1996; Berger 1999). In our case studies, the amounts at stake ranged between US$ 1 and 10 million. However, these 'routine arbitration' proceedings, predominantly conducted under the auspices of the International Chamber of Commerce (ICC), are much more formal and legally sophisticated than it is the case with intra-industry arbitration, for example in the above-described timber trade, where not lawyers but experts or merchants themselves participate as arbitrators.

In the analysed routine arbitration cases, lawyers played a dominant role. Where the contract contains an arbitration clause, the international transactions do not leave the sphere of influence of the law firms at any time. Lawyers draft the often-complex contracts, they advise their clients on all matters concerning the interpretation of the contract, they assist in party negotiations, and they take part in the arbitration proceedings as party representatives or arbitrators. The law firms are often linked to each other by networks within and outside of the arbitration system, and the cited F-connections here work among the lawyers involved.

The state, with its public legal system, is still visible in this context, but not as a central figure exercising a legal monopoly as in a domestic setting (Flood 2005). By means of choice of law, the parties to an international transaction may freely select the applicability of any national private law. Under Article 28 of the 1985 UNCITRAL Model Law on International Commercial Arbitration, which was transposed in many national laws (Sanders 2005), and under Article 17 of the 1998 ICC Arbitration Rules (Derains and Schwartz 2005), parties may choose 'rules of law' as applicable, for instance so-called private codifications such as the UNIDROIT Principles of International Commercial Contracts (Bonell 2005). In addition to the thus created competition of public and private norms, parties may establish complex contracts that leave little room for resort to the applicable law, a fact significantly reducing the influence of the state legal systems.

However, in our case studies, national private law was often used by arbitrators to complement other sources of law. Moreover, arbitrators strictly adhered to mandatory national and international law, because any neglect of such mandatory rules renders the arbitral award unenforceable under the 1958 New York Convention on the Recognition and Enforcement of Foreign Arbitral Awards (Redfern and Hunter 2004). Each arbitral award released under the auspices of the ICC, therefore, is screened for its enforceability in a final scrutiny procedure conducted by the ICC Court of International Arbitration (Derains and Schwartz 2005). Typical instruments attributed to an autonomous law merchant, such as general principles of law and trade usages (Berger 2001; Zumbansen 2002), are of crucial importance for international arbitration, but in the analysed routine arbitration proceedings they only complemented other sources of law, such as the contract itself, national and international law and discretionary powers of the arbitrators. An overview is given in Table 5.2.

When comparing arbitration with litigation in state courts (Benson 1999), the decisive advantage in the praxis of routine arbitration does not seem to lie in the use of completely new legal structures, such as a truly transnational law merchant (Zumbansen 2002, 2006), but rather in the employment of experts who are experienced in the creative use of existing public and private legal structures with due flexibility. These experts are capable of finding pragmatic solutions through consideration

Table 5.2: Sources of law used in routine arbitration proceedings

Type of transaction	Type of contract	Choice of law	Resort to state law	General principles	Discretionary power	Extra-legal expertise
Construction of a fibre-optic network	Complex	Spanish		Good faith, *pacta sunt servanda*	Express discretion in several contract clauses	Construction expert
Sales contract, non-performance	Standardized	German	§326 BGB/Art. 81, 82 EC Treaty	Contract interpretation	Discretionary decision with regard to loss of profit	
Licensing agreement	Standardized, complex clauses	German	§89 b HGB/Art. 81, 82 EC Treaty		Discretionary decision on compensation	
Shareholder agreement	Complex	German		Contract interpretation	Discretion with regard to use of general principles	Expert report from a tax consultant
Stock purchase agreement	Complex	New York	Principle of *res iudicata*			Tax consultant, two Spanish professors (both tax)
Supply of cotton	Standardized			Trade usage, custom between the parties		Technical expert for cotton quality
Purchase of machines	Standardized, complex clauses	CISG				Technical expert
Purchase of railway tracks	Standardized, complex clauses	Mauritanian	Art. 284 Code des Contrats et Obligations	Trade usage, custom between the parties	Discretionary decision on compensation	Three technical experts
Purchase of company shares	Complex	Spanish		Good faith/*culpa in contrahendo*	Discretion with regard to use of general principles	Financial expert

Notes: BGB = Bürgerliches Gesetzbuch (German Civil Code); EC = European Community; HGB = Handelsgesetzbuch (German Commercial Code); CISG = UN Convention on the International Sale of Goods.

of the technical, economic and social context factors of a transaction. Awards are based on rules of national private law, complex contracts, general principles of law and trade usages. Moreover, non-legal expertise plays a crucial role in most decisions. Thus, more particularistic solutions that are better suited to the parties' interests and provide a higher level of fairness may be reached, a reason why it was suggested to perceive 'transnational law' as a 'method of decision making' rather than an autonomous 'legal system' (Gaillard 2001). The openness of arbitration for particular solutions leads to a transfer of not only operational, but also of regulatory responsibility from the level of normative 'programmes' to the level of 'roles' (Luhmann 1983), as lawyers are the key players in this system (Sosa 2008).

To sum up, routine arbitration includes elements of both public and private governance. However, the *recombinant governance* mode observed by us in the praxis of routine international commercial arbitration implies a fundamental transformation in the production of the normative good of legal certainty. In the domestic legal field the state acts as a quasi-monopolist on the regulatory level, and lawyers are reduced to the role of a helping hand in the process of the implementation of state law on the operational level. When it comes to international commerce, in turn, the regulatory authority of the nation state is questioned by the availability of competing public and private governance mechanisms. State law here is reduced to the status of a 'raw material' for arbitral awards; it is simply one supplement in a larger toolbox, out of which lawyers compose tailor-made governance solutions. Furthermore, on the operational level, the responsibility is almost entirely transferred to private actors, except for the small – and with regard to its efficacy disputed (Tannock 2005) – role of the state in enforcing arbitral awards.

Transnational commercial law: Résumé and the way forward

In total, the case studies revealed a high relevance of private governance mechanisms for the production of the normative good of legal certainty in international commerce. As indicated above, however, private governance plays a major role as well in the shadow of efficacious rules of commercial law created and enforced by the nation state. Domestic software development contracts, for instance, are quite similar to those entered into across borders, except for the arbitration clauses; the private regime of the timber industry was originally developed for national and regional trade, before it was extended to meet the needs of globalization; and arbitration is a viable alternative to litigation in certain domestic transactions as well, in which national arbitration institutions such as the German DIS (Deutsche Institution für Schiedsgerichtsbarkeit) offer comparable services as the ICC does for international commerce. Consequently, the relevant difference between domestic and international commerce is not the existence of private governance mechanisms as such, but rather the reduced functionality of the state legal system as a support structure.

Thus, it is quite difficult to derive a clear-cut result from our case studies with regard to the validity of our hypotheses on the transnationalization of commercial law. It seems to be fair to say, though, that private governance in an international context is subject to a functional transformation. While domestic business may or may not use one or the other private governance mechanism as an add-on to legal certainty provided by the state, the function of private governance is fundamentally different when it comes to cross-border commerce. In a situation of relative lawlessness, private governance has to substitute for state-created legal certainty. Although under special circumstances it may still suffice to employ bilateral governance mechanisms such as relational contracting, generally the bundling of a plurality of trilateral governance mechanisms such as private norms, arbitration and social sanctions into effective private governance regimes (Teubner 2004) or private legal systems (Bernstein 2001), is essential in order to get anywhere in terms of production of legal certainty. This is to say that private governance on the transnational plain becomes much more comprehensive, systematic and ubiquitous.

Purely private legal systems are very rare though in praxis. In our case studies, we predominantly observed an institutional mix of public and private governance mechanisms. In view of their hybrid character in terms of the public–private divide, we refer to the regimes resulting from this recombinant governance mode as 'transnational civil regimes' (Calliess 2008). Our case studies have shown that the composition of these regimes in terms of the individual weight of private and public governance mechanisms varies substantially. The optimal institutional mix is not only a variable of the nature of the governed transactions, but depends on the *extent of lawlessness* involved in a specific transaction. While transactions inside the European Internal Market are quite highly regulated, cross-border contracts between parties from different OECD countries with well-functioning national legal systems, for instance between Europe and the United States or Japan, are subject to an intermediate level of legal uncertainty. Due to a lack of judicial cooperation between these states, arbitration may be advisable, but the enforcement of arbitral awards by these states is quite certain.

The situation is different if one partner to the transaction comes from a developing country or a transformation state with a relatively weak legal system. Here one can observe an imbalance between the parties with regard to the availability of public governance mechanisms. While, for instance, a software supplier from India could sue its German client under German law in a German court and have a resulting judgment enforced in Germany, the same is not true vice versa. The Indian court system generally is held to be unreliable and slow (Dixit 2004). Thus, a German court ruling may not be enforceable in India, and although India signed the 1958 New York Convention on the Recognition and Enforcement of Foreign Arbitral. Awards, it might be not worthwhile trying it in practice, so that the German business is forced to fully rely on private governance mechanisms (Dietz and Nieswandt 2008).

To sum up, we observed a substantial, enduring, and in the context of economic globalization, even accelerating trend towards the private governance of international commercial transactions. This transnationalization of commercial law predominantly takes the form of diffusion instead of a shift of responsibility for the production of the normative good of legal certainty. This is because the nation state in OECD countries continues to effectively regulate domestic commercial transactions, while at the same time it never was in a position to perform an equivalent function for cross-border commerce. Transnational civil regimes, therefore, do not take over the outcome, regulatory, or operational responsibility of the modern Western state, but simply take an essential operational as well as regulatory role in the production of the normative good of legal certainty for commerce on the international plain. The extent to which such diffusion of responsibility is interlocked with or disconnected from the state, is a function of the degree of lawlessness involved, which depends on the domicile of the parties to the transaction.

This having been said, the question arises how this trend towards the transnationalization of commercial law could be explained and also whether it will and should continue. Our future research will be directed to both descriptive and normative factors that might influence the global evolution of commercial law. On the basis of our findings, we believe that the probable options are not black or white, and neither a complete privatization nor a full restatement of commercial law will take place. Rather the recombination of public and private shares in the governance of commercial transactions might be subject to an evolutionary change. Four crucial factors in particular are worth addressing by future research.

The recombinant governance mode is characterized by a functional and instrumental approach to the use of public and private governance mechanisms. Therefore, at a more descriptive level, we believe that the competitive capacity of private and public governance mechanisms is decisive for the evolution of the institutional mix. On the one hand, private governance might improve its efficacy through the increased use of information and communication technology (ICT), especially with regard to the costs of creating effective information networks (Factor 1). Good examples are the online feedback mechanism of eBay (Baron 2002; Schultz 2005) or online dispute resolution systems (Calliess 2006b). On the other hand, the relative weight of public governance mechanisms might rise if states engage in creating efficient legal services for international commerce (Factor 2). In 2005, for instance, the Hague Conference on International Private Law adopted a Convention on Choice of Court Agreements, which is intended to have the same effect on the global enforceability of state court judgments as the 1958 New York Convention had for arbitral awards (Calliess 2006a: 147). In addition, a proposed European regulation permits parties to choose private codifications such as the above-mentioned UNIDROIT principles as applicable law (European Commission 2005). Furthermore, in Germany several law reforms aim at making state courts more attractive for commercial transactions (Hein 2003; JuMiKo 2004: 13).

Commercial law, however, is not only concerned with creating legal certainty, its coordinative function, but also aims at safeguarding substantive fairness, especially with respect to weaker contract parties as well as public interests like competition policy or the protection of human rights, that is to fulfil a regulatory function (Calliess 2008). At a more normative level, we therefore believe that the capability of transnational civil regimes to contribute to public policy is essential to the evolution of governance. States will and should support the further transnationalization of commercial law by means of non-intervention or affirmative regulation only if public policy does not suffer. On the one hand, for instance, the structural drift towards a hierarchical organization of global trade implied by private unified governance – multinational enterprises and subcontractor networks – may have detrimental effects on competition policy (Factor 3). On the other hand, if transnational governance regimes would enable the creation and implementation of a truly international public policy, this would constitute a normative argument for further promoting the transnationalization of commercial law. Here, the jurisprudence of alternative dispute resolution bodies in respect of antitrust law as well as human rights is of interest (Factor 4).

After analysing these four crucial factors in much more detail, with the resulting evolutionary theory of transnational commercial law we hope to contribute to the much broader context of a normative theory of a global economic constitution.

Notes

1   The status of the ancient law merchant as a coherent body of substantive rules or even a universal legal system is questionable. The medieval *lex mercatoria* was mainly based on procedural privileges granted to merchants by local rulers, and on the similarity of substantive solutions which emerged from the similarity of the underlying problems and interests of the involved merchants (Cordes 2003; Sachs 2006). However, it seems to be inadequate to judge on the ancient lex mercatoria by comparing it with the formality of modern national legal systems. In the context of our research, it suffices that – albeit the role of local rulers in recognizing the privilege of merchants to be subjected to special court proceedings – indisputably in the late Middle Ages there was no state that took over the full-fledged responsibility for providing the normative good of legal certainty for cross-border commerce.
2   There are regional instruments, such as in Europe the Brussels I Regulation (2000/31/EC) and the 1980 Rome Convention, though, and for inter-state commerce in the United States, where each state has its own private law, the 'full faith and credit' clause of the US Constitution applies (Calliess 2004). However, there are no instruments for mutual recognition and enforcement of judgments between Europe and the United States or Japan.
3   See Deutsche Gesellschaft für Recht und Informatik (DGRI), Conciliation, Information Brochure, October 2002, available at <http://www.dgri.de/service/SchlO-2002-en.doc>, last accessed: 28 February 2007.
4   See, for example, the standard contract form of Escrow Europe, available at <http://www.escroweurope.com/eng/downloads/EscrowContracts.html>, last accessed: 28 February 2007.
5   Since the accession of Romania and Bulgaria to the European Union on 1 January 2007, the Brussels I Regulation (2000/31/EC) on the mutual recognition and enforcement of judgments in civil and commercial matters applies. Problems with the implementation of the *acquis communautaire* in the accession countries notwithstanding, this may change the legal situation in the future.

References

Bar, Christian von and Peter Mankowski (2003) *Internationales Privatrecht Bd. I: Allgemeine Lehren*, 2nd edn., München: C.H. Beck.
Baron, David P. (2002) 'Private Ordering on the Internet: The EBay Community of Traders', *Business and Politics* 4(3), 245–74.
Baumgartner, Samuel P. (2003) *The Proposed Hague Convention on Jurisdiction and Foreign Judgments*, Tübingen: Mohr Siebeck.
Ben-Porath, Yoram (1980) 'The F-Connection: Families, Friends, and Firms and the Organization of Exchange', *Population and Development Review* 6(1), 1–30.
Benson, Bruce L. (1989) 'The Spontaneous Evolution of Commercial Law', *Southern Economic Journal* 55(3), 644–61.

Benson, Bruce L. (1999) 'To Arbitrate or To Litigate: That Is the Question', *European Journal of Law and Economics* 8(2), 91–151.

Berger, Klaus Peter (1999) *The Creeping Codification of the Lex Mercatoria*, The Hague: Kluwer Law International.

Berger, Klaus Peter (2001) 'The New Law Merchant and the Global Market Place. A 21st Century View of Transnational Commercial Law', in Klaus Peter Berger, ed., *The Practice of Transnational Law*, The Hague: Kluwer Law International, 1–22.

Berger, Klaus Peter (2006) 'Contracts with no Governing Law in Private International Law and Non-State Law, Country Report Germany', paper presented at the Conference 'XVIIth World Congress of Comparative Law', Utrecht, The Netherlands, 17–22 July, available at <http://tldb.uni-koeln.de/static/ContratssansLoi.pdf>, last accessed: 27 February 2007.

Berman, Harold J. (1983) *Law and Revolution: The Formation of the Western Legal Tradition*, Cambridge, MA: Harvard University Press.

Bernstein, Lisa (1992) 'Opting Out of the Legal System: Extralegal Contractual Relations in the Diamond Trade', *Journal of Legal Studies* 21(1), 115–57.

Bernstein, Lisa (2001) 'Private Commercial Law in the Cotton Industry: Creating Cooperation through Rules, Norms, and Institutions', *Michigan Law Review* 99(7), 1724–90.

Black, Vaughan (2000) 'Commodifying Justice for Global Free Trade: The Proposed Hague Judgments Convention', *Osgoode Hall Law Journal* 38(2), 237–66.

Bonell, Michael-Joachim (2005) *An International Restatement of Contract Law: The Unidroit Principles of International Commercial Contracts*, 3rd edn, Ardsley: Transnational Publications.

Burdick, Francis M. (1902) 'What Is the Law Merchant?', *Columbia Law Review* 2(7), 470–85.

Calliess, Gralf-Peter (2004) 'Value-added Norms, Local Litigation, and Global Enforcement: Why the Brussels-Philosophy Failed in The Hague', *German Law Journal* 5(12), 1989–98.

Calliess, Gralf-Peter (2006a) *Grenzüberschreitende Verbraucherverträge, Rechtssicherheit und Gerechtigkeit auf dem elektronischen Weltmarktplatz*, Tübingen: Mohr Siebeck.

Calliess, Gralf-Peter (2006b) 'Online Dispute Resolution: Consumer Redress in a Global Market Place', *German Law Journal* 7(8), 647–60; Japanese translation by Kota Fukui, *Osaka Law Review* 56(3), 831–52.

Calliess, Gralf-Peter (2008) 'Transnational Civil Regimes: Economic Globalization and the Evolution of Commercial Law', in Volkmar Gessner, ed., *Legal Certainty Beyond the State: Empirical Studies and Theories of Change*, Oxford: Hart Publishing (forthcoming).

Cordes, Albrecht (2003) 'The Search for a Medieval Lex Mercatoria', Oxford University Comparative Law Forum 5, available at <ouclf.iuscomp.org>, last accessed: 27 February 2007).

Cutler, Claire (2003) *Private Power and Global Authority: Transnational Merchant Law in the Global Political Economy*, Cambridge: Cambridge University Press.

Derains, Yves and Eric A. Schwartz (2005) *A Guide to the ICC Rules of Arbitration*, 2nd edn, The Hague: Kluwer.

Dezalay, Yves and Bryant Garth (1996) *Dealing in Virtue: International Commercial Arbitration and the Construction of a Transnational Legal Order*, Chicago: University of Chicago Press.

Dietz, Thomas and Holger Nieswandt (2008) 'Contract Enforcement in Cross-Border Outsourcing Transactions: The Case of the Global Software-Industry', in Volkmar Gessner, ed., *Legal Certainty Beyond the State: Empirical Studies and Theories of Change*, Oxford: Hart Publishing (forthcoming).

Dixit, Avinash K. (2004) *Lawlessness and Economics: Alternative Modes of Governance*, Princeton: Princeton University Press.

Drobnig, Ulrich (2001) 'Vereinheitlichung von Zivilrecht durch soft law: Neuere Erfahrungen und Einsichten', in Jürgen Basedow *et al.*, eds, *Die Gründung des Max-Planck-Instituts: Aufbruch nach Europa, 75 Jahre Max-Planck-Institut für Privatrecht, Festschrift des Max-Planck-Instituts*, Tübingen: Mohr Siebeck, 45–61.

Eggertson, Thráinn (2005) *Imperfect Institutions: Possibilities and Limits of Reform*, Ann Arbor: University of Michigan Press.

Ellickson, Robert C. (1991) *Order Without Law: How Neighbours Settle Disputes*, Cambridge: Harvard University Press.

European Commission (2005) *Proposal for a Regulation on the Law Applicable to Contractual Obligation (Rome I)*, COM(2005) 650 final, 15 December 2005.

Ferrari, Franco, ed. (2005) *Quo Vadis CISG? Celebrating the 25th Anniversary of the United Nations Convention on Contracts for the International Sale of Goods*, Munich: Sellier European Law Publishers.

Flood, John (1991) 'Doing Business: The Management of Uncertainty in Lawyers' Work', *Law and Society Review* 25(1), 41–71.

Flood, John (2005) 'Rating, Dating, and the Informal Regulation and the Formal Ordering of Financial Transactions: Securitizations and Credit Rating Agencies in Privatising Development', in Michael B. Likosky, ed., *Transnational Law, Infrastructure and Human Rights*, Leiden: Martinus Nijhoff, 147–71.

Friedman, Lawrence (1989) 'Lawyers in Cross-Cultural Perspective' in Richard Abel and Philip Lewis, eds, *Lawyers in Society*, Vol. 3, Berkeley: University of California Press, 1–26.

Furubotn, Eirik G. and Rudolf Richter (2005) *Institutions and Economic Theory: The Contribution of the New Institutional Economics*, 2nd edn, Ann Arbor: University of Michigan Press.

Gaillard, Emmanuel (2001) 'Transnational Law: A legal system or a method of decision-making?', in Klaus Peter Berger, ed., *The Practice of Transnational Law*, The Hague: Kluwer, 53–65.

Gardner, Peter (2003) 'A Role for the Business Attorney in the Twenty-First Century: Adding Value to the Client's Enterprise in the Knowledge Economy', *Marquette Intellectual Property Law Review* 7(17), 17–52.

Gessner, Volkmar (2008) 'The Governance of Business Transactions in Globalizing Economies: Theories of Change', in Volkmar Gessner, ed., *Legal Certainty Beyond the State: Empirical Studies and Theories of Change*, Oxford: Hart Publishing (forthcoming).

Goldschmitt, Levin (1892) *Universalgeschichte des Handelsrechts*, Stuttgart: Enke.

Greif, Avner (2006) *Institutions and the Path to the Modern Economy: Lessons from Medieval Trade*, Cambridge: Cambridge University Press.

Hadfield, Gillian K. (2001) 'Privatizing Commercial Law', *Regulation* 24(1), 40–5.

Hadfield, Gillian K. (2005) 'The Many Institutions that Support Contractual Commitments', in Claude Menard and Mary Shirley, eds, *Handbook of New Institutional Economics*, New York: Springer, 175–203.

Hein, Jan von (2003) 'Die Berufungszuständigkeit der Oberlandesgerichte bei amtsgerichtlichen Entscheidungen mit Auslandsberührung (§119 I Nr. 1 lit. b und c GVG)', *Zeitschrift für Zivilprozeß* 116(3), 335–69.

JuMiKo, Justizministerkonferenz (2004) 'Beschlüsse, Herbstkonferenz, Eckpunkte für eine "Große Justizreform". 3. Konzentration', available at <http://www.berlin.de/imperia/md/content/senatsverwaltungen/justiz/jumiko/h_2004/hbeschluss_oa_3_konzentration.pdf>, last accessed 28 February 2007.

Konradi, Wioletta (2008) 'Lex Mercatoria in the International Timber Trade', in Volkmar Gessner, ed., *Legal Certainty Beyond the State: Empirical Studies and Theories of Change*, Oxford: Hart Publishing (forthcoming).

Konradi, Wioletta and Héctor Fix-Fierro (2005) 'Lex Mercatoria in the Mirror of Empirical Research', *Sociologia del Diritto* 32(2/3), 205–27.

Kronke, Herbert (2001) 'Ziele – Methqoden, Kosten – Nutzen: Perspektiven der Privatrechtsharmonisierung nach 75 Jahren Unidroit', *Juristenzeitung* 56(23), 1149–57.

Kronke, Herbert (2003) 'Unidroit 75th Anniversary Congress on Worldwide Harmonisation of Private Law and Regional Economic Integration: Hypotheses, Certainties and Open Questions', *Uniform Law Review* 8(1/2), 10–30.

Kronke, Herbert (2005) 'Methodical Freedom and Organizational Constraints in the Development of Transnational Commercial Law', *Loyola Law Review* 51(2), 287–300.

Luhmann, Niklas (1983) *Rechtssoziologie*, 2nd edn, Opladen: Westdeutscher Verlag.

Macaulay, Stewart (1963) 'Non-Contractual Relations in Business: A Preliminary Study', *American Sociological Review* 55(1), 86–104.

Macaulay, Stewart (2000) 'Relational Contracts Floating on a Sea of Custom?', *Northwestern University Law Review* 94(3), 775–804.

MacNeil, Ian R. (1980) *The New Social Contract: An Inquiry into Modern Contractual Relations*, New Haven: Yale University Press.

MacNeil, Ian R. (1985) 'Relational Contract: What We Do and Do Not Know', *Wisconsin Law Review* 3, 483–525.

MacNeil, Ian R. *et al.* (2005) 'Panel Discussion: Relational Contracting in a Digital Age', *Texas Wesleyan Law Review* 11(2), 675–706.

McBarnet, Doreen (1994) 'Legal Creativity: Law, Capital and Legal Avoidance', in Maureen Cain and Christine Harrington, eds, *Lawyers in a Postmodern World: Translation and Transgression*, New York: New York University Press, 73–84.

Ménard, Claude and Mary M. Shirley, eds (2005) *Handbook of New Institutional Economics*, Dordrecht: Springer.

Milgrom, Paul R., Douglass C. North and Barry R. Weingast (1990) 'The Role of Institutions in the Revival of Trade: The Law Merchant, Private Judges and the Champagne Fairs', *Economics and Politics* 2(1), 1–21.

North, Douglass C. (2005) *Understanding the Process of Economic Change*, Princeton: Princeton University Press.

Oldham, James (2004) *English Common Law in the Age of Lord Mansfield*, Durham: University of North Carolina Press.

Posner, Eric A. (2000) *Law and Social Norms*, Cambridge: Harvard University Press.

Powell, Michael (1993) 'Professional Innovation: Corporate Lawyers and Private Lawmaking', *Journal of Law and Social Inquiry* 18(3), 423–52.

Redfern, Alan and Martin Hunter (2004) *Law and Practice of International Commercial Arbitration*, 4th edn, London: Sweet & Maxwell.

Sachs, Stephen E. (2006) 'From St. Ives to Cyberspace: The Modern Distortion of the Medieval "Law Merchant"', *American University International Law Review* 21(5), 685–812.

Sanders, Pieter (2005) 'UNCITRAL's Model Law on International and Commercial Arbitration: Present Situation and Future', *Arbitration International* 21(4), 443–82.

Schneider, Jochen (2003) *Handbuch des EDV-Rechts*, 3rd edn, Köln: Otto Schmidt.

Schultz, Thomas (2005) 'eBay: un système juridique en formation?', *Revue du Droit des Technologies et de l'Information* 22(27), 27–51.

Shapiro, Martin (1993) 'The Globalization of Law', *Indiana Journal of Global Legal Studies* 1(1), 37–64.

Silver, Carol (2000) 'Globalization and the US Market in Legal Services: Shifting Identities', *Law and Policy in International Business* 31, 1093–150.

Sosa, Fabian (2007) *Vertrag und Geschäftsbeziehung im grenzüberschreitenden Wirtschaftsverkehr*, Baden-Baden: Nomos

Sosa, Fabian (2008) 'The Role of Midsized Law Firms in Globalized Exchange Processes', in Volkmar Gessner, ed., *Legal Certainty Beyond the State: Empirical Studies and Theories of Change*, Oxford: Hart Publishing (forthcoming).

Tannock, Quentin (2005) 'Judging the Effectiveness of Arbitration through the Assessment of Compliance with and Enforcement of International Arbitration Awards', *Arbitration International* 21(1), 71–90.

Teubner, Gunther (2004) 'Global Private Regimes: Neo-Spontaneous Law and Dual Constitution of Autonomous Sectors?', in Karl-Heinz Ladeur, ed., *Public Governance in the Age of Globalization*, Aldershot: Ashgate, 71–87.

Traynor, Michael (2000) 'An Introductory Framework for Analyzing the Proposed Hague Convention on Jurisdiction and Foreign Judgments in Civil and Commercial Matters: U.S. and European Perspectives', *Annual Survey of International and Comparative Law* 6(1), 1–12.

Trubek, David M., Yves Dezalay, Ruth Buchanan and John R. Davis (1994) 'Global Restructuring and the Law: Studies of the Internationalization of Legal Fields and the Creation of Transnational Arenas', *Case Western Reserve Law Review* 44(2), 407–98.

Ullrich, Hanns and Mathias Lejeune, eds (2006) *Der internationale Softwarevertrag: Nach deutschem und ausländischem Recht*, 2nd edn, Frankfurt a.M.: Verlag Recht und Wirtschaft.

UNCTAD (2002) 'United Nations Conference on Trade and Development, World Investment Report, New York', available at <http://www.unctad.org/en/docs/wir2002overview_en.pdf>, last accessed 28 February 2007.

Williamson, Oliver (1983) 'Credible Commitments: Using Hostages to Support Exchange', *American Economic Review* 73(4), 519–40.

Williamson, Oliver (1985) *The Economic Institutions of Capitalism: Firms, Markets, Relational Contracting*, New York: Free Press.

Williamson, Oliver (2005) 'The Economics of Governance', *American Economic Review* 95(2), 1–18.

Zekoll, Joachim (1998) 'Could a Treaty Trump Supreme Court Jurisdictional Doctrine? The Role and Status of American Law in the Hague Judgments Convention Project', *Albany Law Review* 61(4), 1283–307.

Zitelmann, Ernst (1888) 'Die Möglichkeiten eines Weltrechts', *Allgemeine Österreichische Gerichts-Zeitung* 39, 193–208.
Zumbansen, Peer (2002) 'Piercing the Legal Veil: Commercial Arbitration and Transnational Law' *European Law Journal* 8(3), 400–32.
Zumbansen, Peer (2006) 'Transnational Law', in Jan Smits, ed., *Encyclopedia of Comparative Law*, Cheltenham: Edgar Elgar, 738–54.

6

Breaking the Nation State Shell: Prospects for Democratic Legitimacy in the International Domain

Jens Steffek

The past decades have been marked by a diffusion of political decision-making competence from national governments towards functional international organizations. In this respect at least, the modern nation state is clearly losing ground in world politics. Since international organizations are remote from citizens and dominated by a non-elected elite of diplomats and experts, the concomitant disempowerment of national parliaments has been widely interpreted as a clear loss of democratic legitimacy and accountability (Dahl 1999). Some authors have claimed, however, that at least certain elements of democratic legitimacy may be reproduced beyond the borders of the state. In particular, it has been argued that institutionalizing political participation in international settings is a promising avenue towards enhancing the democratic quality of international and European governance (Nye 2001: 6; Clark 2003: 27; Nanz and Steffek 2004: 323; Scholte 2004: 233). From the vantage point of this debate, this chapter presents the results of a research project that probes into the prospects for the democratic legitimation of international governance through such participatory arrangements.

The first part of this chapter briefly describes the diffusion of political decision-making competence to international organizations and the repercussions that this development has on the provision of democratic self-governance. It emerges from the discussion that the democratic nation state still has the responsibility to provide its constituency with the institutions and procedures necessary for democratic self-governance. In other words, the state still has – or is perceived to have – the outcome responsibility for the provision of this normative good. At the same time, the state is not capable any more of guaranteeing the provision of this good since important decision-making procedures have shifted to international organizations.

The second part of the chapter presents the results of our empirical research project that was designed to assess to what extent civil society participation fulfils the promise of more democratically legitimate governance beyond the state. It presents a catalogue of criteria for empirical research that has been developed to tackle this question (Nanz and Steffek 2005). It also reports some key results of our study on civil society partici- pation in 32 international organizations and informal regimes (Steffek *et al.* 2007). The study reveals that, generally, new forms of civil society consultation are on the rise in most issue areas of global governance. There has also been remarkable progress with regard to the transparency of international governance. Many of these advances in transparency can be traced back to the activities of organized civil society. By means of shaming and blaming, civil society campaigns have challenged those international organizations that were reluctant to open up their policy processes to public scrutiny.

However, with regard to the input dimension of policy making, advances have been quite modest. Very few international organizations grant participatory rights to non-state actors, which would allow them to make a sustained contribution to political deliberation. Most import- antly, highly politicized negotiations in which crucial decisions are made still remain shielded against public scrutiny and critical input by civil soci- ety. Moreover, results from four detailed case studies of decision-making processes show that even when institutional conditions are favourable, input from civil society actors is often marginalized. We therefore conclude that, from the normative point of view, there are important shortcom- ings in many of the existing arrangements for civil society participation in internationalized governance. Their potential for making international governance more democratic has not been realized yet.

The anatomy of the democratic deficit

World politics since the Second World War has been characterized by the rapid proliferation of international institutions. They come in different forms, ranging from loose sequences of intergovernmental conferences over formal international bureaucracies to the supranational architec- ture of the EU. In the course of this great 'move to institutions', to borrow Kennedy's (1987) term, came an unprecedented international- ization of political decision making. This process has weakened what democratic theorists usually call the congruence condition of demo- cratic governance: the stipulation that the authors and the addressees of law should be identical. Citizens are affected by rules that are made beyond the confines of the national polity. They are the ultimate addressees of rules without being, in any meaningful sense, their authors. What is more, the internationalization of politics also has repercussions on the separation of powers within the polity. Intergovernmental multilateralism, as it emerged after the Second World War, clearly privileged the executive over parliamentary bodies (Zürn 2004: 264).

That the internationalization of policy making may be a formidable threat to democratic self-governance was recognized in the 1970s – the period described in this volume as the golden age of the nation state (Kaiser 1971). Scholars realized quite early that the diffusion of political competences to international bodies undermined the state's ability to secure democratic procedures of decision making. However, the 'democratic deficit' of international politics did not become a major issue for political science at that time. It became prominent on the agenda of international studies only in the 1990s. One of the decisive events in this process was the ratification crisis of the Treaty of Maastricht in the European Union (Føllesdal 2006). It brought home to politicians and analysts alike that citizens, when consulted about international integration, were more sceptical than their national elites. With the European integration project in question, other international institutions were equally targeted by critics. In the 1990s, the World Bank, the World Trade Organization (WTO) and the International Monetary Fund (IMF) also became subject to such critical public review that scholars diagnosed a legitimacy crisis (Kaldor 2000; Woods 2000).

Since then, the body of literature on the legitimacy of international governance has grown tremendously. For reasons of space, this chapter cannot provide an in-depth discussion of this debate. It can just refer to recent work in the tradition of international relations (Steffek 2003; Bernstein 2004; Clark 2005), European studies (Lord 2004; Føllesdal 2006) and international law (Stein 2001; Kumm 2004; Esty 2006) that provides good overviews. Nevertheless, we should put due emphasis on two fundamental characteristics of the debate: first, with issues such as democracy, legitimacy and accountability enjoying so much prominence on the agenda, the disciplines of international relations and European studies have taken a remarkable normative turn (Bellamy and Castiglione 2000; Shapcott 2000). The academic study of international politics has opened up to some major debates in political theory and international law. Second, the discussion of legitimacy has reinforced the trend away from the conception of international politics as an intergovernmental affair (Steffek 2007). In fact, the current 'legitimacy crisis' of international governance has been triggered by individual activists and NGOs, not by 'rogue states' or unilateralist superpowers. 'The collision between powerful economic institutions and social movements in many countries has led to a contest over global governance' (O'Brien *et al.* 2000: 2).

With this recent reframing of the legitimacy debate, the traditional narrative, according to which intergovernmental politics is legitimate because it represents a consensus among (elected) representatives of governments, has come under attack. Increasingly, there are calls for a democratization of international politics. This presents a formidable challenge to the democratic nation state. Formally, the state still is in charge of securing the democratic self-governance of its citizens. In practice, however, the internationalization of politics has undermined its capacity to deliver just that. Yet the state has not just been overwhelmed by anonymous forces. It has consciously ceded competencies to international institutions. The state is the author of the democratic deficit, and some would say, quite consciously so. By turning to the international forum, governments may be able to sideline domestic resistance and present desired policy options as externally imposed (Wolf 2000: 92). From the perspective of national governments, the democratic deficit may at times be an attractive feature of international institutions. The state thus is not just a 'victim' of anonymous globalization pressures but the author of these developments.

Therefore, the role of the state in democratizing world politics is ambiguous. While it is in charge of delivering democratic political processes to its citizens, its elite might find it more advantageous to preserve the existing 'democratic deficit'. Even if a country's politicians seek to democratize international institutions, their task remains complicated. Once decision-making competencies have been transferred to international organizations, a single state cannot democratize international politics in its own capacity, even if the government is determined to do so. It will always need the cooperation of other governments to remodel existing international institutions. At least at the global level, many of these potential partners will not be organized democratically at home. Hence, democratically elected politicians might need to rally support from dictators to democratize institutions that their own constituency has found to be undemocratic. Not least for this reason, there has been no 'love at first sight' (Stein 2001) between international political integration and democratic theory. If this diagnosis is correct, what is the remedy?

At the most general level, the choice appears to be quite simple. Either states retreat from international institutions to safeguard democratic self-governance of their citizens; or they strive to democratize the existing institutions and practices of international governance. Many would agree that the first option is hardly an option at all. It is difficult to deny that in the age of global economic and ecological interdependence there is a functional need for international political cooperation (Keohane 1982). The range of problems on the political agenda that transcends national borders is growing and a reversal of that trend is not in sight. If there is no going back to the age before interdependence, we will need to transform the institutions of international cooperation to safeguard democracy.

Probably, the most important question in this respect is: if democracy is to break the tight shell of the nation state, can we rely on states to crack it open? As mentioned above, the state seems to be as much part of the problem as it is part of the solution. Would it be feasible to bypass states as agents of international democratization and to rely on the forces of global civil society instead? This question has fascinated political theorists and empirical social scientists alike. The following section briefly reviews the literature.

How can international governance be democratized?

There is a flurry of proposals for the democratization of international institutions. Although it is impossible to discuss all of these here, I briefly map out the major approaches in order to locate the normative starting point for empirical research. A first set of proposals suggests democratizing international governance through the foundation of transnational par-liaments or equivalent institutions of political representation (Falk and Strauss 2001; Patomäki and Teivainen 2004). These authors suggest reproducing existing national institutions of democratic governance at the transnational level. With the exception of the EU (Rittberger 2005), however, very little has been achieved so far in this regard. It seems unlikely that decision-making power will be handed over to any parlia-mentary institution at the global level in the foreseeable future. A second group of authors suggests more modest institutional reforms, less radical and less ambitious, but certainly more viable for the time being. In many of these proposals, non-state actors or global civil society play a key role. The presumed advantages of civil society participation in internationalized governance can be summarized under the following headings.

Transparency and public accountability

Democratic self-governance requires that citizens are duly informed about the political agenda and possible alternative options for decisions. They should also be in a position to control the executive and the implemen-tation of law. What does this imply for international governance? First decision-making processes would need to be made more transparent in order to create public accountability of decision makers to a transnational constituency of citizens. Scholte (2004: 217) has outlined four contributions of non-state actors to the creation of public accountability: 'by increasing the public transparency of global governance operations; by monitoring and reviewing global policies; by seeking redress for mistakes and harms attributable to global regulatory bodies; and by advancing the creation of formal accountability mechanisms for global governance'. Therefore, the presence of (organized) civil society in international governance may contribute to the emergence of a global public sphere in which policy choices are exposed to public scrutiny, thus triggering transnational political debate (Nanz and Steffek 2004: 328).

Deliberation

Another group of authors finds the clue to the democratization of international governance in deliberative practices (Gerstenberg and Sabel 2001; Brunkhorst 2002; Eriksen and Fossum 2002). Emanating from theories of deliberative democracy, these authors argue that the institutions of international governance should provide a forum for informed and reasoned political debate. They believe that these institutions can be redesigned so as to offer such opportunities. We will come back to this claim in the empirical discussion below. What is important here is that participation of non-state actors is also paramount with a view to the creation of deliberative settings.

Conventional negotiation among diplomats, civil servants and experts cannot secure the inclusion of all relevant concerns of the global constituency into decision making at the global level (Nanz and Steffek 2004: 323). By taking part in political debate, organized civil society may transport new issues, interests and concerns from citizens into global and European governance arrangements. Thus, there is a clear case to be made for institutionalizing civil society participation in international governance.

The design of the empirical research

From the normative point of view there is much to be gained from enhanced participation of non-state actors in global governance. However, this theoretical claim needs some empirical grounding. From all that we know about the functioning of civil society participation in international governance, can we safely say that it is already democratizing world politics? Are existing institutional arrangements fit to enable meaningful participation of non-state actors in internationalized policy making? To answer these questions, we have formulated a research project that uses four theory-driven criteria to assess the democratic quality of such participatory arrangements in international governance: access, transparency, responsiveness and inclusion. These criteria and our research design are discussed briefly in this section (for an extended discussion, see Nanz and Steffek 2005). Our empirical analysis then takes place in two steps. In a first step, we map the participatory arrangements by which civil society is involved in international rule making, as they have developed in 32 international organizations and EU policy fields. Particular attention is paid to the possibility of direct access by civil society organizations (CSOs)[1] to decision-making procedures in international governmental organizations (IOs), and to institutional transparency. In a second step, the core findings from in-depth case studies that were undertaken in the framework of this research project are highlighted.

Access to political decision making

The first criterion for assessing the democratic quality of a procedure is access. It follows from the principle of democratic self-governance that all persons affected by political decisions should have an equal influence on the process of formulating these decisions. Therefore, one core requirement for successful self-governance is that citizens' arguments can enter the process of political deliberation. This is an essential precondition for democratically legitimate decision making. In global and European governance, however, direct citizen access to deliberations in international organizations is extremely difficult to accomplish. We therefore rely on CSOs to communicate arguments from affected or concerned citizens to the sites of global deliberation. It is therefore essential, for a democratic procedure, that CSOs have institutionalized access to these deliberative settings. Only in this way can it be ensured that their concerns can be voiced.

Transparency

In order to take part in political deliberation, all of the actors involved in a rule-making process should have full information about the problem at stake, the options for its solution and the costs and benefits associated with these options. Transparency serves two purposes: first, it enables CSOs to participate directly in the debate equipped with all of the information that governmental actors have. Second, transparency is required for the emergence of a public sphere in which political issues are debated and decisions exposed to wider public scrutiny. The relevant information might come either from the secretariat of the international organization or from government representatives involved in the deliberation.

Responsiveness

Access to political deliberation and the transparency of the policy process are crucial preconditions for civil society participation in policy-making processes. However, they are meaningless for the democratic quality of the procedure if the concerns that are presented by CSOs are not adequately reflected in intergovernmental deliberation and thus cannot affect the resulting decisions or recommendations. The deliberative process must be responsive to these concerns. We distinguish two forms of responsiveness: justification and adjustment. The justification of political proposals and decisions is central to deliberative theories of democracy (Gutmann and Thompson 1996). All proposals made in the deliberative process should be justified with a view to the common good of the constituency and/or in response to the specific concerns voiced by other participants. Thus, justification, understood as giving reasons for positions taken or proposals made, is a major asset to the democratic quality of deliberation.

However, the justification of a proposal can be – and, in fact, in politics often is – an *ex post* rationalization of a fixed position in the light of the criticism that the proposal has received. If justification is just an acknowledgement of criticism without the critical reflection and potential modification of an actor's own position, it contributes little to the evolution of political debate. Therefore, the mere fact that we observe justification on the part of state representatives does not document that civil society input leads to a process of reflection. Since it is difficult to observe such processes of reflection directly in our research, the observable transformation of the actors' articulated positions as a proxy is used. Hence, adjustment means that positions raised by CSOs become adopted, either in part or as a whole, by state actors. An alternative manifestation of adjustment is an adjustment of the agenda. This is the case when new issues raised by civil society are specifically designated for future deliberation.

Inclusion

One of the core principles of democratic political deliberation is that the arguments of all of the people who might be affected by the decision should be included in the process of decision making. Inclusion realizes the principle of political equality and is, therefore, a key issue that affects the democratic quality of decision making. As explained above, we are concerned with the inclusion of arguments, rather than with the inclusion of individuals. However, the two issues cannot be separated completely. The inclusion of arguments is specifically problematical when certain groups of stakeholders are disadvantaged with regard to their resources and their degree of organization. Therefore, the democratic quality of deliberative procedures hinges upon their capacity to include arguments made by all groups concerned.

This is of particular relevance in an international context in which there are enormous differences in the resources available to stakeholders and in their ability to organize their concerns at international level. More specifically, certain groups from developing countries, for example rural populations and indigenous peoples, do not have adequate means for presenting their concerns in international governance. Thus, there is certain probability that the arguments of these people may be excluded from political deliberation. In empirical research, however, it is very difficult to account convincingly for a lack of inclusion at argumentation level. We would have to search for arguments that both exist and are of relevant concern to certain groups, but which are, nonetheless, not voiced in deliberation. We would have to rely on a fairly speculative version of counter-factual reasoning. To avoid this, institutional mechanisms of empowerment are regarded as a proxy for inclusion. The theory-driven requirement is that public organizations make appropriate arrangements for empowering the most disadvantaged stakeholders to take part in deliberative processes. In practice, this can take the form of IOs providing CSOs from developing countries with travel subsidies to attend political meetings. Alternatively, there may be training courses or seminars to improve the technical knowledge of CSO representatives for an adequate understanding of international politics; or IO staff might undertake missions in developing countries to consult directly with affected citizens.

Access and transparency

To account for the empirical situation regarding the criteria listed in the last section, a list of 20 empirical indicators that are discussed in more detail elsewhere (Steffek and Nanz 2007) is developed. While access and transparency could be studied for the complete set of 32 organizations, responsiveness and inclusion required us to conduct some in-depth case studies. With regard to access, it was found that by the year 2005 almost all institutions of European and global governance under study here held consultations with organized civil society in one way or the other. Only two organizations kept their doors tightly shut: the Bank for International Settlements (BIS) and the North Atlantic Treaty Organization (NATO).

The G8 summits also remain completely closed to non-state actors. However, G8 is not an organization, but an informal institution without headquarters or a permanent staff. It is at the discretion of host governments as to whether they wish to consult with civil society in the preparation of the summit. As a rule, they hold a meeting with the representatives of trade unions and business associations. Similarly, the European Central Bank consults with civil society only in the framework of its macroeconomic dialogue, which involves the social partners.

The most decisive regulations for the democratizing effect of civil society participation concern CSO access to political meetings, in which crucial decisions are prepared, discussed and taken. However, access to political meetings is not easy to compare between organizations, as the definition of the term 'political meeting' is unclear. Some organizations studied here, such as the European Commission, have an enormous number of preparatory committees that meet early in the legislative process. Their activity is political in that they discuss concrete legislative proposals, and many of these meetings can be attended by CSOs. However, the EU's intergovernmental negotiation process in the Council cannot be observed by civil society representatives. Other organizations have opened to CSOs select intergovernmental meetings, such as plenary meetings of conferences, without granting access to the preparatory process in committees (in the WTO). In order to account for the differences between types of political meetings, we made the following, more precise calculation: 25 percent of the organizations under study do not allow CSO representatives into any political meeting; in 19 percent of the cases, it was found that CSOs are consulted only in the early phase of the political process, for example, in committees; in 47 percent of the cases, it was found access to both early stage meetings and to intergovernmental bargaining at later stages; and in 9 percent of the cases, access was limited to the late negotiation stages, such as plenary sessions of conferences.

In the vast majority of cases (83 percent), organizations that admit CSOs as observers to political meetings also grant speaking rights to CSOs, subject to various restrictions. The possibility of amending the agenda was found in only three cases. These are the Monitoring Committees of EC Structural Funds, the UN Economic and Social Council (ECOSOC) and the UN Human Rights Commission. Regulations for the circulation of CSO documentation among policy makers vary across organizations. Generally, the right to distribute written material in political meetings – not just outside, in the corridors – coincides with speaking rights in the respective meetings.

With regard to transparency and access to information, clearer rules seem to be on the rise. In almost 90 percent of the cases, it was found that there are clear guidelines on the public release of documents. Information on the work and current projects was found in all cases on the web, but the amount of documentation accessible varies greatly among organizations. Not surprisingly, political documents, for example texts currently under negotiation, are handled much more restrictively than background information. Overall, however, international governance has definitely become more transparent in recent years.

An increasingly common practice observed in many organizations is the inclusion of civil society representatives in governmental delegations. This seems especially widespread in specialized functional organizations, in which members of NGOs participate as experts in national delegations. Evidence of this practice was found in all policy fields except finance, including sensitive issues such as the review of the Nuclear Non-Proliferation Treaty (NPT) and trade negotiations (in the WTO). However, quantifying this phenomenon is very difficult, as the composition of national delegations is at the discretion of the member states and very few international organizations collect respective data. In a survey, the World Health Organization (WHO) found that, during 1998–2000, nine to eleven national delegations to the annual meetings of its governing bodies included (official) representatives of civil society.[2] The delegations of Canada, Cyprus, Norway, Sweden and the United States included civil society representatives in all three years that the WHO analysed. As members of governmental delegations, civil society representatives clearly work under very different conditions and often have access to meetings, including informal meetings, which CSOs cannot attend as observers. They also have the possibility of defending civil society concerns within their own national delegation. However, the fact that they are members of a national delegation, and hence of a governmental structure, compromises their capacity to act as an independent voice in global policy making.

With regard to the formal conditions of civil society access, we noted some interesting differences across policy fields. It appears that, at least to some degree, the chances for organized civil society to consult with an IO depend on the subject matter that the IO deals with. However, within some policy fields, there are surprising exceptions to the rule, which are highlighted in the following paragraphs.

International security

Unlike any other topic in international politics, security has been associated with a need for secrecy. In the realm of international security, one would certainly not expect a great deal of openness towards non-state actors. Yet, it seems that we have, at least partly, to revise our views. Only

NATO thoroughly confirmed our expectations that security organizations are reluctant to interact with CSOs. In similar vein, the EU Common Foreign and Security Policy is also formulated in a secretive manner. Within the UN system, the Security Council for a long time did not regard CSOs as legitimate interlocutors, either. Since the 1990s, however, it has maintained consultations with selected CSOs, mainly in the framework of the so-called Arria formula. This is a series of informal consultations in which Council members meet with CSO representatives, and these consultations are not part of the Council's regular meetings.

A completely different picture was found in the Organization for Security and Co-operation in Europe (OSCE), which reflects significant changes in the agenda of international security policy. The OSCE is a prime example of an organization that focuses on domestic security issues, on stabilization and peace building. To accomplish these tasks, it cooperates intensively with non-state actors. In fact, some of the most pressing challenges to international security today are to build peace in areas of civil war, aid the reconstruction of failed states and to stop ethnic and other forms of tension from turning into open violence. This apparently has repercussions on the way that security IOs deal with civil society. Thus, in the field of international security, we should at least differentiate between classic military alliances on the one hand, and peace-building organizations on the other hand. The relations of a security IO with civil society are likely to be determined by the type of tasks the IO is designed to perform.

Economic cooperation

The tasks of international economic cooperation are manifold, and so are the organizational structures that have developed. It is therefore not surprising that the modes of interaction between IOs and non-state actors also vary in this field of governance. They range from the participatory culture of the International Labour Organization (ILO) to the closed consultations of the G8. The ILO includes representatives of employers' organizations and trade unions as members in its tripartite assembly, but also enters into consultations with many other non-state actors. The G8 marks the other extreme. It remains an exclusive club that does not entertain any institutionalized relationship with non-state actors, although some summit host countries do consult selected CSOs – mainly the social partners – in advance. The other organizations studied are to be found somewhere between these two extremes. The Organization for Economic Co-operation and Development (OECD) maintains privileged relations with only four corporate actors, but relies on ad hoc consultations with the rest of the non-state world. The World Intellectual Property Organization (WIPO) grants more formally secured access to a large number of CSOs, and it is considerably more accessible than the WTO. The treaty setting up the North American Free Trade Area (NAFTA) institutionalized CSO consultation only in a side agreement pertaining to environmental protection. The trade branch of the EC has institutionalized a stakeholder dialogue for an exchange of views in advance of international negotiations, while its decision-making process proper remains closed. The variation in this policy field can again be explained by the specific tasks of the IOs involved. The IOs that are devoted to tariff bargaining remain much more shielded against external scrutiny than those devoted to standard setting.

Environmental cooperation

Arguably, environmental politics is a field in which non-state actors have played an unprecedented role in agenda setting and policy making. This is well documented by the existing literature on epistemic communities and CSO activism (Haas 1992; Lipschutz and Mayer 1996). In fact, all of the regimes analysed in this issue area maintain extensive relations with non-state actors and accept them as legitimate interlocutors. However, with regard to the degree of formalization and legalization of this relationship, there are some interesting variations. In the EU, there is little formalization, while the UN climate change regime grants CSOs far-reaching participation rights in its policy process.

Development

Patterns of participation in this field are characterized by a remarkable gulf between policy making and policy implementation. In the implementation of development projects, organizations rely heavily on non-state actors. In the case of the World Bank, for example, more than 70 percent of all projects are implemented in collaboration with non-state actors. The CSOs are involved in all phases of its project cycle, including evaluation. However, this openness is not reflected at the level of political decision making. Where strategic choices are made, the doors remain closed both to CSOs and to the wider public. Although development agencies in the UN system grant more access to political meetings, there is also a remarkable division between the political and operational level. The same is true for the EU whose (intra-European) structural funds we took as an instance of regional development assistance. Although CSOs are involved in implementation processes on the ground, there is very little guidance on these processes by the Commission, and, consequently, there is remarkable variation both within and across countries as to how CSO consultation is handled in practice. The allocation of the funds is an intergovernmental affair and its decision-making process remains opaque.

Human rights

Similar to environmental protection, the protection of human rights is a policy field in which CSOs are particularly active. Human rights protection is also the *raison d'être* for some intergovernmental organizations, such as the Council of Europe. Hence, one should expect a pattern of highly institutionalized relationships between the two types of actors. Our data confirm that this is true for both the UN human rights regime and the Council of Europe. Both bodies collaborate extensively with civil society, which they need to, in order to identify human rights violations. Without CSOs, they would not be able to monitor compliance with the respective regime. However, the picture changes when we examine the processes of policy making that impact heavily on human rights. In the EU, for example, policy making in the fields of migration and asylum policy is shielded against too much insight and influence by non-state actors.

Financial affairs

International cooperation in the financial sector has been, and still largely is, a pronouncedly intergovernmental affair. Neither the European Central Bank (ECB), nor the Bank for International Settlements, which administers the Basel Accords on banking regulation, have granted CSOs any particular status or consult with them on a regular basis. Similarly, the International Monetary Fund (IMF) has very reluctantly opened up to civil society. It now organizes joint outreach meetings together with the World Bank, although the policy-making process still remains closed. It should be noticed here that, in the financial sector, secrecy has particular justification. With regard to IMF credits, for example, a premature release of information can trigger market speculation that runs counter to the intentions of the Fund.

Responsiveness and inclusion

The empirical analysis conducted for all the organizations in our sample concentrated on the access that civil society actors had to policy-making processes, project implementation and judicial review. In addition, the formal rules governing access to relevant documentation and in this way improving transparency could be investigated for all the organizations under study here. However, responsiveness and inclusion cannot be mapped for a large number of organizations. In order to know if intergovernmental bodies are responsive to CSO input and to spot the potential problems of inclusion, an in-depth study of single organizations and negotiation processes within them is necessary. This could not be achieved for the large set of 32 cases in the framework of this project. We therefore chose examples for our in-depth study, maintaining a balance between the European and global level and between institutional scope conditions that are favourable and less favourable to CSOs.

These in-depth case studies show that responsiveness remains surprisingly low even under most favourable circumstances, such as those offered by the UN World Summit on Information Society (WSIS). As Dany (2007) argues in her case study, the responsiveness of the WSIS process to civil society concerns depended mainly on the interests of governments, the structure of the problems discussed and on the stage of the negotiation process. In fact, when it came to the decision-making stage, CSO arguments that had been formerly accepted were often dismissed again. Another example is highlighted by Ferretti (2007) who studies the consultation of citizens and CSOs by the European Commission in its procedures of authorizing genetically modified organisms (GMO) for marketing or consumption. She reports a striking lack of responsiveness as many of the concerns of 'stakeholders' are in fact dismissed by the public authorities involved in the procedure.

The case studies thus show that power asymmetries between states and non-state actors endure and negatively affect the responsiveness to civil society arguments. Whether or not CSOs are able to significantly influence the course of deliberations still depends on the goodwill of the governmental actors involved. This, once again, confirms our ideas about a persisting intergovernmental core of decision making (Steffek and Kissling 2006). Given the significance of responsiveness for the democratizing force of participatory arrangements, future research should systematically explore the conditions under which responsiveness to civil society's arguments is likely.

Finally, the criterion of inclusion of all citizens presumably affected by a certain decision is meant to give equal influence also to marginalized groups. The results of our analysis, especially of the in-depth case studies, document that in most cases a clear bias towards 'strong' CSOs exists. This group includes well-funded and well-staffed CSOs, such as industry and business associations in the cases of the WTO (Steffek and Ehling 2007) and the EU consultation process (Friedrich 2007). In the WTO case, industry associations at times performed even better than representatives of developing countries' governments. Such findings hint at major asymmetries within organized civil society. First, there are sectoral asymmetries between CSOs, with industry organizations being better able to exert influence. Second, there are geographical asymmetries. The CSOs from industrialized countries are in a more favourable position than those from developing countries, which usually are less well equipped with crucial resources. These imbalances might even aggravate as soon as e-governance begins to play a role, as testified by a study of environmental policy in the EU (Friedrich 2007).

In addition, whenever civil society participation is highly formalized and certain partners become privileged, the problem of cooptation may arise. This may lead to the formation of alliances between governments and established partners against any new voices to be included. Such tendencies were detected in the ILO with regard to the social partners. In the ILO, the privileged partners of governments, namely the social partners, that is employers' and workers' organizations, have the same rights and duties as governments in the 'tripartite' decision-making process. These partners vigorously forestall the introduction of 'quadripartism' within the ILO that would result from associating CSOs more closely to it (Thomann 2007). Hence, the situation at the ILO is a perfect example of how parts of civil society, when closely connected to a governmental forum, defend their privileges. Similar effects can also be observed in EU Regional Policy, in which governmental actors function as 'gatekeepers' and are in principle able to favour certain social and economic partners. As Kamlage (2007) shows for the Monitoring Committee in the German Land of Mecklenburg-Vorpommern, the established social partners managed to tap public resources in order to facilitate their participation in the process.

There is only one case in which we found explicit strategies of 'empowerment' to secure the inclusion of marginalized groups. At the WSIS, the (intergovernmental) International Telecommunication Union (ITU) provided for a restricted number of fellowships, designed to facilitate participation by civil society representatives from least-developed countries (LDCs) and especially women in both the preparatory conferences and the world summit. However, the sum allocated to this purpose was not even utilized to the full extent by CSOs. Although this is just anecdotic evidence, we should take the possibility into account that Eurocentrism and gender inequality may also be rooted in organized civil society itself, and thus marginalize certain voices (Dany 2007). Systematic research on the internal organization and decision-making processes of CSOs and on power relations within transnational civil society should shed more light on this issue.

Conclusion

In this chapter, we investigated the prospects for a democratization of international governance. Is it possible to reproduce the normative good of democratic self-governance beyond the state? We argued in the first section that the nation state is still held responsible for guaranteeing the democratic quality of governance but that it cannot achieve this any more by its own means. Over recent decades, states have delegated political authority to international institutions without ensuring that these institutions operate according to democratic principles. Any initiative for democratizing these institutions needs to be coordinated with other – in some cases non-democratic – countries at the international level. And even if states embarked on a serious endeavour to democratize internationalized policy making, governmental action alone will hardly suffice to remedy the democratic deficit.

As argued in this chapter, organized civil society can make two major contributions to a democratization of world politics. First, it can create public accountability of intergovernmental decision making. Second, by taking part in international governance, it may create alternative avenues for citizen input into decision-making processes at the international level. This is an important asset as the traditional principle of 'one state, one vote' requires an extreme aggregation of interests and hence is unlikely to achieve a balanced representation of citizens' interest and concerns in international governance. If well-informed and inclusive political deliberation is the goal, we will also need civil society representatives as interlocutors.

In the second part of the chapter, we reported the results of a research project that investigated current forms of civil society participation in international governance. The guiding question was: do existing arrangements enable representatives of civil society to make a meaningful contribution to international governance? The evidence was quite sobering. In none of the cases under study here did we find a high democratic quality of participatory arrangements for civil society, as measured by the four criteria that were outlined. The best results were found for the indicator of transparency. In all other dimensions, current participatory arrangements have major shortcomings. The lack of responsiveness to arguments brought forward by civil society appears particularly troubling from the normative point of view. As explained in this chapter, the very idea of democratizing international governance through civil society participation rests on the presumption that arguments voiced by non-state actors will be heard and debated in international negotiation. Existing participatory arrangements have achieved very little in this respect.

Equally disconcerting are the exclusionary tendencies that we found in many participatory settings. Democratic theory requires that all citizens affected by a rule have equal opportunities to influence the course of political deliberation. In many arenas, however, well-organized and well-funded groups, such as industry associations, but also the social partners, have a clear advantage, while organizations from least-developed countries are heavily underrepresented. The global asymmetries in wealth, power, and technical expertise that characterize international politics at the governmental level can also be found within the realm of organized civil society. It would be exaggerated to expect that international organizations resolve such profound problems of inequality, which are deeply rooted in socioeconomic underdevelopment. Nevertheless, some basic measures to facilitate participation, such as the 'fellowships' we found in the case of the WSIS, would not be beyond their reach.

In some cases the reason for a lack of responsiveness can be found in the very design of participatory arrangements. For example, at the WTO, outreach meetings such as public symposia, are not attended by many national delegates. Their capacity to create a dialogue between organized civil society and governmental decision makers is therefore limited. When facing such institutional constraints, CSOs often carry their dissent to other political forums and to the public at large. Rather than searching for dialogue within international organizations or regimes, they take their campaigns to the media and to the streets. We can conclude from the evidence presented in this chapter that participatory practices in international governance are on the rise but they need to be improved if the existing potentials for democratization are to be realized. Compared to democratic states, IOs still are much less able to guarantee the responsiveness of governmental structures to citizens' concerns, and to safeguard democratic equality. These severe shortcomings need to be remedied before we can rely on civil society participation in IOs as a cure to the democratic deficit.

Notes

1   In the literature, the traditional term 'non-governmental organization' for a not-for-profit organization without organizational or financial ties to the state, has been increasingly supplanted by the term 'civil society organization'. We adopt this latter term as it underscores the origin of the non-state actor in the third sector, beyond governmental institutions and the economy. It should be noted, however, that many of the international governmental organizations that we studied do not refer to CSOs, but to NGOs.
2   Source: WHO Civil Society Initiative, CSI Review Series, 'Analysis: NGO participation in WHO Governing Bodies, 1998 to 2002', WHO Doc. CSI/2002/WP3, p. 6.

References

Bellamy, Richard and Dario Castiglione (2000) 'Legitimizing the Euro-"Polity" and its "Regime": The Normative Turn in EU Studies', *European Journal of Political Theory* 2(1), 7–34.

Bernstein, Steven (2004) *The Elusive Basis of Legitimacy in Global Governance: Three Conceptions*, Working Paper Series 04/2, Hamilton: Institute on Globalization and the Human Condition.

Brunkhorst, Hauke (2002) 'Globalising Democracy Without a State: Weak Public, Strong Public, Global Constitutionalism', *Millennium: Journal of International Studies* 31(3), 675–90.

Clark, Ian (2005) *Legitimacy in International Society*, Oxford: Oxford University Press.

Clark, John (2003) 'Introduction: Civil Society and Transnational Action', in John Clark, ed., *Globalizing Civic Engagement: Civil Society and Transnational Action*, London: Earthscan, 1–28.

Dahl, Robert A. (1999) 'Can International Organizations be Democratic? A Sceptic's View', in Ian Shapiro and Casiano Hacker-Cordón, eds, *Democracy's Edges*, Cambridge: Cambridge University Press, 19–37.

Dany, Charlotte (2007) 'Civil Society Participation under Most Favourable Conditions: Assessing the Deliberative Quality of the World Summit on the Information Society', in Jens Steffek, Claudia Kissling and Patrizia Nanz, eds, *Civil Society Participation in European and Global Governance: A Cure for the Democratic Deficit?*, Basingstoke: Palgrave Macmillan (forthcoming).

Eriksen, Erik O. and John E. Fossum (2002) 'Democracy through Strong Publics in the European Union?', *Journal of Common Market Studies* 40(3), 401–24.

Esty, Daniel (2006) 'Good Governance at the Supranational Scale: Globalizing Administrative Law', *Yale Law Journal* 115(7), 1490–562.

Falk, Richard and Andrew Strauss (2001) 'Toward Global Parliament', *Foreign Affairs* 80(1), 212–20.

Ferretti, Maria Paola (2007) 'Participatory Strategies in the Regulation of GMO Products in the EU', in Jens Steffek, Claudia Kissling and Patrizia Nanz, eds, *Civil Society Participation in European and Global Governance: A Cure for the Democratic Deficit?*, Basingstoke: Palgrave Macmillan (forthcoming).

Føllesdal, Andreas (2006) 'Survey Article: The Legitimacy Deficits of the European Union', *Journal of Political Philosophy* 14(4), 441–68.

Friedrich, Dawid (2007) 'Democratic Aspiration Meets Political Reality: Participation of Organized Civil Society in Selected European Policy Processes', in Jens Steffek, Claudia Kissling and Patrizia Nanz, eds, *Civil Society Participation in European and Global Governance: A Cure for the Democratic Deficit?*, Basingstoke: Palgrave Macmillan (forthcoming).

Gerstenberg, Oliver and Charles Sabel (2001) 'Directly Deliberative Polyarchy: An Institutional Ideal for Europe?', in Renaud Dehousse and Christian Joerges, eds, *Good Governance and Administration in Europe's Integrated Market*, Oxford: Oxford University Press, 289–342.

Gutmann, Amy and Dennis Thompson (1996) *Democracy and Disagreement: Why Moral Conflict Cannot Be Avoided in Politics, and What Should Be Done About It*, Cambridge, MA: Belknap Press.

Haas, Peter M. (1992) 'Introduction: Epistemic Communities and International Policy Coordination', *International Organization* 46(1), 1–35.

Kaiser, Karl (1971) 'Transnational Relations as a Threat to the Democratic Process', *International Organization* 25(3), 706–20.

Kaldor, Mary (2000) '"Civilising" Globalisation? The Implications of the "Battle in Seattle"', *Millennium: Journal of International Studies* 29(1), 105–14.

Kamlage, Jan-Hendrik (2007) 'Assessing the Legitimacy of European Regional Policy: The Interplay of Civil Society and State Actors in Sweden and Germany', in Jens Steffek, Claudia Kissling and Patrizia Nanz, eds, *Civil Society Participation in European and Global Governance: A Cure for the Democratic Deficit?*, Basingstoke: Palgrave Macmillan (forthcoming).

Kennedy, David (1987) 'The Move to Institutions', *Cardozo Law Review* 8(5), 841–988.

Keohane, Robert O. (1982) 'The Demand for International Regimes', *International Organization* 36(2), 141–71.

Kumm, Mattias (2004) 'The Legitimacy of International Law: A Constitutionalist Framework for Analysis', *European Journal of International Law* 15(5), 907–31.

Lipschutz, Ronnie D. and Judith Mayer (1996) *Global Civil Society and Global Environmental Governance: The Politics of Nature from Place to Planet*, Albany, NY: State University of New York Press.

Lord, Christopher (2004) *A Democratic Audit of the European Union*, Basingstoke: Palgrave Macmillan.

Nanz, Patrizia and Jens Steffek (2004) 'Global Governance, Participation, and the Public Sphere', *Government and Opposition* 39(2), 314–35.

Nanz, Patrizia and Jens Steffek (2005) 'Assessing the Democratic Quality of Deliberation in International Governance: Criteria and Research Strategies', *Acta Politica* 40(3), 368–83.

Nye, Joseph S. (2001) 'Globalization's Democratic Deficit: How to Make International Institutions More Accountable', *Foreign Affairs* 80(4), 2–6.

O'Brien, Robert, Anne-Marie Goetz, Jan Aart Scholte and Marc Williams (2000) *Contesting Global Governance: Multilateral Economic Institutions and Global Social Movements*, Cambridge: Cambridge University Press.

Patomäki, Heikki and Teivo Teivainen (2004) *A Possible World: Democratic Transformation of Global Institutions*, London: Zed Books.

Rittberger, Berthold (2005) *Building Europe's Parliament: Democratic Representation beyond the Nation-State*, Oxford: Oxford University Press.

Scholte, Jan Aart (2004) 'Civil Society and Democratically Accountable Global Governance', *Government and Opposition* 39(2), 211–33.

Shapcott, Richard (2000) 'Solidarism and After: Global Governance, International Society, and the Normative "Turn" in International Relations', *Pacifica Review: Peace, Security & Global Change* 12(2), 147–65.

Steffek, Jens (2003) 'The Legitimation of International Governance: A Discourse Approach', *European Journal of International Relations* 9(2), 249–75.

Steffek, Jens (2007) 'Legitimacy in International Relations: From State Compliance to Citizen Consensus', in Achim Hurrelmann, Steffen Schneider and Jens Steffek, eds, *Legitimacy in an Age of Global Politics*, Basingstoke: Palgrave Macmillan (forthcoming).

Steffek, Jens and Claudia Kissling (2006) *Civil Society Participation in International Governance: The UN and the WTO Compared*, TranState Working Paper No. 42, Bremen: TranState Research Centre.

Steffek, Jens and Ulrike Ehling (2007) 'Civil Society Participation at the Margins: The Case of WTO', in Jens Steffek, Claudia Kissling and Patrizia Nanz, eds, *Civil*

Society Participation in European and Global Governance: A Cure for the Democratic Deficit?, Basingstoke: Palgrave Macmillan (forthcoming).

Steffek, Jens and Patrizia Nanz (2007) 'Emergent Patterns of Civil Society Participation in Global and European Governance', in Jens Steffek, Claudia Kissling and Patrizia Nanz, eds, *Civil Society Participation in European and Global Governance: A Cure for the Democratic Deficit?*, Basingstoke: Palgrave Macmillan (forthcoming).

Steffek, Jens, Claudia Kissling and Patrizia Nanz, eds (2007) *Civil Society Participation in European and Global Governance: A Cure for the Democratic Deficit?*, Basingstoke: Palgrave Macmillan (forthcoming).

Stein, Eric (2001) 'International Integration and Democracy: No Love at First Sight', *American Journal of International Law* 95(3), 489–534.

Thomann, Lars (2007) 'The ILO, Tripartism, and NGOs: Do Too Many Cooks Really Spoil the Broth?', in Jens Steffek, Claudia Kissling and Patrizia Nanz, eds, *Civil Society Participation in European and Global Governance: A Cure for the Democratic Deficit?*, Basingstoke: Palgrave Macmillan (forthcoming).

Wolf, Klaus Dieter (2000) *Die Neue Staatsräson: Zwischenstaatliche Kooperation als Demokratieproblem in der Weltgesellschaft*, Baden-Baden: Nomos.

Woods, Ngaire (2000) 'The Challenge of Good Governance for the IMF and the World Bank Themselves', *World Development* 28(5), 823–41.

Zürn, Michael (2004) 'Global Governance and Legitimacy Problems', *Government and Opposition* 39(2), 260–87.

7

Governing the Internet: The Quest for Legitimate and Effective Rules

Ralf Bendrath, Jeanette Hofmann, Volker Leib, Peter Mayer and Michael Zürn

More than anything else, the Internet has become a symbol of globalization. Emerging from military and academic efforts in the US to create a highly robust communication system, the Internet is a huge 'network of networks' that links an ever-growing number of computers all over the world and enables the simultaneous and instantaneous flow of immense amounts of information both within and across countries. Through its support of applications and services such as the World-Wide Web (WWW) and electronic mail, the 'Net' has dramatically reduced transactions costs for organizations, groups and individuals situated in different parts of the world. Thus, it has contributed heavily to the unprecedented growth of transborder economic, social, political and cultural interactions that has taken place in recent years. Indeed, the seemingly de-territorialized 'cyberspace' spanned by the Internet, in which ideas are supposed to travel freely with no regard for state borders, has often been celebrated – or deplored – as a powerful repudiation of sovereignty-based claims to social control.

In this chapter, we look at how political actors have responded to challenges posed by the Internet. The most important of those actors is the modern (Western) nation state, which until recently controlled most of the policies that are challenged by the rise of the Internet. This state provided its citizens with a set of *normative goods* of supreme social importance, including peace and physical security, liberty and legal equality, democratic self-determination and economic growth and social welfare. Our goal is to examine the claim that this state is undergoing a far-reaching transformation, possibly indicating the transition from the familiar 'national constellation' to a not yet well understood 'postnational constellation' (Habermas 2001). The suggested transformation has at least two dimensions. First, there are instances in which – previously state-held – responsibilities for securing these normative goods are *internationalized, privatized,* or, if both processes are intertwined, *transnationalized*. Second, in such processes, different *levels* of responsibility are potentially affected: the state may be complemented or supplanted by other public or private organizations with respect to (a) decision making, legislation and oversight (*regulatory responsibility*); (b) the implementation of decisions and the immediate provision of services (*operational responsibility*); or even (c) its socially acknowledged right and duty to step in and take regulatory or operational action if one or several of the normative goods are in jeopardy (*outcome responsibility*). In addition, changes in these dimensions may either involve diminishing the role of the state, that is, public and national responsibilities are lost or *shift* to non-state actors, or the assumption by other organizations of state-like responsibilities may leave the state's powers and range of activities in a given area largely unaffected, that is, statehood is not redistributed according to a zero-sum logic but *diffuses* beyond the state.

On the following pages, we analyse transformations of the state by looking at three policy fields either closely connected to, or deeply affected by, the Internet: (1) the administration of the Domain Name System (DNS), necessary for retrieving information and transmitting messages within the network; (2) the protection of informational privacy; and (3) the taxation of transborder business activities. For each case we ask whether, to what extent and how the emergence and spread of the Internet, particularly since its popularization and commercialization in the 1990s, have spawned or reinforced a transformation of statehood in terms of the shift or diffusion of (previously) public and national responsibilities along either 'spatial' (internationalization) or 'organizational' (privatization) lines or both. The normative goods at stake in our cases vary. However, we are especially concerned in this chapter with a normative good that is involved in all three policy fields: *democratic legitimacy*.

From the point of view of democracy, the Internet has given rise to ambivalent expectations: on the one hand, by virtue of its role as a key driver of globalization in recent years, the Internet is seen as contributing to the weakening of democracy by reinforcing the *incongruence* between the regional or global extension of social interactions and the national scope of democratically legitimized political decision making. On the other hand, the Internet has been acclaimed by many as a potentially crucial device for revitalizing and deepening democratic self-determination both within and across nations. We therefore ask, with respect to the three policy fields, how, if at all, the issue-specific transformations of statehood that we observe affect the normative good of democratic legitimacy. Which legitimacy problems arise and who takes care of them? Does the political responsibility for the provision of democratic legitimacy still rest exclusively with the state?[1] Which part does the Internet have in all that? In looking at these issues, we focus on four criteria that figure prominently in debates about the 'democratic deficit' of global governance, that is *congruence* between social and political spaces, *transparency* of decision making, *accountability* of decision makers to stakeholders and *participation* by stakeholders in decision making.

The administration of Internet names and numbers: global reach of regulatory authority under unilateral supervision

Communication services such as telephony and mail require universal addressing systems in order to work. Addressing systems are sets of globally standardized attributes such as city codes or house numbers that permit messages to reach their destination. Addresses fulfil two functions: they determine the topological position of a communication device (localizing function), and they provide for a unique identity (naming function). Usually, each communication service comes with its own addressing system, and the introduction of a new service will call for a new addressing convention. Accordingly, the emergence of digital data networking in the 1970s created the need for a new address space that would provide users and services worldwide with unique digital identifiers.

National versus global regulation of address spaces

Before the deregulation of postal and telecommunication services in the late 1980s and the 1990s, address spaces formed an integral part of state-run communication services. Telecommunication networks were typically operated as public monopolies with a few selected firms as technical suppliers. This 'ancient regime' (Drake 1994) attributed all three levels of responsibility – for outcomes, rules and operations – to national governments. Incompatible technical standards ensured that both technical infrastructure and services were shielded from international competition. The international telecommunication infrastructure was characterized by fragmentation, and international standard-setting efforts focused on specifying gateways between autonomous, national networks. National sovereignty formed the constitutive principle of international collaboration. The International Telecommunication Union (ITU), a UN agency, based its decisions on the 'one nation, one vote' rule. Participation by companies and non-state experts depended on their government's authorization. Agreements could only be achieved through consensus; countries could not be forced to adopt standards. The sovereignty-based regime slowly faded in the OECD world in the 1990s, but some of its characteristics have persisted. The telephone system's number spaces, for example, are still kept under state regulatory responsibility.

The onset of data networking not only created the need for a new addressing system, but also it brought about new design options, which suggested a departure from the traditional model. It is noteworthy that the Internet's addressing system consists of two parts, numeric addresses and the more user-friendly domain names, for example www.uni-bremen.de, which keep the numeric addresses (in this case 134.102.20.226) hidden from users. The Domain Name System (DNS) differs in several ways from traditional forms of addressing. Most relevant in this context, is that the DNS constituted a global (single, unified) name space from the beginning. The Internet name space does not consist of autonomous, national addressing systems like the telephone network, which subsequently are connected to allow for international calls. Even the reference to the territorial nation state contained in country code top level domains such as '.de' is merely symbolic.

The name space is organized as a tree-shaped hierarchy. The tip of the hierarchy consists of the 'root', the authoritative source from which all Internet users, directly or indirectly, retrieve information on the location of a given website or mailbox. The root thus constitutes a central point of control of the DNS. While the territorial telecommunication regime allocated operational and regulatory responsibility on the national level, the DNS organizes oversight over the root as a central task to be performed *by one single agency*. In the telecommunication world of the past, global connectivity was reached through bilateral contracts between national postal, telegraph and telephone organizations (PTTs). On the Internet, it is the distribution of the authoritative 'root zone file' that provides for global reach of a specific service.

The DNS root was initially administrated by a single person, the Californian computer scientist Jon Postel. The funding of the Internet Assigned Numbers Authority (IANA) initiated and headed by Postel came from the US Department of Defense. In the mid-1990s, after the privatization and commercialization of the Internet infrastructure, this informal arrangement reached its limits. Pressing problems such as escalating speculation with domain names, property rights conflicts over famous names and monopoly profits from skyrocketing domain name registrations made it clear that the DNS needed a more formal regulatory framework. The institutional foundation for the present name space administration was laid in 1998. The US government acknowledged the

Internet Corporation for Assigned Names and Numbers (ICANN) – a private not-for-profit company based on Californian law, but internationally composed – through a memorandum of understanding (MoU). The MoU was initially limited to a period of two years, after which a full privatization of DNS administration was to take place. This was, however, on the condition of ICANN accomplishing several tasks as specified in the MoU: privatizing domain name registration, forming contract-based relationships with various DNS operators and, last but not least, developing a legitimate process of decision making.

Two years after its inception, ICANN initiated a first reform process because the bottom-up process of policy making in the spirit of private self-governance had proven more difficult than expected. Many key actors, such as the operators of root servers – which enable computers worldwide to exchange information with other computers in the network – refused to contract with ICANN, in order to preserve their regulatory autonomy. To date, ICANN has still not fully succeeded in establishing a contract-based regulatory authority over the Internet's name space, and in October 2006, the US Government amended the MoU for the seventh time.

Spatial and organizational transformations of statehood in telecommunications policy

Reviewing telecommunication infrastructures over the past 30 years, we observe major changes, particularly in the spatial dimension of addressing systems, which refers to the level – be it local, national, international – at which decisions are made and implemented. The poly-central, sovereignty-based address space interconnected through multi- and bilateral agreements typical of the 'ancient regime', was dismissed as a model for digital data networking and replaced by a global structure with just one point of control at the tip of its hierarchy. The Internet thus involves a shift of political responsibility away from the national constellation – it is not territorially confined nation states that control the infrastructure, but one government, the United States of America, which holds supervisory authority over a globally acting organization (ICANN). With regard to the organizational dimension, however, the degree of transformation is less clear since the precise role of private and public actors in Internet governance is still a contested issue both in the United States and in intergovernmental forums.

The root, the authoritative heart of the Internet's name space, is subject to regulatory responsibility of the US government, which also claims outcome responsibility. All other governments are relegated to a mere advisory role vis-à-vis ICANN. Regulatory responsibility thus has indeed shifted but not quite in the assumed way. Instead of the heralded complete privatization, we have witnessed the transition from a partly national, partly intergovernmental arrangement to a *unilateral regime* that works through a private organization.[2] Steps towards private, transnational self-governance have been taken with regard to policy development and the implementation of one section of the name space, the so-called generic top level domains such as '.com' or '.org'. (In addition, some of the national registries entrusted with managing the country code top level domains are private entities.) Yet, ICANN, the private agency supervising the generic domain name space, remains itself under tight supervision by the US Government (Goldsmith and Wu 2006: 169). Whereas the spatial shift of digital addressing towards a global system seems to some extent irrevocable, the degree of organizational transformation remains open to negotiation and therefore somewhat unstable.

Legitimacy of transnational regulation under US control

Around the time that the ICANN was founded, state-centred forms of legitimacy were widely dismissed as inadequate for administrating the Internet infrastructure (for a critical account, see Lessig 1998). Private forms of regulation with provisions for direct participation by stakeholders promised to be more efficient and legitimate than 'closed' intergovernmental regimes. The ambitious goal in those years was to compensate the demise of nation state-based legitimacy by creating a bottom-up policy process, which would involve all affected parties present on the Internet, including individual users. It was expected that self-governance by the private sector and civil society would provide for greater transparency in decision making and presumably also for more user-friendly policies than sovereignty-based arrangements. The belief in the superiority of private regulation of the Internet was shared by a coalition of liberalization-oriented governments, the Internet industry and interested users (Mueller 2002).

While the US Government claimed authority to define the basic mechanisms for ensuring the legitimacy of the governing arrangement for the Internet's name space, the task of implementation, in other words the operational responsibility, was delegated to ICANN. Reflecting the MoU between the US Government and ICANN, the latter's original bylaws stipulated that nearly half of its board seats would be filled with individual users while the remaining seats would represent various operative functions of the Internet's address spaces. Governments and international organizations were to participate in a mere consultative capacity through a governmental advisory council. The one exception has been the US Government, which arranged for itself a special supervisory function to be held until the privatization of the DNS administration.

The tasks of ICANN included the creation of a membership mechanism that would represent 'the global and functional diversity of Internet users and their needs' and at the same time ensure accountability (DOC 1998). To that end, in the year 2000, ICANN set up a global organization for individual users, the so-called 'at-large membership', and initiated the first global online elections for five seats of the ICANN board, rather than nine as originally stipulated. However, the legitimatizing impact of the participation of Internet users and online elections on the (semi-) private governance arrangement proved to be a contested issue. On the grounds that users from a few countries had dominated the elections, a majority of the ICANN board and ICANN administration dismissed elections as a mechanism for representing geographic and functional diversity on the Internet. Still in 2000, in the course of ICANN's organizational reform, the ICANN board discarded the concept of a balanced board representation between industry stakeholders and individual users. The ICANN administration's vision of 'ICANN 2.0' was a public–private partnership that would acknowledge and involve in a decision-making capacity governments as true representatives of the public interest.

The idea of a public–private partnership and its failure – governments rejected the offer to share operative responsibility with the private sector – demonstrate some of the dilemmas involved in achieving legitimacy in a transnational setting. The shift of regulatory responsibility from the national and international level to a global private authority – albeit under unilateral state supervision – reopens basic questions of democratic legitimacy that had been settled with the consolidated nation state. These questions concern not only the design of transparent and accountable procedures, but also the adequate definition of the boundaries of the new constituency – who should have a say in the regulation of the Internet's address space and who should not? To date, ICANN still struggles for legitimacy. Practically all developing countries criticize the violation of the principle of sovereignty inherent in the centralized governing arrangement of the Internet. Accordingly, the violation of this fundamental principle of the national constellation undermines the democratic notion of self-determination. The Internet stakeholders, however keep complaining about nontransparent and inefficient procedures. As long as ICANN remains subject to US Government control, the outcome responsibility for its overall performance including its legitimacy will also rest with the US Government, although some ambiguity remains in this regard which may be typical for transnational arrangements under state control.

The emergence of a hybrid global privacy regime

The regulatory idea of protecting citizens' privacy was originally formed with a view to unreasonable police searches of private property, but soon extended to the control of *information about persons* in the hands of governments and private entities (Warren and Brandeis 1890). In 1948, the right to privacy was internationally codified in the Universal Declaration of Human Rights (Art. 12). The idea of 'data protection' in the more narrow sense emerged with the spread of automated data processing in the 1960s. Not only were computers used to store and retrieve vast amounts of personal data, but also they were able to correlate, evaluate and sort these – which in the end came down to sorting persons (Lyon 2003). Although emphasizing different means, both American 'informational privacy' and European 'data protection' policies share the fundamental goal to ensure that individuals know about, and can control, which computer-processed information others have about them. With the growth of transnational trade, the regional integration of markets and the emergence of multinational corporations, a second, derivative goal became an integral part of data protection efforts: permitting the flow of personal data across multiple jurisdictions, while preserving the protection level for individuals.

Since the first data protection law was enacted in the German Land of Hesse in 1970, data protection legislation has spread around the world, mostly through policy emulation and diffusion (Bennett 1998). In the golden age of the nation state, the overall regulatory model was state-interventionist and closely linked to the specific technical structure of the problem. Computers in the 1960 and the 1970s were mainframes in the hands of huge bureaucracies or corporations, and the regulatory model applied was direct government oversight and intervention using instruments such as registration or licensing mechanisms for databases or access controls. While in Europe all processing of personal data was regulated, US privacy regulation only applied to governmental agencies. Moreover, in the American model, there was no counterpart to the European data protection commissioner, an independent public oversight body; instead, courts were relied upon for individual enforcement.

Outcome responsibility for data protection resided with the nation state. Some European countries reacted to this expectation by even including clauses in their constitutions to ensure the privacy rights of citizens, and national courts were the last resort for their enforcement. Regulatory responsibility – the competence to make more concrete rules for data protection – was also borne by the state, although international harmonization efforts, in particular the 1980 OECD Guidelines and the 1981 Council of Europe Convention, foreshadowed a process of internationalization, which culminated in the EU's 1995 Data Protection Directive. Operational responsibility in the early years was held by governmental regulatory authorities. Meanwhile, the German institution of the corporate data protection commissioner – or chief privacy officer – has spread across the globe, giving significant operational responsibility to the private sector itself.

New challenges in protecting online privacy and the transformation of the global privacy regime

When the personal computer hit the market in the mid-1980s, the use and processing of all kinds of data – including personal data – was already growing beyond the reach of effective government oversight. This was aggravated with the advent of the Internet as a mass medium in the 1990s, when the number, diversity and options of data-collecting agents increased dramatically. The types of information collected were no longer restricted to *transactional* data, such as data accruing with purchases or other business exchanges, like credit card numbers, delivery addresses and so on. In addition, users' online *behavioural* data – such as websites visited, search keywords used – could be automatically collected through web servers even without users completing any forms. Specialized customer profiling and advertising companies were able to aggregate user data across several websites and develop fine-grained profiles.

The Internet also made it difficult to apply and enforce national data protection laws. Transnational transfer of personal data between corporations now became possible in a matter of seconds. And it was not clear anymore which law should apply when a European citizen entered his personal data into a website hosted in the United States. If the local PC of the user were regarded the locus of data processing, encompassing European data protection legislation would apply. If the web server were considered the machine where the data collection takes place, the data would only be subject to private sector self-regulation in the United States.

The Internet breakthrough coincided with the adoption of the 1995 EU Data Protection Directive, the third-party rules of which helped create some dynamic in the United States and eventually also in Europe. The EU Commission now could issue 'inadequacy' ratings about countries that lacked comprehensive data protection legislation, thereby prohibiting the transfer of personal data from within the internal market to these countries. Since the United States lacked an omnibus privacy act, the Clinton administration feared that US companies might be locked out of the European market for e-commerce. After protracted negotiations, the EU Commission and the US Department of Commerce in July 2000 sealed a 'Safe Harbor' agreement (Farrell 2003; Heisenberg 2005). This accord links the two regions' regulatory approaches – the European, law-based and comprehensive privacy regulation and the American, private sector-based and sectoral model – by making companies rather than countries the object of 'adequacy' rating. As a result, the United States could keep its data processing industry unregulated by law, and the EU could allow data transfers to American companies provided they subjected themselves to the Safe Harbor agreement principles. Containing regulations on notice, choice, onward transfer, security, data integrity, access and enforcement, these principles roughly mirror the international consensus on fair information and data protection goals and procedures.

In the course of transatlantic negotiations, EU data protection officials came to appreciate the self-regulatory instruments developed in the United States, which since have gained more acceptance in Europe (Farrell 2003). In recent years, several industry associations have developed privacy 'codes of conduct', and many now award 'privacy seals' to websites that publicly declare their adherence to specific data protection standards. Other approaches include privacy contract clauses on personal data flows in transnational business networks. Most of these private governance instruments were introduced on the national level and subsequently transnationalized. Some privacy web seals developed in the United States for a Safe Harbor adequacy rating are now used in East Asia and elsewhere. The latest development is the practice of embedding in a legal framework and certifying by public authorities privacy codes of conduct that were established by business associations. The EU directive mentions this option, but regards it as an exception. Since the Safe Harbor breakthrough, however, European data protection commissioners have turned to actively promoting this form of public–private collaboration in data protection.

The organizational and spatial diffusion of privacy protection

The emerging global or at least OECD-wide regulatory arrangement is a transnational-intergovernmental combination of the European law-based and comprehensive data protection regulation and the American self-regulatory approach. Outcome responsibility still seems to reside with the nation state, although the European Union legally took over this function from its members in 1995. In contrast with the golden age, regulatory responsibility is now organized in a multi-layered, hybrid way. Minimal privacy protection levels are defined internationally, the most important documents being the EU directive and the EU–US–Safe Harbor agreement. But whereas public regulation differs along territorial lines, be it the nation, Europe, or the OECD, private self-regulatory instruments apply to companies or branches and tend to ignore geography, thus making for global regulation within organizational or sectoral limits: DaimlerChrysler's binding corporate rules for privacy are valid globally, yet apply only to the corporation's employees and subcontractors. Operational responsibility is now by default organized through chief privacy officers. They are supplemented by privately organized certification and seal schemes, which have established their own compliance and arbitration mechanisms and only to a lesser extent rely on public oversight authorities or courts.

Altogether, we find a significant growth in importance of transnational mechanisms in the regulation and operation of privacy protection. It is not a complete takeover, though, as the self-governance of privacy continues to take place within national or supranational legal frameworks – privacy laws or laws against unfair and deceptive trade practices – and within a network of international rules that defines minimal levels of protection. The emerging global privacy regime is decentralized, heterogeneous and multifaceted, with the EU directive as its legal core and the Safe Harbor agreement as the dominant model of hybrid regulatory patterns. The general picture is therefore one of a diffusion of statehood in privacy protection, although within the EU responsibilities have partially shifted from the national to the supranational level.

The legitimacy of the new regime

The emerging global privacy regime faces three kinds of legitimacy problems, each of which has been addressed in different ways and by different actors. The first is typical for international policy making. International harmonization generally limits the accountability of the governmental rule makers to their societies through prolonged chains of representation as well as reduced transparency. The Internet helped address this problem by making new forms of transparency and stakeholder participation possible. Drafts of official regulatory instruments are now routinely being made available online, and the EU, the OECD and the Council of Europe regularly conduct online consultations in this policy field.

Interestingly, international organizations seem to be more strongly motivated to provide for transparency and stakeholder inclusion than national governments. They have started online consultations much earlier, their policy development processes are generally more comprehensively documented online than on the national level, and they sometimes actively reach out to civil society groups. This may be taken as an indication that international organizations see the need to compensate for their 'distance' to the ordinary citizen and to some extent assume responsibility for securing or enhancing the democratic legitimacy of international policy making (see Steffek in this volume).

The second legitimacy problem stems from the privatization of former public duties. The private sector privacy instruments are developed by business associations, service providers, or technology vendors, which are neither transparent in their work nor accountable to the public. While some of these forums have recently seen an involvement of privacy advocacy groups, most are closed shops and accessible only to a small number of insiders and experts. Governments and public data protection authorities respond by mandating minimal privacy thresholds for the private instruments, be they technical solutions, codes of conduct, or contractual clauses. They do not take steps to ensure greater transparency, accountability, or participation in these forums. Nor do they seize full operational or regulatory responsibility again, thus subjecting privacy protection (anew) to the state's democratic, parliamentary process. Nor do other actors assume a responsibility for tackling this 'democratic deficit', which may indicate that privacy protection is a policy field in which 'output legitimacy' (effectiveness) dominates 'input legitimacy' (democratic decision making).

The third legitimacy problem is concerned with the congruence of rule makers and rules. Because of the EU's market power, its rules on data transfers to third countries have become the de facto standard for global privacy governance. Other countries face high costs if they ignore the regulations developed in Brussels and put in place rules of their own choosing. Insofar as this is concerned, their autonomy is restricted. Some have therefore openly questioned the legitimacy of the EU rules. The Australian Government, for example, protested that there was 'no need for any externally-imposed test of "adequacy"' (McGinness 2003). Asian countries have developed regional privacy guidelines in the APEC framework, which are considered to correspond more to the 'Asian way', based on encouragement, voluntary mechanisms and no legal obligations (Greenleaf 2005). While this has enhanced regional congruence and therefore legitimacy, it may be short-lived. The countries will still have to adapt to the EU rules if they want to tap into the growing market of e-outsourcing, including for example call centres and other processing of customer data.

The global development of privacy governance takes place in this interplay of regional and global as well as public and private mechanisms. Its legitimacy is challenged, but the relevant public bodies – leading international organizations – are trying to secure it in new ways. The Internet is helpful for ensuring transparency and public participation here.

Electronic commerce and the transformation of the international tax regime

Taxes are the most important resource for the nation state to fulfil its functions. Because taxation means expropriation for the common good, tax rules require high legitimacy. It is hard enough for state authorities to perform their duty to collect taxes in a single territory. Additional difficulties arise whenever two or more countries are involved in the taxation of multinational firms: conflicts are bound to arise about which portion of the profit was produced – and hence is taxable – in which state. The globalization of the economy aggravates the problem that several states may claim the right to levy taxes on the same income. Furthermore, there are different principles of taxation that collide unless they are brought into line by a joint effort. The 'residence principle' aims at the place where a company has its domicile – its identification may be controversial as well – whereas the 'source principle' targets the place where income is created. If states do not coordinate the liability to pay taxes and the principles they apply, double taxation or non-taxation result. Both damage the legitimacy of the tax state. Therefore, the aim of international tax coordination is to grip taxpayers' money only once and to assign the tax base to the respective states according to mutually agreed rules.

Up to the 1970s, the tax state enjoyed a golden age. Fiscal sovereignty was extensive, tax systems were nationally confined, and firms resided in their mother country. Alongside effective national tax systems, an international tax regime, which placed no formal constraints on states' tax policies, had slowly emerged. In the 1920s, the League of Nations promoted the idea of a multilateral treaty against double taxation and tax evasion. Member states, however, wanted to keep their fiscal sovereignty and thus settled for a non-binding document. This 'model convention', which was published in 1928, contained draft models for bilateral tax treaties between states. After the Second World War, the OECD continued the task and published a new Model Tax Convention in 1963, accompanied by a comprehensive Commentary. Thus, the basic architecture of international taxation – a multilateral convention and many bilateral treaties – was confirmed. It is still in place today. The dominant role of national fiscal authorities notwithstanding, the institutionalization of the international tax regime has progressed, and the OECD's Committee on Fiscal Affairs has become the most prominent multilateral forum for international tax policy matters (Rixen and Rohlfing 2005). Participation has widened to non-OECD member countries and to the private sector, which is represented in the Business and Industry Advisory Committee (BIAC). In addition, the International Fiscal Association, a distinguished global organization of tax experts, maintains close contact with the OECD. The Model Tax Convention and the Commentary serve as a standard and are recognized by the whole tax community, including courts. The network of bilateral double taxation agreements has become more and more dense. Normally, the negotiators of an agreement adopt the Convention's text verbatim and add some extra articles. Thus, the OECD Model Tax Convention provides a 'focal point' for the agreements but leaves control at the national level. (Tax policy within the EU is subject to integration and requires separate consideration; see Uhl in this volume.)

The challenge of the Internet and the adaptation of the international tax regime

The Internet came as a threat to the tax state. The prerequisites of taxation – reviewable transactions, identification of involved parties and the nexus to a territory – were put into question by myriads of transborder data flows. The dispersed and ubiquitous network of networks undermined the existing system of territorially confined tax jurisdictions. Governments feared big tax losses in view of the opportunities of doing business in cyberspace. The Internet multiplied the options for legal tax planning and illegal tax fraud. Tax administrators worried about the possibility of e-commerce being carried out from tax havens and thus depriving industrial countries of a large part of their financial resources.

With hindsight, the years 1995–97 appear as a phase of uncertainty, speculation and learning how to come to grips with the Net. It was unclear whether current tax systems could cover the electronic business models or new taxes such as the 'bit tax' on data transfers were needed. While several national task forces were trying to figure out the Internet's effect on taxation, governments refrained from taking legislative action. The aim was to reach an international consensus on taxation of e-commerce before mutually contradictory national laws had been passed (Sprague and Boyle 2001). Policymakers and stakeholders turned to the OECD and its proven and widely accepted procedures of defining tax concepts. This was a remarkable novelty in the tax policy world.

Amid the soaring 'dot.com boom', the OECD began to examine the area. Prospects of how the Internet would transform the economy rocketed high, but tax experts became increasingly confident that the problems of Internet taxation could be tackled with existing taxation rules. The OECD addressed the subject in a series of conferences. At the 1998 Ottawa conference, the Taxation Framework Conditions for Electronic Commerce and a comprehensive post-Ottawa agenda were agreed. The institutions of the OECD's Committee on Fiscal Affairs expanded when several new advisory groups were set up to implement the framework (OECD 2001). National governments supported the efforts because the Ottawa conditions assured fair sharing of tax bases from e-commerce and maintenance of fiscal sovereignty. The position that the Internet could be managed with the established tax concepts became the prevailing opinion. The adaptation phase of tax rules to the Internet took five years and resulted in the adoption of an updated Model Tax Convention and Commentary in 2003. Of course, this revision did not settle Internet tax rules once and for all, but the essential steps were made.

One of the most important issues was how an Internet server should be classified so as to fit in the established tax rules. More specifically, it had to be defined under what circumstances a server is a so-called 'permanent establishment'. This concept refers to the location of a commercial activity and is used to attribute profit to a particular place of business. The tax experts at the OECD worked out a catalogue of qualifications according to which, simply put, a server constitutes a permanent establishment for a firm if it simultaneously meets four conditions: it is owned, controlled and maintained by the firm and is of vital importance for its business. In contrast, a website or other immaterial applications fall short of a permanent establishment. Consequently, it is not so easy to move an e-commerce business to a tax haven. If a company resides in an industrial country and has an online shop hosted on an offshore server, the income from this server will nonetheless be taxed in the firm's home country. Furthermore, even if a server located in a foreign country is recognized as a permanent establishment, the profit attributed to this place of business will be small because the creation of value consists in the development and production of a good or service, not in transmitting data. The location where the revenue is generated is not necessarily the place where it is taxed. This example illustrates how the Internet was integrated in international tax rules.

Although the expert community managed to keep up the principles of taxation, the rise of the Internet fuelled the internationalization of firms, the division of production and intelligent profit shifting. Tax administrations became aware that closer cooperation was necessary. Therefore, the OECD created new transgovernmental institutions to bring together tax administrators of member and non-member countries and of international organizations. The agenda comprises information exchange, use of technology and best practice in tax administration. Notably, the use of the Internet has become an important tool for tax collectors, too.[3]

Transformation of the tax state?

At first glance, the adaptation to the Internet effected little change in the international tax regime. The main features remained unaltered: national fiscal sovereignty, a multilateral convention and a network of bilateral tax treaties. So far, there is little evidence to support the prediction that e-commerce will lead to a shift of taxing authority to a new global tax arrangement (Paris 2003: 177). Nevertheless, the fact that, in the phase of uncertainty, nation states did not act on their own but called on the OECD to handle the problem, brought up the view that tax policy making on e-commerce made the OECD an 'informal "world tax organization" ' (Cockfield 2006). So, does a closer look reveal some kind of transformation of the tax state? As mentioned above, states preserved their fiscal sovereignty, that is, outcome responsibility remained at the national level. But the OECD's definition of the Internet issues for taxation and their incorporation in the updated Model Tax Convention and the Commentary show that regulatory responsibility for tax matters has partly moved to the international level. The new bodies set up in the process strengthened the OECD's Committee on Fiscal Affairs. This institutional empowerment amounts to a diffusion of statehood. Since representatives of national governments form an essential part of the OECD's tax institutions membership, the regulation of e-commerce taxation is interlocked with the respective government departments. The operational responsibility of national tax administrations as such is not challenged. Change occurred, however, with respect to the means and procedures of tax collection and tax computation. The function to provide the state with money stayed at the national level, but transgovernmental cooperation of tax authorities has intensified. Again, this points to a (tentative) diffusion of statehood in tax matters. In sum, the internationalization caused by the need to regulate e-commerce taxation was a reaction of the states to the Internet, formulated by an intergovernmental organization, implemented at the international and the national level and triggering an ongoing transgovernmental process.

States ensure the legitimacy of international taxation

Just as the international tax regime did not change significantly in response to the Internet, its legitimacy was not impaired. In some respects it may be said to have increased. Like other international organizations, the OECD – the institution facilitating and shaping international tax cooperation – has enhanced transparency by documenting its work online. The website contains many documents on taxation but no minutes of meetings. The Internet's communicative possibilities were sparsely used in the formulation of the rules, whereas networked computers became more important for the exchange of information between tax administrators. The OECD has established stakeholder relationships since the 1960s, especially to business and industry but recently also to consumer groups. Thus, the groups directly affected by practical tax matters were enabled to take part in the formulation of the e-commerce taxation framework.

The tax regime's architecture of multilateral standard setting and bilateral negotiations provides for the congruence of political and social spaces in international tax policy. Thus, the efforts of states to avoid double taxation and to reduce tax evasion are legitimate in the sense that they aim at taxpayers that have a link to the territory of the involved states. Although the democratic accountability of the OECD's committee members is only indirect, the involvement of national government officials makes the process accessible to parliamentary controls. Nevertheless, bilateral tax treaties can only be approved or rejected as a whole – a well-understood legitimacy problem that parliamentary democracies have to put up with. The fears that e-commerce would cause tax losses and unequal taxation of the online and offline economy were dissolved by the rules adopted by the international tax community. The states' abstinence from producing an incomprehensible diversity of national laws in favour of a common OECD standard for e-commerce taxation reflects their awareness that the Internet requires international solutions to some extent, but not necessarily a 'world tax organization'. Overall, states have stabilized their position as main actors in tax policy by international and transgovernmental cooperation and as providers of legitimacy to the international tax regime.

Conclusion

Nothing comes closer to a completely denationalized social space than cyberspace. This makes the Internet and policy areas that are in one way or another strongly impacted by it a 'most-likely case' (Eckstein 1975) for the hypothesis that globalization pressures cause the modern Western nation state to transform by internationalizing or privatizing some of its wide-ranging responsibilities. In the three cases reviewed in this chapter, we indeed found evidence to support this hypothesis, although the extent of the transformation is smaller and more variable than might have been surmised. Thus, in each of our cases international institutions – including supranational (EU), intergovernmental (OECD) and transnational (ICANN) bodies – gained in importance since the advent of the Internet, eliminating, circumscribing, or qualifying the autonomy of the nation state in the issue area at hand. Moreover, in two cases, 'DNS' and 'data protection', the (self-)regulatory efforts of private corporations and associations are now much more critical than before for the provision of the normative good in question. In both cases, this resulted in the emergence of a hybrid mixture of public and private arrangements and authorities – taking the shape of a unilateral-transnational regime in 'DNS' and of a multilayered intergovernmental-transnational regime in 'data protection'.

Outcome responsibility usually remains with the nation state, although the United States claims the role of a global warden over the Internet's name space, and the members of the EU have delegated their sovereignty in the area of privacy protection to the supranational level. Both regulatory and operational responsibilities in the three policy fields are no longer monopolized by the nation state, as they indeed were in the 1960s and the 1970s. At the same time, nowhere has the state ceased to make and implement rules altogether – the single partial exception being the DNS, in which, in the case of generic top level domains, privatization – under the auspices of the US Government – has prevailed 'all the way down'. At both levels of responsibility, international and private actors now play important roles in the provision of the normative good in question. As to the nature of the reconfiguration of statehood, the bulk of the reshuffling of responsibilities that can be observed is more adequately described as a diffusion than a shift, that is the powers and efforts of the nation state in these areas tend to be complemented rather than replaced. Again, 'DNS' turns out a special case, though: taking the 'ancient regime' of international telecommunications as a baseline, nation states, except for the United States, have indeed lost most of their responsibilities with respect to a specific part of the telecommunications infrastructure to a private institution with global reach (ICANN).

The three cases vary significantly with regard to the extent of transformation that has taken place. The most radical deviation from the *status quo ante* of the golden age occurred within the policy field of international communications, in which we focused on the administration of a new name space, the DNS. Not only is this the case where the role of the nation state, in general, has been most drastically curtailed, but also it is here that we find the most innovative, though ill-fated, experiments with novel ways of securing legitimacy for a transnational authority, culminating in the 2000 global online elections of Internet users' representatives to its oversight body. By contrast, despite the widespread fears for, and speculations about, the future of the tax state that were aroused by the advent of the Internet in the mid-1990s, comparatively little has changed in the way that states, individually and collectively, seek to secure access to their tax base and to avoid double taxation or non-taxation in international commerce. The international tax regime appears to have 'absorbed' the shock that came with the rise of e-commerce, although the OECD's regulatory responsibility has slightly increased and transgovernmental cooperation to improve states' ability to exert operational responsibility has intensified in the process. Finally, 'data protection' occupies a middle position that witnesses both continuity and change in prevailing practices of statehood.

These differences can be accounted for by a combination of closely related factors: first, the observed variation reflects the policy – typological differences between the three cases and the degree of 'intrusiveness' that comes with them: 'market-making' policies such as 'DNS' tend to be less conflict-prone than 'market-braking' policies such as 'privacy protection' or even 'market-correcting' endeavours such as 'taxation' (Streeck 1995); therefore, states will guard their sovereignty and their means of social control less jealously in such fields and institutional arrangements will be more flexible. Second, the three issue areas differ considerably in their 'age', with 'taxation' being the oldest and 'DNS' being the youngest. This is significant and helps to explain the variation observed in that 'older' policy fields will tend to have given rise to stronger path dependencies, habits and vested interests that resist change. Third, it seems plausible to assume that the novel features of the Internet which, as many observers pointed out, have a considerable potential for reorganizing and democratizing politics, will play out the more strongly the 'closer' and more 'essential' a policy area is to the Internet. Again, this correlates nicely with the features of our three cases.

It is part of the logic of most-likely case studies that we expect the hypothesis to pass the test posed by the selected cases clearly and unambiguously and that whenever it fails to do so we should become more cautious about it. Against this background, it is important to reiterate that the transformations of statehood we observed in our cases were less far-reaching and pronounced than might have been expected – and indeed often was expected only a few years ago. What is more, there are indications that the transformation may have topped out and we are witnessing a *return of the state.*

Thus, the nation state has recently begun to intervene more vigorously in private self-regulation activities in the area of 'data protection', and during the World Summit on the Information Society, many states, including the EU, voiced concerns about the unilateral character of present-day Internet governance that clearly breathed nostalgia for some of the constitutive features of the 'ancient regime'. (There is no such trend in 'taxation', for the simple reason that here the nation state had never shown signs of retrenchment.) Interestingly, this return of the state has been facilitated by the difficulties the new post-national arrangements faced securing the normative good of *democratic legitimacy.* This is somewhat ironic given that issue-specific transnational arrangements were often expected to be more congruent, transparent, participatory, and accountable to stakeholders and also to be more effective in terms of problem solving than traditional intergovernmental regimes. As our review of the three cases has indicated, the political arrangements in the three fields are – and, in varying degrees, are perceived to be – wanting in each of these respects, although some advances have been made in recent years, not least thanks to the Internet, in particular with regard to transparency. Moreover, disappointments about the legitimacy (DNS) and doubts about the effectiveness (privacy protection) of the privatized regimes currently in operation have contributed to the nation state now being in a position to reclaim increased responsibilities in the respective issue areas. Even though it seems safe to be predict that a restoration of the 'national constellation' will not take place, the future division of labour between the nation state, private bodies and international institutions in these three Internet-impregnated policy fields is far from settled and hence the search for a new stable order is likely to continue for some time to come.

Notes

1 Obviously, it is the people who grant or deny legitimacy to the state; at the same time, the state may have the socially acknowledged and legally enshrined obligation to provide for the institutions (e.g., elections) which enable the people to exert their right to democratic self-determination. It is in this sense that we talk of the golden-age nation state's responsibility for the provision of the normative good of democratic legitimacy.
2 Note, however, that not all regulatory functions related to the DNS are centralized. The country code top level domains, while in principle dependent on

the central root zone file, are operated and administered more or less autonomously on the national level, notwithstanding ICANN's Internet-wide authority claims.
3   Due to restrictions of space, the chapter leaves aside sales taxes or value added taxes, which cause similar problems in transborder e-commerce. As with income tax, officials responded by developing closer transgovernmental cooperation.

References

Bennett, Colin J. (1998) 'Convergence Revisited: Towards a Global Policy for the Protection of Privacy?', in Philip E. Agre and Marc Rotenberg, eds, *Technology and Privacy: The New Landscape*, Cambridge MA: MIT Press, 219–41.

Cockfield, Arthur J. (2006) 'The Rise of the OECD as Informal "World Tax Organization" through National Response to E-commerce Tax Challenges', *Yale Journal of Law and Technology* 8(2), 136–87.

DOC (1998) 'Memorandum of Understanding between the U.S. Department of Commerce and Internet Corporation for Assigned Names and Numbers', available at <http://www.ntia.doc.gov/ntiahome/domainname/icannmemorandum.htm>, last accessed: 23 November 2006.

Drake, William J. (1994) 'The Transformation of International Telecommunication Standardization', in Charles W. Steinfield, Johannes Bauer and Laurence Caby, eds, *Telecommunications in Transition: Politics, Services, and Technologies in the European Community*, Thousand Oaks: Sage, 71–96.

Eckstein, Harry (1975) 'Case Study and Theory in Political Science', in Fred I. Greenstein and Nelson W. Polsby, eds, *Handbook of Political Science*, Reading, MA: Addison-Wesley, 79–138.

Farrell, Henry (2003) 'Constructing the International Foundations of E-Commerce: The EU–US Safe Harbor Agreement', *International Organization* 57(2), 277–306.

Goldsmith, Jack L. and Tim Wu (2006) *Who Controls the Internet? Illusions of a Borderless World*, New York: Oxford University Press.

Greenleaf, Graham (2005) 'APEC's Privacy Framework: A New Low Standard', *Privacy Law and Policy Reporter* 11(5) available at Online: <http://www.austlii.edu.au/au/journals/PLPR/2005/1.html>, last accessed: 23 November 2006.

Habermas, Jürgen (2001) *The Postnational Constellation: Political Essays*, Cambridge, MA: MIT Press.

Heisenberg, Dorothee (2005) *Negotiating Privacy: the European Union, the United States, and Personal Data Protection*, Boulder, CO: Lynne Rienner.

Lessig, Lawrence (1998) 'Governance', Keynote: CPSR Conference on Internet Governance, 10 October, available at <http://www.lessig.org/content/articles/works/cpsr.pdf>, last accessed: 23 November 2006.

Lyon, David (2003) *Surveillance as Social Sorting: Privacy, Risk, and Digital Discrimination*, London: Routledge.

McGinness, John (2003) 'What's up in the Asia-Pacific? APEC Privacy Initiatives', paper presented at the Conference 'Privacy Issues Forum', Wellington, 28 March, available at <http://www.knowledge-basket.co.nz/privacy/media/ McGinness.pdf>, last accessed: 23 November 2006.

Mueller, Milton (2002) *Ruling the Root: Internet Governance and the Taming of Cyberspace*, Cambridge, MA: MIT Press.

OECD (2001) *Taxation and Electronic Commerce: Implementing the Ottawa Taxation Framework Conditions*, Paris: OECD.

Paris, Roland (2003) 'The Globalization of Taxation? Electronic Commerce and the Transformation of the State', *International Studies Quarterly* 47(2), 153–82.

Rixen, Thomas and Ingo Rohlfing (2005) *The Political Economy of Bilateralism and Multilateralism: Institutional Choice in International Trade and Taxation*, TranState Working Paper No. 31, Bremen: TranState Research Centre.

Sprague, Gary D. and Michael P. Boyle (2001) 'Taxation of Income Derived from Electronic Commerce: General Report', *Cahiers de Droit Fiscal International* LXXXVIa, 21–63.

Streeck, Wolfgang (1995) 'From Market-Making to State-Building? Reflections on the Political Economy of the European Social Policy', in Stephan Leibfried and Paul Pierson, eds, *European Social Policy: Between Fragmentation and Integration*, Washington, DC: Brookings Institution, 389–431.

Warren, Samuel D. and Louis D. Brandeis (1890) 'The Right to Privacy', *Harvard Law Review* 4(5), 193–220.

8

The Internationalization of Education Policy: Towards Convergence of National Paths?

Kerstin Martens and Ansgar Weymann[1]

Education policy is today considered a classic prerogative of the modern nation state. As a means to *integrate* the nation state and as a key tool to improve *economic growth,* it denotes a core element of its *sovereignty* and *autonomy*. Today, however, steps towards the *internationalization* of education policy can be observed (Bascia *et al.* 2005; Daun 2005; Mundy 2005; Zajda 2005). With initiatives such as the 'Programme for International Student Assessment' (PISA; directed by the OECD) and the Bologna process (in the EU context), international organizations (IOs) have increasingly become important actors in education policy. But how did education policy become transferred to the international level? Why are states willing to share control of their sphere of this policy field? In this chapter, we show that the reasons for this diffusion of statehood in education policy lie in the domestic domain itself: as states are increasingly unable to solve their problems individually, they turn to international organizations and ask them to develop internationally applicable solutions. However, by transferring responsibilities for education policy to international organizations, states triggered *institutional dynamics* within the IOs leading to the progress of internationally adopted standards and the harmonization of systems. These developments have a strong impact on national paths in education policy as they can lead to convergence between states.

In the first part of this chapter, we introduce the analytic grid for assessing convergence by relying on the concept of isomorphism. Subsequently, we go through the different phases of educational isomorphism from (a) the medieval times under the canopy of Christian curriculum and clerical regimes to (b) humanism, Reformation, Enlightenment and to incorporating education in the course of modern state building, turning it into one of its policy prerogatives. These days (c), we can observe the third step towards a new global isomorphism of education policy, driven by national problems but shaped by international organizations. By identifying these three distinct periods of education policy making – pre-national, national and international – we essentially argue that internationalization carries on prior developments in the history of education policy: by involving international organizations into education policy making a further level of isomorphism in this policy field comes into reach after religious and national homogenizing forces. In this chapter, we focus on international standard-setting activities as exercised by the EU and the OECD.

Forces of historical convergence and isomorphism

In present, as a result of an extended historical development, education forms part of the normative good of welfare, the provision of which became constitutive for the modern state. It developed into a useful instrument of the *intervention state* to provide for economic growth and to decrease and, at the same time, legitimize *social inequality*.[2] By and by, the emerging modern state took responsibility for the provision of education at each of the three levels – *outcome, regulation and operation*. In the case of Germany, to give an example, *outcome responsibility* can be traced back to the first medieval universities that needed the Emperor's 'privilege'[3] to be academically acknowledged. *Regulatory responsibility* was introduced as an element of early state building, for example in terms of school statistics and by supervision over curricula and personnel of local and clerical schools. *Operational responsibility* of the state was introduced, among others, with the payment of state salaries for professors since the Reformation.

Given that education is such an old and important element of the modern nation state, how can the present trend towards internationalization of education policy be explained? What are the driving forces behind it? We try to understand the current transformation of this national prerogative into international education policy by looking back to the historical constitution of education policy as an integral part of statehood. As theoretical explanation of the force driving historical convergence once towards modern statehood and today into the internationalization of education policy we refer to institutional isomorphism. The key argument for explaining why isomorphism occurs is that institutions and organizations – organizations being the corporate form of institutions – need to be culturally accepted within their institutional context to be effective and efficient. For these reasons, organizations tend to implement those cultural values, norms and rules that are institutionalized in society (DiMaggio and Powell 1983). Consequentially, there is a general tendency in history towards conformity of institutions and organizations, that is, towards isomorphism.

In a universal perspective, Max Weber once coined the term 'occidental rationalism' to designate the key aspect of convergence of institutions in the course of European modernization. Based on the assimilation of ideas and the competition of organizations, the occidental type of rational institutions became dominant in the world – primarily represented by the bureaucracy and capitalist firms, the legal system, science and education. The more dominant the culture of occidental rationalism in the world, the more numerous the number of isomorphic rationalized organizations on the globe will be (Meyer and Rowan 1977: 358). Premodern political actors were unable to prevent the isomorphic transformation of institutions into the modern nation state; similarly, the modern nation state will be unable to call a halt to the transformation into isomorphic international institutions. In the face of decreasing national power, the nation state's sovereignty and autonomy, paradoxically, are best protected if former national prerogatives such as education policy are partially delegated to the international level, that is, to intergovernmentally controlled policy actors.

Isomorphism of education has slowly developed over extended historical times. In China, India, Egypt and ancient Europe, education was quite dissimilar with respect to ideas and organization (Collins 2000). A first step towards isomorphism in Europe was the introduction of Christianity and the institutions of Christendom. A second step was taken with the formation of the state since about 1500. Modern states began to govern education with respect to ideas and goals and by means of curricula and isomorphic organizations. The rationale was the *social integration* of the population and the assumed positive effect of education on national *economic development*.[4] The third step, global isomorphism of education, was originally launched by exporting western educational policy in the wake of European and North-American expansion. Today, especially transnational and international organizations provide networks of global elites that install *global isomorphic patterns of education* and science (Finnemore 1993).

We regard international organizations in this respect as institutional entrepreneurs who foster the trend of internationalization. They are brokers in an organizational field that have manifold advantages compared to other members, in particular single states: due to their central position, they can act strategically and move in a field transparent to them, while other actors might perceive the field as opaque or hazy (Dorado 2005). Moreover, IOs, as central actors in the field, are engaged in constructing means-end frames which make them a source of information for other field members and stabilizes the field (Borum 2004). They become successful education policy entrepreneurs – in particular through their ability to establish strong linkages and exchange between their member states and to deliver common goals, problems and solutions.

Pre-national education policy – the idea of Christianity and the institutions of Christendom

In Athens, education was an individual endeavour aiming at intellectual and aesthetic improvement. The Roman idea of education focused on virtues, not at least military virtues, and to some extent on craftsmanship. Higher education was a copy of the *Hellenistic tradition* of the learned individual. But with the fall of the Roman Empire non-religious education almost ceased to exist in Europe. Migrating tribes and nations embraced Christendom one after the other. Christendom and Christianity became the main forces of cultural and institutional isomorphism in Europe (Mann 1986). In terms of curricula, education became religious education primarily. Only rarely were antique traditions of education kept alive. For example, Charlemagne re-established a non-religious sector of education at his 'School of the Palace', and asked archbishops and abbots to offer elementary education for the common people at the parish level and studies of fine arts at their regional capitals for sons of high origin – as seen, for example, in 787 in letters to bishop Lullus of Mainz and abbot Bangulf of Fulda (Durkheim 1977: 42).

The medieval European university is 'Christian' and often developed out of well-esteemed monastery or bishop schools. Within the boundaries of the 'Holy Roman Empire of German Nation' the first university 'privileged' by the Emperor in 1236 was Bologna, followed by Prague (1346), Vienna (1365), Heidelberg (1386) and Cologne (1389), all of these institutionally shaped after the model of Paris University. Before the Reformation, 18 universities were founded and privileged. As a rule, students received access to universities after graduation from a municipal 'Latin school'. In the 15th century, municipalities of 1,000 inhabitants and more had established such schools for children of higher social standing. From the beginning, universities not only enjoyed good reputations but also self-governance as well as several tax and juridical exemptions. The imperial privilege of 1158, the *Authentica Habita,* guaranteed protection of autonomy, for example, against local forces. In terms of organization, universities were divided in four faculties: the higher studies theology, law and medicine, and the lower studies of the arts, subdivided into *trivium* (grammar, rhetoric, logic) and *quadrivium* (arithmetic, geometry, astronomy, music) (Hammerstein 2003).

Students of arts graduated with a master's degree, students of the higher studies with a doctorate or with the more affordable licentiate. The first layer of study was finished with the bachelor. Master's students earned their living by teaching bachelor students. On average, about 3,000 students enrolled per year. The imperial privilege was costly but inevitable. It proved the acknowledgement of academic degrees of graduates within Christian Europe. Graduates were licensed to teach everywhere. The curricula were based on approximately thirty canonized volumes. Faculties were small, comprising 11 professors on average. The faculty had to be paid for by means of a regular salary or by means of prebends, benefices or sinecure. Within the German empire, the territor- ial states were in charge of providing the living (Hammerstein 2003). Up to today, in federal Germany, the *Länder* are in charge.

Thus, the main forces of institutional isomorphism of universities in the era of pre-national, medieval education policy were the culture of Christianity and the institutions of Christendom. Organizationally, universities were divided into four faculties. Latin was the lingua franca. A German peculiarity was the strained relation among territorial authorities and the imperial privilege. In this historical period, there was little state responsibility over education because the state itself is poorly developed.

Education policy in times of state-building – a case study on Germany

In times of nation building, convergence and isomorphism developed further. Step by step, education turned into a normative good of statehood, transcending the boundaries of Christendom, feudal territories and local authorities. From the 15th and the 16th centuries onwards, education was increasingly used by the emerging modern state, confronted with religious conflicts and clashes, to integrate the multi-centred population by means of literacy, religious lectures, basic arithmetic, a national language and narrative. Since the middle of the 18th century, the state became the most important 'container' of modern society. The state was taken as a stronghold of civilization, progress and protection and was seen as a key instrument of rational economic decision making, as the tool of political power elites, as the backbone of welfare and social policy and as the most important social construction of community.

The state in turn bred the nation, nurturing nationalism, ethno-symbolism and political Messianism as secular religions and ideologies (Smith 1998). Education – already used as an instrument of distinction and individual human capital investment for status admission in the clergy, guilds and professions – was turned into a mercantilist instrument of the state to improve industrialism and human capital of the sovereign's people collectively (Smith 1974). Finally, in the 19th century, education became a prime tool of the democratic welfare state, and began to be conceived as a social right (Marshall 1992). In the end, we have the full-fledged state responsibility over education that we know today.

Education policy in times of early modern state building

With respect to ideas and curricula, an important impetus was given by Humanism in the 15th century. Humanism replaced the *reductio artium ad theologiam* by *reductio artium ad humanitatem* – the reduction of the arts to theology by the reduction of the arts to humanity (Buck 1996; Hammerstein 1996). Humanism, which originated from the early rising bourgeoisie of the Italian cities, represented an ideal of the learned. Life conduct of the learned was based on moral philosophy and aesthetics. Humanism spread all over Europe, deeply influencing education and universities. In terms of organization and power, the German university in the 16th and the 17th centuries became more and more closely supervised by the territorial states. The latter gained sovereignty and autonomy at the expense of the empire and its institutions as a consequence of the Reformation in the Passau Treaty of 1552[5] and the Thirty Years' War. Regular salaries became the rule. Universities were operated to improve common literacy, economic and legal relations, rational bureaucratic administration, science and the professions. University extension triggered the increase of university-trained men in many fields. Civil law emancipated from religious law and became a fundament of civil service. Medicine took advantage from the developing sciences.

In the 18th century, often called a century of education, education turned into a universal means of policy. In terms of ideas, it was the century of the Enlightenment, of scientific and social progress. There was a profound belief in the benefits of educating the entire population, preferably by public institutions of education (Herrmann 2005a; Stollberg-Rilinger 2005). Again, Enlightenment like humanism, was a universal European ideal. The spread of the trust in the benefits of education went hand in hand with early industrialization, the rise of the bourgeoisie in capitalist commerce and industry and the rise of the citizen, the *citoyen*, in public administration and professions. At the end of the 18th century, we can observe a complete and state-maintained system of public education operated by elementary schools for the lower and *Gymnasien* (Latin or grammar schools) for the upper classes.[6] Mass education transformed cultural, mental, political and economic values as well as attitudes and habits of the population. Education was believed to support social progress, human and civil rights, political self-determination, participation and the acceptance of meritocratic norms as legitimate standards of inequality in modern civil society.

The new bourgeois class of citizens seized and filled positions in bureaucracies and professions creating a meritocratic society based on individual achievements and acquired credits. Although there was no formal class barrier by birthrights – in contrast to the precedent feudal society of medieval standings – the new rising class was characterized by a high rate of self-reproduction. The meritocratic principle forced everybody, including the lower aristocracy, to submit their offspring to competition for credits and positions. But, at the same time, this democratic principle de facto excluded the proletariat and 'mob' from being successful competitors. University education attracted more students than ever, providing an oversupply of academics at the end of the century. At the close of the 18th century, Germany hosted 22 Catholic and 18 Protestant universities, more than any other European country. Jewish students were admitted to doctoral studies as well (Hammerstein 2005). German completely replaced Latin and the law faculty ranked highest.

As compared to higher education at universities and Latin schools, the condition of the lower education was much worse. As before, children of the lower classes, especially from farms, small shops and craftsmen's families, were integrated into family work and trade. School evasion was a – prosecuted – consequence (Neugebauer 2005). Elementary school teachers were often subject to local social powers. However, state supervision and inspection of the outcome of the lower school system improved continuously. General school statistics developed. Only vocational education resisted state responsibility.[7] It remained mainly a practical education by means of observing the performance of an experienced master and submitted to the rule of the guild master (Bruchhäuser 2005: 414). Furthermore, education policy much more than before turned into an instrument of welfare and social care policy (Albrecht 2005). In this field, education aimed at enabling self-sustenance of the citizen or – in case of long-lasting unemployment – at teaching honesty to the poor. Education was to provide the competence necessary to earn one's living honestly. Finally, migration and vagrancy were already objects of education policy. Educational measures were to prevent the spread of poverty and violence. Release from tuition and sometimes even allowances above market income for daily work were to prevent school avoidance of endangered youth. Step by step, school attendance became a question of family honour and self-esteem for the lower classes of the population, too.

Towards the golden age of the nation state's education policy

State building executed pressure on the convergence of education and education policy – even under a particularistic constitution as in the case of Germany with its 'fatherlands' below the level of the nation (Green 2001). In the 19th century, the modern nation state fully developed. Legal regulations, organizations, professions and curricula further converged into isomorphic forms of the 'education state' (Jeismann 1987). Education turned into a means of nation building in modern European societies (Gellner 1983; Smith 1998; Hechter 2000). The rising metropolitan classes perceived themselves as representatives of society and the nation, and of the ideological, economic and political sources of social power (Mann 1993). In Germany, the number of students enrolled in universities multiplied in the period from 1815 to 1870. For women, teacher training colleges and professions became a major track of social advancement from 1800. Universities attracted more and more social climbers from the petit-bourgeoisie but much less from the proletariat. At the same time, universities remained elite institutions.[8]

The bourgeois society ambiguously stood for the democratic principle of universal inclusion on the one hand and de facto exclusion on the other hand, making its image ambivalent and controversial. Between the classes and within the classes, institutions of education served as important means of social differentiation, distinction and social reproduction (Lenger 2003: 221). Humboldt's university reform at the beginning of the 19th century integrated research and teaching, introduced permanent research competition, and made the *Abitur* (final secondary-school examinations) a general precondition of university enrolment (König 2000). These measures enormously raised the quality of university education but had exclusionary effects as well. Mass education and the use of mass media spread over society, providing the basis for efficient political mass organizations, various special interest groups and the general public debate (Berg and Hermann 1995: 17; Berghahn 1994).

Historians underline the general isomorphism of developments in the 19th century in Europe. In Germany, for example, industrialization began late compared to England but early compared to other European nations. In 1914, net incomes of German workers were the highest in Europe. Demographic growth was above the European average. Similarly, the

German nation state developed later than the English and French, but earlier than most others in Europe. Parliaments and democracy developed steadily. Universal suffrage, the principle of 'one man [not woman], one vote', was introduced during 1867–71, and for women in 1918. Rule of law, constitutionalism, the continuity of the party systems and a strong corporatism were salient (Collins 1995). In sum, the German path is not a peculiarity but a variety among varieties of a universal European development (Kocka 2001: 141).

In brief, nation building replaced or at least diminished the priority of traditional loyalties with respect to religion, clan, family, class and gender. For entrepreneurs, the modern state functioned as an excellent economic instrument, guaranteeing basic institutions of the market. For the new political elites, state institutions of administration, law, science and military became a prime tool of power. But the modern state supplied much more: a secular religion, a fictitious community, a container for a common culture, public goods like infrastructure, rational administration, safety and security, participation, legality and personal freedom. In this transformation process, isomorphic curricula and institutions of education played a key role. The metropolitans, entrepreneurs and politicians needed large markets and large administrative units. It was in their interest to govern the educational system. Education had to convert the growing deracinated urban proletariat into literate and arithmetic citizens. But, the introduction of a national curriculum and of isomorphic organizations by the central elite again and again elicited resistance of the geographical and social periphery as well as of the church. The metropolitan bourgeois class had to realize the paradox of education: better education can create the basis for more sophisticated strategies of opponents in distributional and power conflicts, and elicit cultural self awareness and counterculture.

The process of nation building led to fully fledged responsibility of the state over outcome (in terms of numbers and competences of graduates), over regulations (in terms of laws, professional status, acknowledgment of organizations and curricula) and over operation (at least in the field of public education).

Transforming the nation state prerogative in education – international convergence through international organizations?

Thus, over the recent centuries, the state has progressively managed to incorporate education into its realm of sovereignty. But in the present period of spatial and organizational transitions of the state, we can observe a weakening of this sovereign responsibility over education. Education as an element of culture and as a means of economic prosperity is increasingly moved onto the international level. In particular, international organizations function as policy entrepreneurs that try to strengthen interaction, increase information flow and facilitate interorganizational cooperation and communication on shared goals – processes that constitute the conditions for an organizational field between states (DiMaggio and Powell 1983). We look at two international organizations active in education policy: the OECD and the EU.[9] In both cases, we show that states initiated the process of internationalization and that during its course state-like responsibilities diffused to the intergovernmental level and became interlocked with international institutions.[10]

The OECD as shaper of standards in education

Although education was not mentioned explicitly in its establishing convention, the Organization for Economic Co-operation and Development (OECD) has been involved in education policy since its inception in 1961. In its early phases, the IO was strongly influenced by modernization theory, giving priority to the promotion of technology, mathematics and the natural sciences. Consequently, education policy aimed at promoting the 'human factor' as a prerequisite for technological and economic progress. Education planning was seen as a precondition for the production of a sufficient number of well-trained natural scientists and technicians (Papadopoulos 1994: 21; Interview OECD #26, 2004). During the 1970s, education policy became more closely linked to the labour market. At the same time, social objectives and education ideals moved to the fore, with discussions on equality of opportunity becoming an established part of OECD policies. Several education programmes were launched at the time, broadening the scope of activities at the organization.

The onset of the oil crisis, however, ended the expansion of education policy. In 1978, the first ministerial conference of education ministers on the future of education policy emphasized the 'changing social and economic context' of education (Henry *et al.* 2001: 64). Rising unemployment rates, especially among adolescents, a lack of public funds and demographic changes increasingly dominated the OECD programmes relating to education policy during the 1980s. Likewise, increased attention was devoted to the linkages between education and economic growth. With the demise of the Soviet Union, the states of Eastern Europe approached the OECD during the 1990s, which welcomed several as new members. As a result, OECD programmes – including those on education policy – have become yet more diverse over the years, with non-OECD states increasingly being integrated into OECD projects.

The OECD's breakthrough as *the* educational organization, however, came with the 'Programme for International Student Assessment' (PISA), first conducted in 2000. PISA is an internationally standardized survey of 15-year-old school students assessing 'how far students near the end of compulsory education have acquired some of the knowledge and skills that are essential for full participation in society' (OECD 2005). PISA covers reading, mathematical skills and scientific literacy, and is conducted in cycles of three years with a particular emphasis on one of these subjects in each assessment cycle. More and more countries are joining the PISA project: whereas in 2000 the survey was conducted in 43 counties, 57 participated in the third assessment in 2006 and 62 countries have signed up to take part in the fourth assessment in 2009. The reach of PISA goes far beyond the OECD membership – almost half of the participating countries in 2006 are not OECD members. Through PISA, the OECD is today able to shape standards in education that affect national policy making in this field.

The findings of the assessments resulted in the so-called 'PISA shock' in countries that had always believed their education systems to be good. The German system, for instance, was shown to have failed in evening out achievement gaps due to differences in socio-economic background, and in integrating children from immigrant families. The poor PISA results therefore prompted a wide discussion about reforming the German educational system. In fact, education has moved to the very top of the *Länder* governments' agendas and plays a crucial role in local and regional elections today. PISA has also triggered discussions about the Danish education system: investing considerably more money and resources into education than other countries, the Danes were irritated to find their PISA results only insignificantly above average. In the UK, the poor results of British pupils in the latest PISA test became a *politicum* and led the government to withdraw their publication, based on the questionable justification that an insufficient number of tests was taken.

Through this path-breaking work on education statistics and indicators, the OECD has acquired the status of an *éminence grise* of international education policy (Rinne *et al.* 2004), surpassing even such renowned education organizations as the United Nations Educational, Scientific and Cultural Organization (UNESCO) in reputation and policy influence. Compiling statistical information on education, however, was not new for the IO; in fact, it started in the 1960s, when interest in the use of statistical information for education planning grew: national policy makers needed a basis for gathering and comparing statistics in this policy field for increased efficiency. However, the quality of these statistics was 'catastrophic': they 'were not at a serious level for an organization like the

OECD, practically they were second, third level statistics, coming out very late, not comparable at all' (Interview OECD #20, 2004). At that time, the OECD was not generating data itself but was entirely dependent on what countries were supplying; and it never questioned the national data it received, even if there were obviously dubious figures (Interview OECD #25, 2004). As a result, its work on educational statistics was criticized as being too simplistic and primitive, such that the project was in fact partially abandoned during the 1970s (Rinne *et al.* 2004: 460).

In the mid-1980s, however, some individual states revived the indicator project within the OECD context and thus initiated the self-transformation of the education state. Particularly, the United States and France wanted the OECD to conduct more statistical work on education indicators. For very different reasons, both countries were concerned about their respective national education systems: the United States feared losing the technology race of the cold war; France's left-wing government was concerned about educational opportunities for socio-economically disadvantaged children. Education suddenly gained prominence on the US political agenda in 1983, after a report entitled 'A Nation at Risk: Imperatives for Educational Reform' had been published (National Commission on Excellence in Education 1983). It described the appalling state of education in the United States in an alarming language, triggering broad public concern and identifying the need for the monitoring of schools and personnel. With Sputnik still in mind, US pupils' poor science performance was considered tantamount to 'committing unilateral disarmament' at the height of the cold war (Interview OECD #16, 2004).[11] With changes in the French cabinet in the mid-1980s, the new socialist Minister of Education Jean-Pierre Chevènement also set new priorities for education policy. His aim was to arrive at a more egalitarian education system that enabled equal access to education and the resulting opportunities, independent of social background. Chevènement wanted figures on student performance to prove that the elitist French system fostered poor performance. As a result of the pressure from the United States and France, regulatory responsibility diffused to the level of the OECD which gradually modified its programme of work to develop standardized applicable education indicators (Interview OECD #20, 2004). Through a series of conferences, new and more feasible approaches to developing comparative statistics were discussed over the following years, and OECD member states agreed on a small set of indicators which could be collected in the participating countries.

States thus set in motion a process through which the OECD's activities in education policy became more institutionalized within the organization.

Most importantly, from the late 1980s onwards, the International Indicators of Educational Systems (INES) project became established – of which PISA is only the latest offspring, entirely developed within and through the OECD. With institutional backing through INES, the nature of OECD indicators changed significantly in quantitative and qualitative terms: they became more regular, more reliable and more meaningful sources of data. Since 1992, the OECD has published, for example, its famous *Education at a Glance* (EAG) each year, widely recognized in the field as an – if not *the* most – important source of educational indicators. Through its 36 indicators, it provides education data about OECD members and enables comparison and contrast over time and across countries (Interview OECD #21, 2003). Moreover, the OECD's work on education statistics also went through other significant changes in content due to the establishment of INES. Most importantly, the project today emphasizes 'outcome measures' rather than 'input measures'. Until the mid-1980s, the statistics mainly recorded what governments and individuals invested into the educational process in the form of private and public spending, staff expenditure, enrolment, number of staff and so on. With EAG and especially with PISA, the OECD today focuses instead on system effectiveness, recording elements such as subsequent labour force participation, education and work among the youth population.

In brief, it was not until the 1990s that the OECD became one of the most significant players in matters of education. Today, the statistics that the IO collects and generates, and the indicators for education it develops and analyses, all belong to the most recognized works in international education policy (Cussó and D'Amico 2005: 207). Although states – in this case the United States and France – intentionally approached the OECD and initiated the internationalization of education policy, they did not anticipate the institutional dynamics they set free within the international organization. Especially with PISA, it was the OECD itself which created a 'framework of assessment ... where we can look at education systems in the light of the efficiency of other education systems' (Interview OECD #9, 2003). By doing so, states are increasingly under pressure to conform to internationally accepted standards and adhere to shared values and adapted 'best practices'.

The EU as harmonizer of education institutions[12]

In the EU context, higher education was reserved to intergovernmental decision making only, as the Treaty of Rome did not provide any Community competencies in this field. However, linking this field to general economic issues – for which it had direct competencies – enabled the Community to gradually become involved in education. Involvement of the European Commission with education policy started with vocational training in order to enhance the free movement of labour in the common market. Although the European Court of Justice in the mid-1980s supported a Commission proposal to include higher education under its purview, any such aspirations were tamed by the governments of the member states in the 1992 Maastricht Treaty. This stressed the principle of subsidiarity also for education matters (Corbett 2003: 326), which in consequence left few options for the European Commission to interfere with national education systems. Articles 126 and 127 of the Maastricht Treaty clearly limited the Commission's legal competencies in education and training to mere support functions and stressed the value of responsibility at state level and of cultural diversity.

The initiative for a European Higher Education Area was instead developed outside of the EU framework. In 1998, education ministers from France, Germany, Italy and the UK agreed in the 'Sorbonne Declaration' on the harmonization of the European higher education system, aiming at 'remov[ing] barriers and ... develop[ing] a framework for teaching and learning, which would enhance mobility and an ever closer cooperation' (Sorbonne Declaration 1998). One year later, higher education ministers of 29 European states signed the 'Bologna Declaration', with the goal of creating a barrier-free and harmonized European space for education until 2010. The process triggered by the Bologna Declaration led to ministerial follow-up conferences every two years which further developed the policy goals and a common agenda, sharpened the conceptual guidelines and defined strategies and instruments for their practical implementation and evaluation. Over the years, the number of states that have formally acceded to the Bologna Declaration has risen steadily up to 46.

Although the process was initiated outside of the institutional framework of the EU, the European Commission has become increasingly involved in 'Bologna' since 2001, when it was accepted as a full member of the process. The European Commission even counts as the coordinating body behind the scene, providing impetus for its goals and administering its progress: under its auspices, the Bologna process has led to the progressive harmonization and structural convergence of national higher education systems, with the Anglo-American bachelor's and master's degree system as a common frame of reference, and with mechanisms of quality assurance, student mobility, and employability of graduates. Consequently, some of the participating countries, such as Germany and Italy, will have to completely restructure their current education systems, which presents the greatest reform process in decades (see also Balzer and Martens 2005).

Thus, with the introduction of the Bologna process, participating governments initiated their self-transformation towards *Europeanizing* their education systems. They were united by diverse domestically motivated interests in gaining leverage for reforms in their respective countries by going onto the European level. The French Government, for example, was keen on a common initiative, since it was seeking support from other states to reform its higher education system (Interview EU #3, 2003): in 1997, the Minister for National Education, Research and Technology Claude Allègre had commissioned a report on streamlining the diversity of degrees in France and making the system more transparent (Interview EU #5, 2004). The resulting Attali Report (1998) suggested a restructuring of the French system towards a 3-5-8-year programme of studies (bachelor's degree – master's degree – PhD) to bring it closer to that of other European countries. The French minister 'got the impression that the only way to make changes in the French system would be to blame it on Europe' and therefore wanted to link domestic reform to the European sphere (Interview EU #3, 2003). The German Federal Government encouraged an international initiative in order to gain leverage within Germany and put pressure on domestic opposition: because responsibility for higher education generally rests on the level of the *Länder* in Germany (*Kulturhoheit*), the Ministry of Education and Research needed to mobilize international pressure for reforms in higher education to overcome the unwillingness and incapability of the individual *Länder* to agree on any substantial reforms (Interview EU #1, 2003; Interview EU #5, 2004).

The European Commission was made a full member of the Bologna process only later, when basic policy goals already seemed to have been fixed and when its inclusion was deemed instrumental for promoting these goals. Moreover, the Commission covered promotion costs. Controlled inclusion of the Commission thus allowed the respective national governments to institutionalize and strengthen the external pressure on their domestic settings. It functioned like 'a tool to explain at home that you need to change and ... as a guarantee that change introduced at home will actually be coherent with other countries ... . It provided a strong political argument which has been used by all governments' (Interview EU #3, 2003).

However, during the course of developments, the Bologna process and other education activities of the EU became increasingly intertwined. For example, at the European Council meeting in Lisbon in 2000, education was given a high standing. It was seen as a means for making Europe the world's leading knowledge-based economy. The Bologna process, although not explicitly related to that Declaration, inspired 'some key people who drew up the Lisbon message' (Interview EU #3, 2003). Most importantly, education policy was now firmly integrated into the EU context (Interview EU #7, 2004). In addition, with the Open Method of Coordination (OMC), the EU gained a new tool for pursuing commonly agreed upon goals, even though to some this seemed like 'the creeping hostile takeover [of education policy] by the Commission' (Interview EU #1, 2003). Thus, even though the EU had first been deliberately excluded from the process, during its course, state responsibility – especially regulatory and to some extent operational responsibility – gradually diffused to the European level.

As a result, the EU now plays a much larger role in higher education than the ministers had envisioned when they first started the process. Their intention was to create an intergovernmental process without any substantial EU involvement. But they needed the European Commission during the further course in order to put into action their envisioned goals. Today its part in education policy clearly goes beyond that of an instrumental 'scapegoat' or mere financer. It is able to contribute 'the impetus, the ideas ... [of] what should be done, what the priorities are, discussing each and every article' (Interview EU #3, 2003). Thus states intentionally initiated the Europeanization of education policy and, by involving the EU, fostered increasing system harmonization. The EU now has more undisputed options and responsibilities in the field of education policy due to the Bologna process, although it was deliberately excluded from the process at the beginning (see also Balzer and Rusconi 2007).

Conclusion

Over the course of centuries, the modern state gradually achieved responsibility over outcome, regulation and operation in the field of education. It was a process of deliberate and enforced transformation of the polycentric medieval regime into modern statehood, driven by metropolitan elites of the rising bourgeois classes in the economy, in state administration and professions as initiators and managers of transformation. Further phases of state building turned the state from the absolutist military state of the 17th and the 18th centuries to the civil democratic intervention state of the 19th and the 20th centuries (Mann 1993). The corridor of sub-national paths became smaller, leading to *national isomorphism* of modern statehood and a convergence of educational curricula and institutions.

Since the 1990s, however, consecutive steps towards *global isomorphism* have been taken which in the long run may lead to further convergence of national paths in education. States increasingly approach international organizations for solutions for commonly shared domestic problems. States thus initiated a process of internationalization in the field of education. As a result, they *unintentionally diffused responsibility* over regulation – and some sort of operation as in the case of the EU – to the *intergovernmental level*. Today, the OECD influences national education policy as the shaper of standards in education, while the EU affects educational institutions by exerting pressures for harmonization. However, these processes are still too recent to ascertain their ultimate consequences. To what extent states really adapt to international pressures and to what extent their development remains path dependent are unanswered questions that need further research.

Notes

1   The historical part of this chapter was prepared by Ansgar Weymann during his stay as visiting Professor at Max Weber Kolleg Erfurt in 2005.
2   This article focuses on education as part of the normative good of welfare – leaving aside the fact that education serves as well as a social right of the constitutional state, as a fundamental of democratic self-determination and even as a means of providing security.
3   A privilege grants special rights, benefits or exemptions to a person or institution based on private law 'privilegium' of the emperor.
4   The latter may partially be a myth (see Chabbott and Ramirez 2000; Schofer *et al.* 2000: 848ff).
5   The Peace of Augsburg of 1555 extended the Emperor's privilege to Protestant universities.
6   Prussian-German common law (*Allgemeines Preußisches Landrecht*) stipulated that 'schools and universities are provided for by the state' (Herrmann 2005b: 547).
7   Vocational training is still a 'dual system'.
8   Enrolment statistics show 45 percent offspring from academic background, 15 percent from the aristocracy. The effects of recurrent demand and supply crisis on social change in the years 1780 to 2000 are analysed by Tietze (2004) as Kondratieff cycles.
9   Some of the empirical data underlying this part were generated through semi-standardized expert interviews with politicians, bureaucrats and consultants who participated in the development of education policy in the OECD and EU context. The OECD interviews were conducted by Kerstin Martens, and EU interviews by Carolin Balzer. The interviews were conducted between December 2003 and August 2004. To protect the anonymity of interviewees, a coding scheme is applied.
10 For an elaborated analysis of states' motives for involving the OECD and EU in education policy, see also Martens and Wolf (2006).
11 The report showed, for example, a steady decline in science achievement scores over the preceding decade; 23 million American adults and about 13 percent of all 17-year olds in the United States were considered functionally

illiterate, and among minorities the figure ran as high as 40 percent. Most alarming was that the average achievement of high school students on most standardized tests was lower than 26 years before when Sputnik was launched (see National Commission on Excellence in Education 1983).
12   This part draws on Martens & Wolf (2006).

References

Albrecht, Peter (2005) 'Fürsorge und Wohlfahrtswesen', in Notker Hammerstein and Ulrich Herrmann, eds, *Handbuch der deutschen Bildungsgeschichte, Band II: 18. Jahrhundert. Vom späten 17. Jahrhundert bis zur Neuordnung Deutschland um 1800*, München: C.H. Beck, 421–41.

Attali, Jacques (1998) 'Pour un modèle européen d'enseignement supérieur', available at (Online: <http://www.amue.fr/Telecharger/RapportAttali.pdf>, last accessed 29 May 2006.

Balzer, Carolin and Kerstin Martens (2005) 'International Higher Education and the Bologna Process: What Part does the European Commission Play?', *epsNet Kiosk Plus – THE NET Journal of Political Science* 3, 15–24.

Balzer, Carolin and Alessandra Rusconi (2007) 'From the European Commission to the Member States and back: A Comparison of the Bologna and the Copenhagen Process', in Kerstin Martens, Alessandra Rusconi and Kathrin Leuze, eds, *New Arenas of Education Governance: The Impact of International Organizations and Markets on Educational Policymaking*, Basingstoke: Palgrave Macmillan, 57–75.

Bascia, Nina, Alister Cumming, Amanda Datnow, Kenneth Leithwood and David Livingstone, eds (2005) *International Handbook of Educational Policy*, Dordrecht: Springer.

Berg, Christa and Ulrich Herrmann (1995) 'Industriegesellschaft und Kulturkrise. Ambivalenzen der Epoche des Zweiten Deutschen Kaiserreichs (1870–1918)', in Christa Berg, ed., *Handbuch der deutschen Bildungsgeschichte, Band IV: 1870–1918. Von der Reichsgründung bis zum Ende des Ersten Weltkriegs*, München: C.H. Beck, 3–56.

Berghahn, Volker (1994) *Imperial Germany, 1871–1941: Economy, Society, and Politics*, Oxford: Berghahn Books.

Borum, Finn (2004) 'Means-end-frames and the Politics and Myths of Organizational Fields', *Organization Studies* 25(6), 897–921.

Bruchhäuser, Hanns (2005) 'Berufsbildung', in Notker Hammerstein and Ulrich Herrmann, eds, *Handbuch der deutschen Bildungsgeschichte, Band II: 18. Jahrhundert. Vom späten 17. Jahrhundert bis zur Neuordnung Deutschland um 1800*, München: C.H. Beck, 401–19.

Buck, August (1996) 'Der italienische Humanismus', in Notker Hammerstein with the collaboration of August Buck, eds, *Handbuch der deutschen Bildungsgeschichte, Band I: 15. bis 17. Jahrhundert. Von der Renaissance und der Reformation bis zum Ende der Glaubenskämpfe*, München: C.H. Beck, 1–56.

Chabbott, Colette and Francisco O. Ramirez (2000) 'Development and Education', in Maureen T. Hallinan, ed., *Handbook of the Sociology of Education*, New York: Kluwer Academic Press, 163–87.

Collins, Randall (1995) 'Bashing the Germans', *Zeitschrift für Soziologie* 24(1), 3–21.

Collins, Randall (2000) 'Comparative and Historical Patterns of Education', in Maureen T. Hallinan, ed., *Handbook of the Sociology of Education*, New York: Kluwer Academic Press, 213–39.

Corbett, Anne (2003) 'Ideas, Institutions and Policy Entrepreneurs: Towards a New History of Higher Education in the European Community', *European Journal of Education* 38(3), 315–30.

Cussó, Roser and Sabrina D'Amico (2005) 'From Development Comparatism to Globalization Comparativism: Towards more Normative International Education Statistics', *Comparative Education* 41(2), 199–216.

Daun, Holger (2005) 'Globalisation and the Governance of National Education Systems', in Joseph Zajda, ed., *International Handbook on Globalisation, Education and Policy Research*, Dordrecht: Springer, 93–107.

DiMaggio, Paul and Walter W. Powell (1983) 'The Iron Cage Revisited: Institutional Isomorphism and Collective Rationality in Organizational Fields', *American Sociological Review* 48(2), 147–60.

Dorado, Silvia (2005) 'Institutional Entrepreneurship, Partaking and Convening', *Organization Studies* 26(3), 385–414.

Durkheim, Emile (1977) *The Evolution of Educational Thought: Lectures on the Formation and Development of Secondary Education in France*, London/Boston: Routledge & Kegan Paul.

Finnemore, Martha (1993) 'International Organizations as Teachers of Norms: The United Nations Educational, Scientific, and Cultural Organization and Science Policy', *International Organization* 47(4), 565–97.

Gellner, Ernest (1983) *Nations and Nationalism*, Oxford: Oxford University Press.

Green, Abigail (2001) *Fatherlands: State-Building and Nationhood in Nineteenth-Century Germany*, Cambridge: Cambridge University Press.

Hammerstein, Notker (1996) 'Die historische und bildungsgeschichtliche Physiognomie des konfessionellen Zeitalters', in Notker Hammerstein with the collaboration of August Buck, eds, *Handbuch der deutschen Bildungsgeschichte, Band I: 15. bis 17. Jahrhundert. Von der Renaissance und der Reformation bis zum Ende der Glaubenskämpfe*, München: C.H. Beck, 57–101.

Hammerstein, Notker (2003) *Bildung und Wissenschaft vom 15. bis zum 17. Jahrhundert*, München: R. Oldenbourg Verlag.

Hammerstein, Notker (2005) 'Universitäten', in Notker Hammerstein and Ulrich Herrmann, eds, *Handbuch der deutschen Bildungsgeschichte, Band II: 18. Jahrhundert. Vom späten 17. Jahrhundert bis zur Neuordnung Deutschland um 1800*, München: C.H. Beck, 369–400.

Hechter, Michael (2000) *Containing Nationalism*, Oxford: Oxford University Press.

Henry, Miriam, Bob Lingard, Fazal Rizvi and Sandra Taylor (2001) *The OECD, Globalisation and Education Policy*, Oxford: IAU Press/Pergamon Press.

Herrmann, Ulrich (2005a) 'Erziehung und Bildung. Pädagogisches Denken', in Notker Hammerstein and Ulrich Herrmann, eds, *Handbuch der deutschen Bildungsgeschichte, Band II: 18. Jahrhundert. Vom späten 17. Jahrhundert bis zur Neuordnung Deutschland um 1800*, München: C.H. Beck, 97–133.

Herrmann, Ulrich (2005b) 'Schlussbetrachtung. Das 18. Jahrhundert als Epoche der deutschen Bildungsgeschichte und der Übergang ins 19. Jahrhundert', in Notker Hammerstein and Ulrich Herrmann, eds, *Handbuch der deutschen Bildungsgeschichte, Band II: 18. Jahrhundert. Vom späten 17. Jahrhundert bis zur Neuordnung Deutschland um 1800*, München: C.H. Beck, 547–55.

Jeismann, Karl-Ernst (1987) 'Zur Bedeutung der "Bildung" im 19. Jahrhundert', in Karl-Ernst Jeismann and Peter Lundgreen, eds, *Handbuch der deutschen Bildungsgeschichte, Band III: 1800–1870. Von der Neuordnung Deutschlands bis zur Gründung des Deutschen Reiches*, München: C.H. Beck, 1–21.

Kocka, Jürgen (2001) 'Das lange 19. Jahrhundert. Arbeit, Nation und bürgerliche Gesellschaft', in Bruno Gebhardt, ed., *Handbuch der deutschen Geschichte*, Vol. 13, 10th edn, Stuttgart: Klett-Cotta.

König, René (2000) *Vom Wesen der deutschen Universität*, Opladen: Leske & Budrich.

Lenger, Friedrich (2003) 'Industrielle Revolution und Nationalstaatsgründung 1849–1870er Jahre', in Bruno Gebhardt, ed., *Handbuch der deutschen Geschichte*, Vol. 15, 10th edn, Stuttgart: Klett-Cotta.

Mann, Michael (1986) *The Sources of Social Power. Volume I: A History of Power from the Beginning to A.D. 1760*, Cambridge: Cambridge University Press.

Mann, Michael (1993) *The Sources of Social Power. Volume II: The Rise of Classes and Nation-States, 1760–1914*, Cambridge: Cambridge University Press.

Marshall, Thomas H. (1992) *Citizenship and Social Class*, London: Pluto Press.

Martens, Kerstin and Klaus Dieter Wolf (2006) 'Paradoxien der Neuen Staatsräson – Die Internationalisierung der Bildungspolitik in der EU und der OECD', *Zeitschrift für Internationale Beziehungen*, 13(2), 145–76.

Meyer, John W. and Brian Rowan (1977) 'Institutionalized Organizations: Formal Structure as Myth and Ceremony', *American Journal of Sociology* 83(2), 340–63.

Mundy, Karen (2005) 'Globalization and Educational Change: New Policy Worlds', in Nina Bascia, Alister Cumming, Amanda Datnow, Kenneth Leithwood and David Livingstone, eds, *International Handbook of Educational Policy*, Dordrecht: Springer, 3–17.

National Commission on Excellence in Education (1983) *A Nation at Risk: The Imperative for Educational Reform*, A Report to the Nation and the Secretary of Education, United States Department of Education.

Neugebauer, Wolfgang (2005) 'Niedere Schulen und Realschulen', in Notker Hammerstein and Ulrich Herrmann, eds, *Handbuch der deutschen Bildungsgeschichte, Band II: 18. Jahrhundert. Vom späten 17. Jahrhundert bis zur Neuordnung Deutschland um 1800*, München: C.H. Beck, 213–61.

OECD (2005) 'What PISA Assesses', available at <http://www.pisa.oecd.org/pages/0,2966,en _32252351_32235918_1_1_1_1_1,00.html>, last accessed 15 September 2006.

Papadopoulos, George (1994) *Education 1960–1990: The OECD Perspective*, Paris: OECD.

Rinne, Risto, Johanna Kallo and Sanna Hokka (2004) 'Too Eager to Comply? OECD Education Policies and the Finnish Response', *European Educational Research Journal* 3(2), 454–85.

Schofer, Evan, Francesco O. Ramirez and John W. Meyer (2000) 'The Effects of Science on National Economic Development, 1970 to 1990', *American Sociological Review* 6(65), 688–887.

Smith, Adam (1974) *The Wealth of Nations*, Harmondsworth: Penguin Books.

Smith, Anthony D. (1998) *Nationalism and Modernism: A Critical Survey of Recent Theories of Nations and Nationalism*, London: Routledge.

Sorbonne Declaration (Ministers in Charge of France, Germany, Italy and United Kingdom) (1998) *Joint Declaration on Harmonisation of the Architecture of the European Higher Education System*, Paris, 25 May.

Stollberg-Rilinger, Barbara (2005) 'Politische und soziale Physiognomie des aufge-klärten Zeitalters', in Notker Hammerstein and Ulrich Herrmann, eds, *Handbuch der deutschen Bildungsgeschichte, Band II: 18. Jahrhundert. Vom späten 17. Jahrhundert bis zur Neuordnung Deutschland um 1800*, München: C.H. Beck, 1–32.

Tietze, Hartmut (2004) 'Bildungskrisen und sozialer Wandel 1780–2000', *Geschichte und Gesellschaft* 30(2), 339–72.

Zajda, Joseph (2005) *International Handbook of Educational Policy*, Dordrecht: Springer.

9
The Role of the Nation State in the Internationalization of Accounting Regimes

Jochen Zimmermann

One of the nation state's main tasks is the provision of welfare. Its optimal level is often achieved through market transactions. In the case of market failures, however, private actors will attain lower than possible welfare levels. The state therefore intervenes in the organization of otherwise inefficient markets by redistributing resources or by improving allocation through regulatory efforts. Across all OECD states, capital markets are an object of regulatory intervention, which is a result of the widely accepted premise that capital markets suffer from information asymmetries, which potentially harm their smooth functioning. With an every-increasing importance of capital markets, their malfunction would severely depress the welfare levels in an economy, which makes it necessary to develop mechanisms to reduce information asymmetries. Timely and accurate information to market participants can achieve this. One of the key mechanisms to furnish markets with the necessary information is accounting.[1]

Accounting is the process of how (results of) business transactions are recorded, verified and disseminated to wider business and investment audiences, which use accounting information for their decision making. As financial reports are the 'end products' of the accounting process, the term 'financial reporting' is used interchangeably with the term 'accounting' in this context. Financial reports are a major source of information for equity financial markets (Scott 2003: 135–64), and because the financial markets are believed to be forerunners of globalization, the tensions between national regulatory efforts and pressures from global business should become most visible.

This chapter analyses the role of the nation state in establishing accounting rules for financial reporting in capital markets: this is the arena of standard setting for listed groups. Two national regimes of accounting standard setting are scrutinized in some detail: the more 'market-driven' system of the UK and the more 'state-driven' system in Germany. These regimes are 'archetypes' and can therefore be regarded as role models. For both, major developments since the early 1970s, the golden age of the nation state, are traced. While both systems start with different allocations of operational and regulatory responsibilities, they are subject to similar internationalization tendencies. In particular, the influence of the European Union reduces degrees of freedom in the design of accounting rules, and statehood is shifted to existing transnational and emerging transgovernmental bodies.

Organizing state responsibilities in accounting

This section discusses how different types of responsibility for accounting can be distributed in the nation state. This is the groundwork for taking a closer look at the empirical setups in a later section.

Levels of responsibility in welfare production: the case of accounting

There are three categories into which the nation state's responsibility for providing welfare in capital markets can be subdivided: operational responsibility, regulatory responsibility and outcome responsibility. Operational responsibility means that the nation state runs the institutions and agencies that are necessary to provide the normative good 'welfare'. Regulatory responsibility means that nation states set the relevant legislative standards for welfare provision. While the nation state might take on operational and regulatory responsibility to varying degrees, outcome responsibility marks whether the nation state is an addressee for producing the normative good in the first place. When outcome responsibility is ascribed to the nation state, market participants demand remedial action from the state if the provision of the normative good falters.

This general taxonomy of state responsibilities needs to be adapted to accounting. As part of the normative good 'welfare', this chapter explores more precisely the smooth functioning of the capital markets that is achieved by furnishing the markets with an appropriate level of timely and accurate information. The level of information is set by disclosure rules, which are the accounting standards used for financial reporting. There are different ways to set these standards.

When the state takes on both regulatory and operational responsibility, it develops all necessary disclosure rules and enforces them accordingly. This means that the nation state provides a framework and detailed standards that determine what kind of transactions have to be reported and in which fashion. For instance, the state not only decides that the net worth of a firm is to be disclosed, for example by prescribing the publication of balance sheets, but also develops detailed valuation (accounting) rules for each particular class of asset. Specifications are made by parliament, state agencies, courts and, to a smaller extent, by bodies under public law, for example bourses or chambers.

By contrast, when a state restricts itself to regulatory responsibility, it withdraws from providing detailed accounting rules. It either delegates these functions or accepts results from – possibly already existing – arrangements outside of the state. In this case, operational responsibility is exercised by communitarian (or societal) institutions such as private standard setters, unofficial de facto standard setters, or the academic literature. When the regulatory responsibility still rests with the nation state, it has to ensure that the developed standards provide the capital markets with sufficient information. This may be done in three different ways. The state may establish some type of 'framework legislation' with which the standards have to comply. It may also consider each standard on its individual merits and lend 'authoritative support'. Or the nation state relies on procedural features and supports an official or factual standard setter without scrutinizing accounting rules in detail. In the context of standard setting, all of these arrangements have been employed to various degrees and they will be therefore considered in more detail later.

The distribution of responsibilities in the golden age

National systems of accounting standard setting fall into two broad categories. The first category consists of primarily state-driven systems of standard setting in which the state takes on operational responsibility. Examples for these systems are mainly continental European: Germany, France and Italy are among them. The second category of setting national accounting standards can be thought of as market driven. In these systems, private bodies such as 'standards boards' or institutions of the accounting profession serve as standard setters. In this communitarian setting (for an early classification in accounting, see Puxty *et al.* 1987), one finds that the nation state takes on (at best) the regulatory responsibility. The United Kingdom and the (early) United States are its primary exponents.

These differences in accounting regimes may be reflections of varying organizational structures among Western economies. These varieties are discussed in several contexts, such as the organization of labour markets, social security, or business systems (Esping-Andersen 1990; Whitley 1999; Manow 2001; Yamazura and Streeck 2003; Crouch 2005). More closely related to accounting, Leuz and Wüstemann (2004) identify economies that predominantly use an arm's length financing of the equity style and those that rely on insider financing based on debt instruments.[2] This dichotomy overlaps with that developed by Hall and Soskice (2001), not only with respect to the constituting countries, for example the UK and Germany in their respective groups, but also in regard to the predicted dynamics under the process of economic globalization: both works stipulate a shift towards an arm's length financing style typical for liberal market economies with regard to large (internationally significant) companies. If this is the case, different accounting systems should therefore converge and display a reduced involvement of the nation state.

Standard setting and the shifting of responsibilities in accounting

The following sections describe the development of two model accounting regimes: the UK and Germany. In the golden age, both regimes differed substantially. In Germany, the state had assumed both operational and regulatory responsibilities; while the UK had reluctantly accepted regulatory responsibility. When the nation states were the addressees of the first wave of European accounting harmonization in the mid-1980s, both countries found a system-specific response. The second wave of accounting harmonization began in the early 2000s, when substantial decision-making authority was shifted from the nation states to the EU. Both developments are addressed on the following pages. The picture would be incomplete, however, without taking note of the intertwined history of the International Accounting Standards (IAS), which emerged in the early 1970s, well before the first wave of European harmonization. The IAS was an initiative of private actors, mainly accounting bodies, to create unified accounting standards worldwide. Its impact on the European process differed: while the first wave of harmonization ignored the initiative, the second wave largely relied on IAS standards.

Primarily market-driven systems: the UK example

In the United Kingdom, the state traditionally took a back seat in the development of accounting standards. While the concept of 'true and fair view' accounting, namely producing annual reports that provide an understandable picture of the firm, appeared in the Companies Act 1947, the disclosure requirements for firms were minimal and remained virtually untouched until the Fourth, Seventh and Eighth Council Directives had to be transposed into national law (Roberts *et al.* 2005). Before 1970, there were no mandatory requirements outside of the company law.

This left the market to operate freely, and as a result accounting practices varied considerably over time and over industries. Sometimes, the results were inconsistent within one annual report and the treatment was considered as inappropriate (Lee 1984). Private bodies such as the Institute of Chartered Accountants in England and Wales (ICAEW) made recommendations on accounting practice, but these were not binding: the response of the respective professional bodies to a wide array of accounting questions remained varied (Leach 1981).

To provide a more consistent approach to accounting matters, the ICAEW issued a 'Statement of Intent on Accounting Standards in the 1970s' (Nobes and Parker 1979). The Institute of Chartered Accountants of Scotland, the ICAEW's sister institution, and the Institute of Chartered Accountants in Ireland co-sponsored the initiative, which therefore had the three most influential professional accounting bodies in the UK and Ireland on board. A year later, the Chartered Institute of Management Accountants and the Chartered Association of Certified Accountants joined, and so did the Chartered Institute of Public Finance and Accountancy in 1976. This group of professional bodies became known as the Consultative Committee of Accounting Bodies (CCAB).

As a result of this joint action, the Accounting Standards Committee (ASC) was established in 1970. It was a committee of part-time volunteers. The task of the ASC was, *inter alia,* to keep under review the practices of financial accounting and reporting, to propose standards to the councils of the CCAB, and to consult with government, industry and commerce on financial reporting matters (Turley 1992). This means that there was no unified body to set accounting standards, rather there was convergence in the sense that the decision-making bodies of the CCAB members would accept the recommendations of the ASC. Thus, a converging accounting practice emerged.

The European Community did not exert any influence on accounting until the early 1980s. Even though the Treaty of Rome of 1957 had already established 'a formal reason for the harmonization of accounting systems across Europe' (Haller 2002), there was no impact on national accounting legislation. Major steps towards a Europeanized accounting law were taken only in 1978 and 1983, when two European Council Directives – henceforth the Fourth and Seventh Council Directive[3] – were passed. In the UK, the Fourth Council Directive was transformed into national law through the Companies Act 1981, and the Seventh Council Directive through the Companies Act 1989. With the transposition of the Fourth Council Directive into British law, the number of detailed legal prescriptions multiplied. The standard setters and the preparers of accounts found their freedom to act significantly constrained as European legislation specified in some detail which accounting treatments were applicable and how a financial report was to be structured. Contrasting the previous national practice with the new European approach, this constituted a major interference by the law and a substantial extension of the nation state's role.

The Companies Act 1989, transforming the Seventh Directive into national law, gave for the first time a legal recognition of accounting standards. In Section 256, it was defined that accounting standards mean 'statements of standard accounting practice issued by such ... bodies as may be prescribed by regulations'. This legal development met with several initiatives by the CCAB, and the transformation of the Seventh Council Directive proved a catalyst for a major overhaul in standard setting.

Three major reports had previously been considered by the CCAB, namely the Watts Report, the McKinnon Report, and the Dearing Report. While the McKinnon Report of 1983 successfully addressed some issues in the procedures of standard setting, the two others dealt with institutional reforms. The 1981 Watts Report, for example, suggested very early on some structural improvements; however, most of the issues raised remained unresolved until the Dearing Report in 1988, which somewhat coincided with the timing to transpose of the Seventh Directive into national law. Therefore, the Dearing Report provided the blueprint for some sweeping reforms in the arena of standard setting (Whittington 1989).

With the full implementation of EC accounting regulations, the accountancy profession opted for a major structural transformation but held on to the societal way of standard setting. The idea to incorporate standards into the body of law – having emerged when the Fourth Directive had strengthened the nation state's operational responsibility – was again shelved. The Dearing Report stated in paragraph 10.2 that '[making standards part of the law] inescapably requires a legalistic approach and a reduction in the ability of the financial community to respond quickly to new developments'. To tackle issues of legitimacy, the standard-setting process was to reach out into the wider policy arena. It was suggested to involve the whole community of interests and to use separate professional capabilities to translate policy into standards. For this purpose, the Financial Reporting Council (FRC) should be set up, the chairman of which was to be appointed jointly by the government (the Department of Trade and Industry) and the financial sector (the Bank of England). Moreover, the ASC was to be transformed from a part-time committee of volunteers into a permanent body, and to be renamed the Accounting Standards Board (ASB). With this change in standing, the ASB should be authorized to issue standards out of its own authority, no longer requiring approval from the decision-making bodies of the CCAB. All of these recommendations were subsequently implemented. The ASB, for example, became operative in 1990, as a subsidiary of the FRC, which was founded a year earlier. With the implementation of the Seventh Council Directive, the state therefore more clearly acknowledged its regulatory responsibilities, while leaving the operational responsibilities with private (communitarian) actors. However, with the assumption of regulatory responsibilities, the state tightened its grip on the new standard setter, the ASB.

In brief, during the golden age of the nation state, the UK had opted to develop accounting standards by a private body. Not only did the UK leave the operation of the standard setting to private bodies, but also it did not regulate or supervise the standard-setting process or its outcomes. European integration shifted the balance of regulatory responsibility towards the state. The nation state was required to enact certain stipulations as a kind of framework legislation – necessitated by the Fourth and Seventh Directive – that were previously observed only as current practice. This already led to an increased involvement of the state. The institutions responsible for the operative aspects of standard setting remained, however, national, and they remained private: in this respect, the UK saw no major institutional reforms.

Primarily state-driven systems: the German example

Traditionally, financial accounting in Germany was regulated by codified law with the first, simple rules dating back to 1794 (Born 2002). Respective legislation[4] was put forward by the ministries and had to be approved by the parliament. State rule setting had been a long-standing tradition that survived two world wars and several economic crises. The interpretation of the law falls in the competency of courts. Tax jurisdiction became particularly relevant; since the 1920s, financial reports are the starting point for determining taxable income. Thus, tax jurisdiction became de facto a highly relevant source of accounting rules unlike in the UK where financial reporting and taxation are decoupled. In Germany, its influence has been further increased by the comparatively low importance that accounting and financial reports have in an 'insider economy' system.

Although the state used to play a predominant role in standard setting, there has also been substantial involvement of private actors. The relevant legislation did by no means contain all-embracing provisions and determined instead that financial reports had to be rendered according to 'principles of proper bookkeeping'. Although these principles were slightly different from what in the UK and the United States context has become known as 'generally accepted principles', I henceforth refer to them as German 'Generally Accepted Accounting Principles' (GAAP). They consisted, and still consist, of inputs from different sources that are neither clearly defined nor published as an anthology. In a common understanding, GAAP comprise jurisprudence, regular commercial practice, academic input and professional opinions. In particular, the latter exerted a significant influence on financial reporting practice. Auditing standards issued by the Institute of Auditors (*Institut der Wirtschaftsprüfer:* IdW) interpreted relevant regulations and filled regulatory gaps. Although they were not law, they were binding auditors by a litigation mechanism and were therefore highly likely to be complied with (Marten *et al.* 2003).

This tradition of nation state standard setting was still in practice in the early 1980s. A first limit to the might of the nation state occurred with the beginning European harmonization (e.g., Flower 1997). Germany dealt with the Fourth and Seventh Council Directives differently than the UK and enacted both directives simultaneously in 1985.[5] This transposition caused a shift of many regulations partly from GAAP but mostly from specific company laws into the commercial code. The commercial code's paragraphs concerning financial reporting skyrocketed, but at the same time the provisions in the company law were reduced. The immediate legislation now applied to more firms. Qualitatively, however, the accounting system remained unchanged.

Unlike the UK, Germany witnessed no institutional reforms with the transposition of the directives. And although the Council Directives had to be implemented into each member state's law, the national parliament's power to set accounting law in its sole discretion was only seemingly curtailed. The most contentious issues in European accounting could still be decided by national parliaments as the directives contained much scope for choice. Thus, de facto, formulating accounting rules still remained the responsibility of state institutions, especially courts, and not of any private actors. In 1998, however, this setting changed in two respects in Germany.

First, with the Supervision and Transparency Act of 1998 (*Gesetz zur Kontrolle und Transparenz im Unternehmensbereich*, KonTraG), an amendment to the commercial code, the Federal Ministry of Justice was allowed to accredit a privately organized standard-setting institution. In the same year, a contract was signed with the newly founded private standard setter, the German Accounting Standards Committee (GASC). Its board (GASB), staffed with academics as well as users and preparers of financial reports, was authorized (1) to develop recommendations for group accounting; (2) to advise the Ministry of Justice in accounting legislation projects; and (3) to represent Germany in international standardization committees.

In the standardization contract, the Ministry of Justice committed itself to involve the board in all legislation projects concerned with accounting. The major task of the GASB was to independently develop accounting standards for consolidated financial statements. However, such standards do not represent official accounting rules until the Federal Ministry of Justice reviews and publishes them. The German GASB and the British ASB thus have a similar structure, but while the ASB can issue standards in its own authority, the GASB still depends on final approval from the national government.

Second, while the national government did not bestow any ultimate authority on the national standard setter, it admitted international outsiders into the accounting arena to a surprising extent. Also in 1998, the Capital Raising Facilitation Act (*KapitalaufnahmeErleichterungsgesetz*: KapAEG) was adopted. The KapAEG allowed listed (parent) companies to publish their consolidated financial statements following recognized international accounting standards, which means in practice International Accounting Standards or US GAAP. These provisions of the KapAEG were a trial solution and had a set expiry date of 2004. They were supposed to enhance German firms' abilities to access foreign capital markets, especially in the United States, as reconciliation statements – technical information provided to 'translate' a balance sheet or income statement prepared under German GAAP into, say, US GAAP – had proven costly for preparers and puzzling for users. As US GAAP statements of US firms were accepted in Germany even before, the German parliament saw its act as an abolishment of discrimination against domestic companies. Furthermore, the act was intended to strengthen the German capital market by introducing investor-oriented accounting reports. Retrospectively, the first intention turned out to be less important, because only a small number of firms used the new opportunity for listings in the United States. The second reason was more relevant: large listed groups had in earlier times repeatedly and with increasing emphasis expressed their concerns that German accounting rules were insufficient for satisfying investors' information needs (Thiele and Tschesche 1997; Schildbach 2002). In fact, many companies used the opportunity they had lobbied for (Born 2002) and applied IAS or US GAAP after the KapAEG was passed.

The decision not to require group accounts according to German GAAP any longer was accompanied by strong objections from jurisprudence: critics pointed first to a lack of legitimacy of the externally set rules and second to the impossibility of influencing further standard setting (Ebert 2002: 53–6; Kirchhof 2002; Schildbach 2004; Bratton 2007). Accounting literature castigated the declining comparability among German group accounts – some being rendered according to German laws and GAAP, others according to IAS or US GAAP (e.g., Börsig and Coenenberg 1998). As standards for group accounting totally eluded from the influence of German authorities,[6] private standard setting reached its climax during the period in which this legislation was valid. From 2005, this has become a matter of EU regulation, precluding a further extension of the KapAEG.

In sum, Germany had adopted the state model of standard setting in the golden age and the state had taken on operational as well as regulatory responsibility for standard setting, Germany abandoned its state tradition in 1998. For German GAAP, the nation state gave up operational responsibility by establishing a standards board for group accounting, but it held on tightly to its regulatory responsibility: each individual pronouncement of the GASB was scrutinized by the Ministry of Justice. The nation state controlled the process for German GAAP much more closely than did the UK. This response with regard to German GAAP contrasts sharply with the legislator's initiative regarding third-party standards: in the same year, Germany allowed – alternatively, to be decided by the preparer of financial statements – the most sweeping model of internationalization by giving up operational and regulatory responsibility for capital-market-oriented standard setting altogether. Any respectable third-party standards could be used. As a national legislator, Germany had no influence over them.

A parallel structure: international accounting standards

In 1973, accounting bodies from nine countries founded the International Accounting Standards Committee (IASC). Among the founding members, three had a more state-orientated tradition of standard setting (France, Germany and Japan), the others following a more market-driven approach (Australia, Canada, Ireland, Mexico, the Netherlands, the UK and the United States). The IASC had the goal of harmonizing worldwide accounting practices and eventually to establish a common set of standards (Flower 2004). These activities were driven by communitarian actors, primarily accounting bodies. Nation states and the EC did not get involved.

In the first phase of its existence, the harmonization efforts of the IASC were merely additive. The published standards were not intended to replace certain accounting methods that were deemed less useful or inappropriate. Rather, the newly established International Accounting

Standards were a mix of observed practice in the constituent countries. Therefore, nearly all published financial reports conformed to IAS. Unification work began in 1987, when the comparability project was started. The project, led by a steering committee, aimed at abolishing accounting choices and at achieving comparable financial reports, which was helped when the IASC developed a framework for setting accounting standards in 1989. This framework comprises a set of accepted theoretical principles, which, in turn, allow the evaluation of existing standards and the development of new standards. The conceptual framework defines which events should be accounted for and how they should be measured and communicated to the user. In June 1990, the 'Statement of Intent on Comparability of Financial Statements' signalled that the IASC would work towards a substantial reduction in accounting treatments, for instance by reducing the number of available valuation methods for assets. Additionally, certain methods would not be outlawed immediately but should be labelled 'preferred treatments', also referred to as 'benchmark method', or 'allowed alternative treatments' with a view to the latter's demise in the longer term.

The IAS had to compete against national standards, which were already in accordance with the binding legal environment, for example the Fourth and Seventh Council Directive in Europe. To gain acceptance, the IASC sought cooperation with the International Organization of Securities Commissions (IOSCO). The IAS aimed at a globalized financial market, and therefore the securities regulators, not the legislators for company law, seemed an appropriate entrance route. Finally, in 2000, the IOSCO recommended a core set of IAS to their national constituents as being acceptable for listings on a stock exchange. However, not all national regulators followed suit: for the particularly important US market, the national standards still prevail.

A certain amount of scepticism with regard to the IASC's professionalism, independence, and competence led to the rebuilding of the international standard-setting institutions. In 2001, the International Accounting Standards Committee Foundation (IASCF) was founded. It is incorporated in the US state of Delaware, was charged with establishing a set of high-quality standards in the public interest to assist users in capital markets in their decision making. The operative tasks were delegated to the International Accounting Standards Board (IASB), which consists of 14 members. Five members are chosen from the accounting profession, three are previous preparers, three are users, and one member comes from academia. The main qualifications for membership of the IASB are independence, professional competence and practical experience. Each full-time or part-time member of the IASB has to agree contractually to act in the public interest and to observe the IASB framework in deciding on setting up new and revising existing standards. To mark the new start, all future accounting standards promulgated by the IASB were to be known as International Financial Reporting Standards (IFRS) while the old IAS would remain in force.

A second wave of harmonization: the European approach

When the equity markets around the globe moved towards their peak in the beginning of the new millennium, US GAAP seemed to become the prevalent set of standards worldwide. However, US GAAP combine in a somewhat arcane way the market-driven and the state-driven approaches. They are, on the one hand, set by private institutions as are the UK standards; on the other hand, they seem to be heavily influenced by the state-driven legalistic prescriptions known, for example in Germany. Moreover, if global accounting standards were to be set by Americans, the European governments would have no influence over core reporting models for their businesses unless they wished to impose onerous burdens of dual reporting – as was witnessed in the German case.

European efforts in financial integration were stepped up after the EU's Lisbon Special Summit in 2000. In November 2000, the 'Initial Report of the Committee of Wise Men on the Regulation of European Securities Markets' (Lamfalussy Report) was published, and this highlighted the need for a better integration of the European financial markets. Building on these developments, the EU Commission put forward a regulation that all listed European companies had to use IAS for their consolidated accounts. In 2002, both the European Parliament and Council decided that

> '[f]or each financial year starting on or after 1 January 2005, companies governed by the law of a Member State shall prepare their consolidated accounts in conformity with the International Accounting Standards adopted ... if, at their balance sheet date, their securities are admitted to trading on a regulated market of any Member State'.[7]

Unlike the accounting directives, the IAS regulation had not to be transformed into national law as EU regulations directly apply to all constituents in the member states (Hix 2005).

When delegating authority to the IASB, Europe recognized the risk of being faced with policy outcomes that could differ from the favoured policy choice. To ensure at least some political oversight, the IAS Regulation

(Art. 2, 2) established a screening mechanism. Each individual standard has to be endorsed by the European Commission in accordance with specific committee procedure to become European law (Schaub 2005). This procedure consists of a two-tier mechanism: the IASB develops the rules, while the European Union possesses the ultimate decision-making authority in adopting them.

In this process, the Commission receives input from two bodies: the European Financial Reporting Advisory Group (EFRAG), and the Accounting Regulatory Committee (ARC). The EFRAG was founded in 2001 so that experts could be included in the EU endorsement mechanism from the very beginning (Scheffler 2004). It is a private-sector expert-level body that delivers input to the IASB and gives endorsement advice to the European Commission. The ARC is a regulatory committee that was set up according to the IAS Regulation. The Committee provides opinions on Commission proposals to endorse an international standard. The ARC consists of representatives from the member states' governments.

The current procedure of standard setting is as follows. When an International Financial Reporting Standard has been adopted by the International Accounting Standards Board, the European Commission will ask the EFRAG for its view on whether a particular standard should be endorsed. The latter then carries out a review process, mainly consulting sponsoring organizations and the European national standard setters. When a positive position of the EFRAG has been received, the Commission moves for the standard's adoption by preparing a proposal and submitting it to the ARC. Here, a qualified majority is required for endorsement. If the proposal is rejected, the Commission takes it to the Council. If the EU Council has no opinion on the standard in question, the Commission will endorse the standard. In case of rejection, the Commission can change or amend it. An adopted standard is published in the official languages of the Community and thus becomes European law, which also means that the European Court of Justice has jurisdiction over them.

In brief, with the initiatives on the European level, standard setting for the accounts of listed groups has moved from the nation state. By means of the IAS directive, standards that are set by the IASB apply. The IASB is a transnational body, but its pronouncements do not automatically extend into European law. Its standards must be endorsed in a comitology procedure. As the IASB sets out detailed standards, it carries the operational responsibility that is now internationalized. So is the regulatory responsibility. The Accounting Regulatory Committee decides if the operational regulation is of an appropriate level, and on this basis it takes its decision to endorse standards into European law. The ARC is composed of representatives from member states, which makes it a transgovernmental body. This setup is somewhat similar to the solution which Germany found for its domestic GAAP: it established a standards board, whose recommendations came under the individual scrutiny of the Ministry of Justice. The European approach is therefore more reliant on governmental arrangements than the UK approach, which allowed communitarian standard setting within the framework of the Fourth and Seventh Directives and without any further state involvement.

However, outcome responsibility still rests with the nation state. This is most clearly documented by the so-called 'accounting scandals' in the early 2000s. Here, several large corporations defrauded the capital markets by using dubious accounting procedures. The ensuing reaction was prompt – and it came from national legislators. Germany, for instance, enacted control provisions in the Financial Statement Monitoring Act in 2004 (*Bilanzkontrollgesetz*: BilKoG), and the UK remodelled the Financial Reporting Council into an 'independent regulator'. People were still calling upon the national legislator to take action. The EU tried to assume this responsibility when the European Commission developed new initiatives on corporate governance and enforcement, but its suggestions were widely neglected, and little progress has been made on the EU level since.

As the capital markets are also a pillar of the common market project of the European Union, the Commission proposed some initiatives in financial reporting and company law, but there has not been any significant progress neither on the European level nor on the level of national governments. This also shows (current) limits of internationalization, in particular when it comes to outcome responsibility: the nation state remains the foundation for the provision of welfare as a normative good even in the Europeanized context of capital markets.

The role of and the future scope for the state

Financial reporting for capital markets had long been a preserve for national policies. Market imperfections were mitigated by national interventions in accounting. The increased involvement of private and international actors implies a major change for the nation state, which is articulated both in process and outcome. From a process perspective, one needs to ask how autonomously the state acted in transforming its structures. Was it the initiator of change? Or did it involuntarily retract as a result of unintended change? From an outcome perspective, one needs to ask about the degree of the transition that has taken place. Have responsibilities shifted or are they merely shared?

A perspective on self-transformation

The nature and extent of the state's contribution to its own transformation largely depends on the prior institutional setting. In this context, the contrast between the state-driven and the market-driven systems is helpful because the state's role varies with the respective system as well as over time. In the first wave of Europeanization of accounting regimes, Germany enacted the European Directives without any institutional reforms and was at best a manager of (not much) change. In the UK, the nation state's role was slightly more pronounced as the transposition of the Seventh Directive was used to strengthen the regulatory responsibility of the nation state. However, as the initiatives to augment the responsibilities of the state were started in Europe rather than in the UK, the state acted as a manager, too. This assessment is also underlined by the immediate delegation of many powers to a newly created private standard setting body, the Accounting Standards Board.

The second wave of internationalization in the 1990s was mainly driven by a political agenda. Not only does the 'globalization' of financial markets stem from their (politically willed) liberalization, but also the decisions to embrace change came from the national governments themselves. Internationalizing accounting rules, in turn, is a response to the underlying internationalization processes in the financial markets. This does not mean that the nation state is a promoter of change throughout. Again, judgements depend on the role models under consideration. In the UK, the transfer of standard-setting responsibilities was seen with equanimity, because the Accounting Standards Board had already started to implement International Financial Reporting Standards as national standards in a convergence project. The transformation was largely left to the private sector with the nation state as a bystander. Even the role of change manager would suggest too active of a role.

In Germany, there is a mixed response that is hard to interpret. In 1998, the state shed its operational and regulatory responsibilities on an experimental basis. This was largely forced upon the nation state and already the title of the law enacting the change, 'Capital Raising Facilitation Act', has signalled that it is a result of lobbying activities by internationally active firms. This view would help explain why the preferred choice of institutional setup, the GASB (German Accounting Standards Board), emphasized more strongly the role of the state. But even this solution was not greeted with much enthusiasm. Overall, the reforms dragged Germany in line with other national regulatory systems. The following reallocation of standard setting to an international body was seen critically, but again it was unavoidable in the European context.

The German nation state was therefore an object of transformation to a much greater extent than being a transformer itself.

Another indicator for the role of the state in these changes is based on the following consideration: if the process is not fully driven by transnational developments, such as globalized markets, there must be scope for autonomous decision making in the nation state. This leeway is best assessed by looking at 'corridors' of institutional arrangements. The smaller the variance between institutional arrangements across nations, that is, the smaller the 'corridor', the more likely the nation state has lost scope for autonomous involvement in accounting matters. In accounting, the nation state indeed loses options for regulation. The interventionist scope narrows and the corridor between nation states closes. This is particularly true for the institutions of standard setting that concern themselves with listed groups and operate under the regulatory umbrella of the EU.

Statehood: shifted or diffused?

Concerning itself with accounting for listed groups, this chapter finds substantial changes in statehood. The operational responsibility of setting accounting standards has been transferred to a transnational body, the International Accounting Standards Board. The regulatory responsibility of setting standards now rests with the EU, in particular with the Accounting Regulatory Committee, which is a transgovernmental body. There is no place left for the nation state – apart from carrying the outcome responsibility which the EU tried to assume but failed to conquer. This constitutes a strong case for arguing that a shift in statehood has occurred.

However, the nation state still has to decide how to deal with accounting rules for company accounts and for non-listed groups in the framework of the Fourth and Seventh Council Directive. Here, the responses vary: in the UK, the national standard setter remains responsible for these firms, but it has been decided that the national rules will be duplicating the IFRS. This means that while there is still a notional responsibility within the nation state, the practical operational responsibility has been shifted.[8] In Germany, the nation state remains the standard setter for company accounts and non-listed firms. The reason for this is that the national legislator feels that the IFRS does not serve the interests of the stakeholders that need to be protected in company law: accounting responsibilities have diffused. However, there is an increasing debate on whether such an approach is tenable in the long term. If company law becomes more harmonized or structural differences between economies disappear further – which is increasingly the case – there seems very little scope for specific national solutions.

Conclusion

The analysis of two accounting regimes allows important insights into the remaining power of the nation state: from a widely diverging starting point, the integration of capital markets – in this case mainly driven by the European Common Market project – has forced the hands of a reluctant German Government towards system convergence. The UK system, which had seen a strengthened role of the nation state in the early phases of European integration, adapted more easily to the internationalization of accounting regimes. The analysis finds the role of the nation state in providing operating standards (operational and regulatory responsibility) diminished, but its responsibility for the effective organization of capital markets (outcome responsibility) widely intact.

Although the chapter focuses only on two 'role models', many observations can be extended to the OECD world as a whole. The German and the UK systems of standard setting were integrated into a European structure that balances transnational with transgovernmental institutions. Often, the analysis of standard setting is confined to the transnational body, the International Accounting Standards Board (IASB). The IASB develops the operative accounting solutions, and it now cooperates with the national standard setters of all OECD countries. But only the implementation of standards into applicable regulations reveals the overall role of the state. This is why the European solution is of special interest. It allows the provision of appropriate accounting standards for commerce and industry that also serve the public interest. The European solution re-balances business and public interests more transparently than, for instance, the US system, which relies on a precarious relationship between the national standard setter, the Financial Accounting Standards Board (FASB), and the Securities and Exchange Commission (SEC) as the regulator. In this arrangement, operational and regulatory responsibilities are intertwined, and the SEC may reassume the delegated operational responsibilities at any moment.

However, there is always tension between setting the rules and their actual application. This is why most national regimes of OECD countries have enforcement mechanisms in place. The most common enforcement mechanism is the statutory audit, which falls into national jurisdictions. Additionally, many states have now established an 'enforcement agency', which is twinned with the standard setter (UK), linked to the securities regulator (USA), or operates independently (Germany). The respective national legislatures decide on how these bodies work and which powers are conferred on them. This implies that the quest for global standards may ultimately be thwarted because standards are not uniformly enforced. A new round of regulatory convergence is therefore not entirely unlikely.

Notes

1 As this chapter concerns itself with the provision of information to capital markets, group accounting forms the focus of attention. Company accounts, which are not intended to supply capital markets with information but serve to solve conflicts such as the distribution of residual claims, are not considered.
2 A similar approach is taken by Vitols (2005), who distinguishes between 'market-based' and 'bank-based' financial systems.
3 Formally, these Directives refer to Art. 54.3(g) of the Treaty of Rome. The Fourth Directive of 25 July 1978 (78/660/EEC) relates to the annual accounts of certain types of companies; the Seventh Directive of 13 June 1983 (83/349/EEC) relates to consolidated accounts, and the Eighth Directive of 10 April 1984 (84/253/EEC) deals with persons responsible for carrying out the statutory audits of accounting documents.
4 Found in the Commercial Code (*Handelsgesetzbuch*) and the Stock Companies Act (*Aktiengesetz*).
5 In Germany, the Fourth, Seventh and Eighth Council Directives were transferred into national law with the *Bilanzrichtliniengesetz* of 1985.
6 However, there is also a German member on the International Accounting Standards Board (IASB), who authors the IFRS, and the GASB cooperates with the IASB as one of its liaison standard setters.
7 Cited from regulation (EC) No. 1606/2002 of the European Parliament and of the Council of 19 July 2002.
8 There will be exemptions for small- and medium-sized enterprises (SME), but these may again be superseded if the IASB decides on its own SME standard.

References

Born, Karl (2002) *Rechnungslegung International, Einzel- und Konzernabschlüsse nach IAS, US-GAAP, HGB und EG-Richtlinien*, Stuttgart: Schäffer-Poeschel.
Börsig, Clemens and Adolf G. Coenenberg (1998) *Controlling und Rechnungswesen im internationalen Wettbewerb*, Stuttgart: Schäffer-Poeschel.
Bratton, William W. (2007) 'Private Standards, Public Governance: A New Look at the Financial Accounting Standard Board', *Boston College Law Review* 48(1), 5–53.
Crouch, Colin (2005) *Capitalist Diversity and Change: Recombinant Governance and Institutional Entrepreneurs*, Oxford: Oxford University Press.
Ebert, Elke (2002) *Private Normsetzung für die Rechnungslegung: Möglichkeiten und Grenzen*, Sternfels: Verlag Wissenschaft und Praxis.
Esping-Andersen, Gøsta (1990) *The Three Worlds of Welfare Capitalism*, Cambridge: Polity Press.
Flower, John (1997) 'The Future Shape of Harmonization: The EU versus the IASC versus SEC', *The European Accounting Review* 6(2), 281–303.

Flower, John (2004) *European Financial Reporting: Adapting to a Changing World*, Basingstoke: Palgrave Macmillan.

Hall, Peter A. and David Soskice (2001) *Varieties of Capitalism*, Oxford: Oxford University Press.

Haller, Axel (2002) 'Financial Accounting Developments in the European Union: Past Events and Future Prospects', *European Accounting Review* 11(1), 153–92.

Hix, Simon (2005) *The Political System of the European Union*, Basingstoke: Palgrave Macmillan.

Kirchhof, Paul (2002) 'Gesetzgebung und private Regelsetzung als Geltungsgrund für Rechnungslegungspflichten?', *Zeitschrift für Unternehmens- und Gesellschaftsrecht* 29(1), 681–92.

Leach, Ronald (1981) 'The Birth of British Accounting Standards', in Ronald Leach and Edward Stamp, eds, *British Accounting Standards: The First 10 Years*, Cambridge: Woodhead-Faulkner, 3–11.

Lee, Geoffrey Alan (1984) 'Accounting in the United Kingdom', in H. Peter Holzer and Derek T.Bailey, eds, *International Accounting*, New York: Harper and Row, 235–71.

Leuz, Christian and Jens Wüstemann (2004) 'The Role of Accounting in the German Financial System', in Jan Pieter Krahnen and Reinhard H. Schmidt, eds, *The German Financial System*, Oxford: Oxford University Press, 450–77.

Manow, Philip (2001) *Comparing Welfare Capitalism: Social Policy and Political Economy in Europe, Japan and the USA*, London: Routledge.

Marten, Kai-Uwe, Reiner Quick and Klaus Ruhnke (2003) *Wirtschaftsprüfung: Grundlagen des betriebswirtschaftlichen Prüfungswesens nach nationalen und internationalen Normen*, Stuttgart: Schäffer-Poeschel Verlag.

Nobes, Christopher W. and Robert H. Parker (1979) 'The Development of Company Financial Reporting in Great Britain 1844–1977', in Thomas A. Lee and Robert H. Parker, eds, *The Evolution of Corporate Financial Reporting*, Walton-on-Thames: Nelson, 197–207.

Puxty, Anthony G., Hugh C. Willmott, David J. Cooper and Tony Lowe (1987) 'Modes of Regulation in Advanced Capitalism: Locating Accountancy in Four Countries', *Accounting, Organizations & Society* 12(3), 273–91.

Roberts, Clare B., Pauline Weetman and Paul Gordon (2005) *International Financial Reporting: A Comparative Approach*, Harlow: Prentice Hall.

Schaub, Alexander (2005) 'The Use of International Accounting Standards in the European Union', *Northwestern Journal of International Law and Business* 25(3), 609–29.

Scheffler, Eberhard (2004) 'Der europäische Endorsement-Prozess – Europäischer Einfluss auf die Fortentwicklung der International Financial Reporting Standards', in Thomas A. Lange, Wolfgang Arnold and Jürgen Krumnow, eds, *Rechnungslegung, Steuerung und Aufsicht von Banken: Kapitalmarktorientierung und Internationalisierung; Festschrift zum 60. Geburtstag von Jürgen Krumnow*, Wiesbaden: Gabler, 55–72.

Schildbach, Thomas (2002) *US-GAAP: Amerikanische Rechnungslegung und ihre Grundlagen*, München: Vahlen.

Schildbach, Thomas (2004) 'Rechnungslegung im Spannungsfeld zweier Kulturen der Regulierung: Gute Gründe für die Kombination privater mit obrigkeitlicher Regulierung', *Der Schweizer Treuhänder* 78(3), 159–72.

Scott, William R. (2003) *Financial Accounting Theory*, Toronto: Prentice Hall.

Thiele, Stefan and Frank Tschesche (1997) 'Zur Bilanzierungspraxis der DAX-Unternehmen im Geschäftsjahr 1996: Mehr "Einblick" durch internationale Rechnungslegungsnormen?', *Der Betrieb* 50(50), 2497–502.

Turley, Stuart (1992) 'Developments in the Structure of Financial Reporting Regulation in the United Kingdom', *European Accounting Review* 1(1), 105–24.

Vitols, Sigurt (2005) 'Changes in Germany's Bank-Based Financial System: Implications for Corporate Governance', *Corporate Governance: An International Review* 13(3), 386–96.

Whitley, Richard (1999) *Divergent Capitalism: The Social Structuring and Change of Business Systems*, Oxford: Oxford University Press.

Whittington, Geoffrey (1989) 'Accounting Standard Setting in the UK after 20 Years: A Critique of the Dearing and Solomons Reports', *Accounting and Business Research* 19(2), 195–205.

Yamazura, Kozo and Wolfgang Streeck (2003) *The End of Diversity? Prospects for German and Japanese Capitalism*, Ithaca: Cornell University Press.

10
The Transformation of the Golden-Age Nation State: Findings and Perspectives

Achim Hurrelmann, Stephan Leibfried, Kerstin Martens and Peter Mayer

It can hardly be denied that the state remains a political institution of utmost importance. Throughout the Western world, states collect taxes and deploy large parts of the national income, operate armies and fight wars, regulate markets and organize the legal infrastructure for economic exchange; they provide education and social services, hold democratic elections and constitute forums for citizen engagement. Nevertheless, in recent decades, both external and internal pressures have put state structures under strain. Economic, political and cultural globalization has undermined the boundaries between national spheres of authority; new public and private actors have appeared in domestic and international politics that challenge the autonomy of state institutions; new political problems such as global terrorism, climate change, and societal aging constitute risks to which most states have yet to find a response.

All of these developments have called into question the ability of the Western state – as a distinctive regime form – to adequately provide the normative goods that have traditionally been used to justify its existence: peace and physical security, liberty and legal certainty, democracy and self-determination, economic growth and social welfare. At the same time, the new challenges seem to have unleashed a trend towards an internationalization of state functions, meaning that responsibility for the provision of these four normative goods is increasingly transferred to – and shared with – institutions beyond the national level.

Against this background, we have asked in this volume: What has become of the Western state? In which respects is it being transformed? Are we witnessing the emergence of a new state, or post-state, constellation in global politics? The eight case studies assembled here, each primarily focusing on one of the four normative goods, explore and map out the extent to which the responsibility for providing these goods has been transferred from the state to international institutions. They each employ an analytical grid, laid out in the Introduction, which distinguishes:

(1) the level of responsibilities for the provision of normative goods that might be subject to change;
(2) the type of institutions at the international level that might gain responsibilities;
(3) the extent to which responsibilities are being demonopolized;
(4) the type of state involvement in setting these changes in motion; and
(5) the reaction of states once the implications of transformative processes have become observable, possibly leading to a convergence or divergence of various states (corridor effects).

This conclusion draws together the most important findings of the individual chapters, concentrating on the overall patterns that emerge. By doing so, we seek to assess whether the recent transformations of the state can best be described as an unravelling of state functions, implying that the former 'bundling' of responsibilities within a coherent and synergetic regime is coming apart, or whether a new equilibrium is on the horizon.

Levels of state responsibility – and their transfer

To describe the degree of operational involvement of the state – or any other institution – in the provision of a normative good, we distinguished three levels of political responsibility: *outcome* responsibility means that an institution is the ultimate guarantor for the provision of the normative good; *regulatory* responsibility means that an institution decides about the processes through which the good is provided; and *operational* responsibility means that an institution performs the tasks necessary for putting these decisions into practice.

All of the case studies in this volume confirm that in the 1960s and the 1970s, the Western nation state came close to exercising a monopoly over all of these responsibilities, and with respect to all four normative goods studied here. They thus corroborate findings presented in an earlier volume, originating from the same research context and using a similar analytical framework (Leibfried and Zürn 2005): In the 1960s and the 1970s, a period rightfully referred to as its 'golden age', the state was indeed a *territorial state* that controlled the essential resources for the protection of its citizens' physical security, a *constitutional state* that guaranteed legal certainty and the rule of law, a *democratic state* with institutions that provided for the citizens' self-determination, and an *interventionist state* that actively promoted social welfare. What is more, it did not have any serious competitors with respect to any of these functions. Whenever physical security, legal certainty, democratic self-determination, or social welfare were at issue, state institutions – and only state institutions – would step in, both by taking the necessary legislative decisions and by performing the crucial operative services.

The contributions to this volume reveal only few deviations from this general pattern: *Calliess et al.*[1] (Chapter 5) point out that legal certainty in international trade has always relied to a large extent on the private regulatory and enforcement mechanisms of *lex mercatoria*; and *Zimmermann* (Chapter 9) argues that even in the golden-age nation state, one variant of accounting regimes, namely the British model, placed regulatory and operational responsibilities in the hands of private organizations. In the overwhelming number of cases examined here, however, all three levels of responsibility were exercised by state institutions. For the territorial dimension, *Uhl* (Chapter 2) affirms that the state had almost exclusive responsibility for creating, collecting and administering taxes, while *Mayer and Weinlich* (Chapter 3) remind us that modern statehood unquestionably implied exclusive state control over military force. As concerns the rule of law and democracy, *Herberg* (Chapter 4), *Steffek* (Chapter 6) and *Bendrath et al.* (Chapter 7) show that during the golden age, the state was the principal – if not the sole – lawmaker and provider of institutions for collective self-determination. With respect to the intervention dimension, finally, *Martens and Weymann* (Chapter 8) explore how the state gradually gained and increasingly incorporated responsibilities for regulating social integration by means of education policy.

To be sure, even in the 1960s and the 1970s, states were not the only actors in international and domestic politics. But the international institutions that existed at the time rarely challenged state sovereignty, because their tasks remained confined to regulating the interfaces between states, hardly ever touching upon behind-the-border issues (Zürn 2004: 268–9). Similarly, private institutions, though closely involved in political decision making especially in corporatist states, did not threaten the ultimate capacity of state institutions to intervene directly and to make autonomous decisions about the provision of normative goods (Streeck and Schmitter 1985: 19–26).

As this volume clearly demonstrates, the state monopoly over the provision of physical security, legal certainty, democratic self-determination and social welfare is a thing of the past. To a considerable extent, state responsibilities have been transferred to the international level. However, the various levels of responsibility are affected by this transfer to different degrees. Most importantly, the studies in this volume find little evidence that the state has relinquished its *outcome responsibility*. There seems to be hardly any doubt in public discourse that the state is the institution to be blamed, and that is expected to take remedial action when a normative good is jeopardized.

That such expectations might, in principle, be subject to change is hinted at in the chapter by *Mayer and Weinlich*, who point out that the international community as a whole – and not any particular state – is increasingly charged with a responsibility to protect the physical security of citizens in less-developed states against human rights abuses. Yet for the time being, this partial transfer of outcome responsibility to the international level is clearly an exception.

An entirely different matter is whether the state still possesses the means for effectively exercising its outcome responsibility. A number of contributions to this volume, most explicitly the chapters by *Uhl* and *Steffek*, raise the question whether the transfer of *regulatory and operational responsibilities* away from the state has gone so far as to turn outcome responsibility into little more than rhetoric, since its social and legal bases have been undermined by international interdependencies. The relevance of this question, to which we shall return later in this chapter, is highlighted by the fact that all contributions to this volume find evidence for some kind of transfer of regulatory and operational responsibility to the international level. This means neither that the state becomes irrelevant in any of the policy fields considered, nor that international institutions gain anything like the autonomy that the state once possessed. Nevertheless, it is apparent that regulatory and operational responsibility no longer constitute state monopolies.

As for *regulatory responsibility*, the contributions map a number of far-reaching changes affecting all four normative goods: international institutions restrict the state's scope for generating core resources as well as employing these resources for enhancing physical security, as *Uhl* as well as *Mayer and Weinlich* report; non-state law making at the international level becomes a crucial mechanism to secure legal certainty in globalized economic exchange, as *Herberg* and *Calliess et al.* argue; the internationalization of political decisions is accompanied by the emergence of (proto-)democratic procedures in international organizations, as *Steffek* and *Bendrath et al.* outline; the growth of international policy regimes increasingly conditions state rules for welfare provision in the wider sense, as *Martens and Weymann* as well as *Zimmermann* observe, even though earlier studies have shown that the welfare state's 'core' (for example pension and health policy) is relatively unyielding (Obinger *et al.* 2005a; Rothgang *et al.* 2005).

Operational responsibility seems to be affected in broadly similar ways, but the studies in this volume suggest a somewhat greater resilience of the state in this respect. For instance, the chapters by *Uhl* and *Mayer and Weinlich* focusing on the territorial dimension of the modern state plus those by *Martens and Weymann*, as well as *Zimmermann*, dealing with the intervention dimension all argue that international bodies have gained a role in overseeing the execution of policies, but they also point out that front-line implementation generally remains with state agencies. Similarly, the chapters on the state's constitutional dimension by *Herberg* and *Calliess et al.* show that while informal legal rules governing economic exchange are often implemented by private actors such as law firms or industrial panels, state courts remain important as arbitrators of last resort. In the democratic dimension, finally, attempts to actually fill with life the democratic procedures that are provided for in international organizations have in part been so disappointing that there have been calls for a 'return to the state' which to some extent have already been heeded, as *Steffek* and *Bendrath et al.* observe.

The 'state-scape' that emerges is thus different from that outlined for cases of privatization at the domestic level, in fields such as the provision of welfare services (health care, pensions) or the maintenance of infrastructures (public transport, energy and so on). Here, the state often hangs on to its regulatory responsibility, while operational responsibility is transferred to private actors (Obinger *et al.* 2005a; Rothgang *et al.* 2005; Zohlnhöfer and Obinger 2005; Starke 2007). By contrast, internationalization processes, which are in focus here, are characterized by a different logic: State agencies often remain indispensable for the exercise of operational responsibility, especially when it comes to front-line implementation, whereas regulatory responsibility is more easily internationalized.

International institutions gaining responsibilities

Does this pattern have anything to do with the characteristics of the institutions at the international level that profit from internationalization processes? Put differently, which institutions acquire the responsibilities that the state once monopolized? As we outlined in the Introduction, such institutions can be *intergovernmental* (members being states), *transgovernmental* (members being state bureaucracies), *supranational* (members being international public servants), or *transnational* (members being private actors).

All four types of institutions are in fact mentioned in this volume as beneficiaries of transformation processes. In the state's territorial dimension, *intergovernmental* institutions such as the UN Security Council and the EU Council of Ministers and, closely interconnected with them, *supranational* institutions such as the UN Secretariat and the European Commission tend to be the main beneficiaries, as the chapters by *Uhl* and *Mayer and Weinlich* reveal. In the constitutional and democratic dimensions, by contrast, the case studies by *Herberg* and *Calliess et al.* demonstrate the influence of *transnational* institutions such as business corporations or law firms involved in making and applying (para-)legal rules for global economic exchange, or, as the case studies by *Steffek* and *Bendrath et al.* show, of civil society organizations and private corporations expected to bolster the democratic legitimacy of international organizations and regulatory regimes. However, *Herberg* and *Bendrath et al.* also mention *transgovernmental* institutions, such as networks of environmental protection agencies in the context of Agenda 2000 or the regularized cooperation between national tax authorities within the OECD. The state's intervention dimension, finally, displays the greatest variety of international institutions that profit from transfers of responsibility. Here, as the chapters by *Martens and Weymann* and *Zimmermann* reveal,[2] *intergovernmental* (EU Council of Ministers, OECD), *supranational* (EU Commission), *transgovernmental* and *transnational* institutions (cooperation between accounting specialists from public and private institutions) now exercise political responsibilities once 'bundled' at the state level.

If we analyse which types of international institutions tend to gain which kinds of responsibility, no clear pattern emerges. There is, for example, no indication that regulatory responsibilities are particularly likely to be transferred to institutions in which national governments retain some control (inter- or transgovernmental bodies), or that a transfer of operational responsibilities always implies an increased involvement of private actors (transnational bodies). Rather, it seems that all kinds of responsibilities can, in principle, be moved to all kinds of institutions. Against this background, the greater difficulty of transferring operational responsibilities away from the state is unlikely to be an artefact of the specific set of institutions that profit from such transfers, but rather seems to point to a general weakness of all institutions at the international level. With few exceptions, they simply do not possess the same operational resources for the front-line implementation of political decisions that national institutions – bureaucracies, armies, courts, parliaments, schools – have. It is these resources that in many respects make the nation state, still today, indispensable for the provision of the four normative goods examined here.

Extent of demonopolization

This indispensability of state institutions can also be observed if we examine the extent to which regulatory and operational responsibilities are transferred away from the state. Our conceptual framework in this respect, as outlined in the Introduction, is based on the distinction between a shift of responsibilities, which implies that the transfer of responsibilities detracts the same amount of power from the state that international institutions gain (zero-sum logic), and a diffusion of responsibility, which means that practices of providing for the normative goods of modern statehood emerge beyond the nation state without diminishing state responsibilities (variable-sum logic). We further distinguish between partial and complete shifts with respect to the relevant level of responsibility; and between forms of shift and/or diffusion that are *disconnected* from or *interlocked* with states.

The contributions to this volume find more instances of diffusion than of an outright shift of state responsibility. Only the case studies on taxation in the EU by *Uhl*, administration of the Domain Name System (DNS) for the Internet by *Bendrath et al.*, and accounting regulation by *Zimmermann* unearth *partial or complete shifts* of responsibilities. In these cases, nation states relinquish regulatory and – to a lesser extent – operational responsibilities that they once held, which are reallocated either to supranational and intergovernmental institutions (EU Commission and Council) or to transnational and transgovernmental actors (ICANN in Internet governance, IASB and ARC in accounting regulation).

In all other examples covered in this volume, states do not lose regulatory and operational competencies, but only the *monopoly* over their exercise. This means that they now have to factor in additional sources of decision making on the provision of normative goods, and, to a lesser extent, also additional institutions involved in their operational provision. In most of these instances of diffusion, however, states remain *interlocked* with these new loci of responsibility, either because they retain an important voice in them, as in the case of intergovernmental and transgovernmental institutions, as shown by *Mayer and Weinlich* and *Martens and Weymann*; or because they have actively sought, with considerable success, to re-incorporate forms of transnational rule making and rule adjudication into the existing state structures, as brought to light by

Herberg and *Calliess et al*. In this respect, our study confirms the recent findings by Levy (2006), whose volume – although focusing on comparative political economy rather than the domestic/international interface – also shows that state activism has shifted, not simply eroded.

Nevertheless, the case studies in this book also stress that there remain substantial forms of international activity that cannot be fully controlled by the state. In addition to the examples discussed above that demonstrate a shift of responsibilities, this is the case if processes of diffusion have empowered supranational institutions, or intergovernmental institutions, in which forms of majoritarian decision making are used (as in the EU Council of Ministers if qualified majority voting rules apply), or transnational institutions whose activities the state has not successfully managed to re-incorporate. Thus, although our results by no means point to a demise of the state, it would be wrong to deny the significance of the changes that have taken place. Again, we can corroborate results reported in the earlier volume by Leibfried and Zürn (2005): States in the Western world have not ceased to be active at all levels of the provision of physical security, legal certainty, democratic self-determination and social welfare, but they have increasingly lost their autonomy in guaranteeing for these goods' provision.

State involvement in the process of transformation

What role have state institutions themselves played in bringing about these changes? To tackle this question, we differentiated between three types of state involvement: (1) the state acts as a direct or immediate *initiator* of its own transformation if it actively brings about a transfer of responsibilities to enhance governing capacities; (2) it acts as an indirect *promoter* of transformation if state activities are at the root of changes to a state's material and social environment that later come back to haunt it; and (3) it acts as a *manager* of transformation if state institutions deliberately channel and mold external pressures. In all of these instances, the state is in one way or another involved in a process of *self-transformation*. Only if none of the above applies is it literally overpowered by external developments, or remains completely passive towards them.

Most of the chapters in this volume indeed reveal evidence for one or more forms of state involvement. However, there are differences between policy areas, and between the various normative goods affected. Both chapters on the state's territorial dimension, *Uhl* dealing with taxation as well as *Mayer and Weinlich* studying control over military power, stress that steps towards internationalization have been consciously initiated by states themselves. This is consistent with the expectation that states would keep careful control over their key resources and vital means to secure physical security, and allow internationalization only if it was perceived as being in their manifest interest.

The state's constitutional and democratic dimensions show quite a different trajectory. Here, the relevant chapters suggest that states were at best promoters of internationalization by encouraging the global processes of economic exchange and political decision making that came to challenge the sufficiency of their own mechanisms for securing legal certainty and democratic self-determination. In other words, as *Herberg, Calliess et al., Steffek* and *Bendrath et al.* show, states supported processes of economic and political globalization, often in the hope that this might allow a more effective protection of normative goods like physical security or social welfare, but they remained inactive when it came to the implications of such processes for the rule of law and democracy. The state's self-transformation in this respect, hence, was largely unintentional, although in some cases states later did attempt to regain control as managers of change. In the intervention dimension, finally, the impression is a mixed one. The case study on educational governance by *Martens and Weymann* stresses the role of the state as initiator of internationalization processes, while the chapter on accounting regimes by *Zimmermann* describes the state's role as oscillating between that of promoter, manager and 'bystander' of change.[3]

While one should certainly be cautious in drawing generalizations from the cases discussed in this volume, our results suggest that the state's self-transformation has been marked by a higher degree of intentionality when policy-making competencies crucial to citizens' physical security and social welfare were at issue, while problems of legal certainty and democratic self-determination only caught the state's attention as unintended consequences of other, more policy-related decisions. This indicates that the implications of internationalization for the provision of these two normative goods might be particularly troublesome. Another result that needs to be stressed is that all of the case studies find that the state played some role in its own transformation, and none would justify describing it as an utterly powerless object exposed to pressures entirely beyond its control.

Responses to transformative processes, and corridor effects

Just as state institutions play a role in their own transformation, they also have the power to react to unwanted aspects of change. They may, for example, try to regain control over the provision of normative goods at the *international level* by deliberately influencing international institutions. Or they may choose to reform institutions or policies at the *national level* in order to better accommodate internationalization. Such state reactions ultimately determine whether transfers of responsibility lead to a convergence or divergence of various states, that is, a broader or narrower *corridor* between them.

Unsurprisingly, the chapters assembled in this volume find deliberate state reactions to internationalization processes especially in cases where states have not themselves been initiators of such processes, but rather played a less active role. In the constitutional dimension, for example, both *Herberg* and *Calliess et al.* examine attempts by various states to reaffirm their role as providers of legal certainty by consciously adapting national institutions for conflict resolution to the needs of globalized markets. In the democratic dimension, legitimacy deficits of international institutions primarily seem to have encouraged calls for a greater role of the state in international governance, and the case study on data protection by *Bendrath et al.* shows that these calls have contributed to more vigorous state intervention into private self-regulation. In addition, *Steffek* demonstrates how international institutions increasingly try to devise their own strategies for overcoming democratic deficiencies without necessarily relying on the state, for instance by upgrading their relations with civil society organizations.

With respect to *corridor effects*, those chapters that address this issue tend to find a narrowing of the corridor, that is, a convergence of various states, a tendency already observed earlier in case studies on the welfare state (Obinger *et al.* 2005a; Rothgang *et al.* 2005; Obinger and Starke 2007). Examples include the growing similarity of European tax regimes in the face of increasing EU constraints, studied by *Uhl*, the 'isomorphism' of national educational systems in reaction to EU and OECD rules, researched by *Martens and Weymann*, as well as the convergence of accounting standards encouraged by EU level regulation examined by *Zimmermann*. These findings indicate that even where nation states have retained their regulatory and/or operational responsibility in full or in part, internationalization processes generally imply a loss of national autonomy, resulting in a 'blurring' of once idiosyncratic national regimes.

Implications: a new synergetic constellation?

Where have these transformations left the state in its post-golden age? One notable result of the analysis in this volume is that the basic characteristics of the Western state have not changed. It can still be characterized as territorial, constitutional, democratic and interventionist; it continues to be committed to the normative goods of physical security, legal certainty, democratic self-determination and social welfare; it is still actively involved in the provision of each of these goods. What *has* changed, however, is that the state no longer exercises a *monopoly* over the provision of the four normative goods. While it still tends to be perceived as the *ultimate guarantor* of these goods (outcome responsibility), important areas of decision making about their provision (regulatory responsibility) and to a lesser extent also operational services for putting these decisions into practice (operational responsibility), have *diffused* (or even shifted) to the international level.

Has this diffusion of responsibility endangered the provision of the normative goods, and turned the state's outcome responsibility for their protection into a mere chimera? The analyses in this volume call for a differentiated response to this question. At least in the territorial and intervention dimensions, internationalization processes have mainly been initiated by states themselves, have most often implied a transfer of powers to institutions in which states continue to have a say (intergovernmental and sometimes transgovernmental institutions), and have not fundamentally challenged their operational responsibility with respect to front-line implementation. Undeniably, as *Uhl's* chapter makes clear, states now often operate under severe constraints. But one can nevertheless argue that in the territorial and intervention dimensions, they retain a large array of instruments to make good on their outcome responsibility, and to protect their citizens' physical security and social welfare.

With respect to the constitutional and especially the democratic dimensions, by contrast, there is more reason for concern. For one thing, the internationalization of responsibilities for ensuring legal certainty and democratic self-determination appears to have been promoted by the state rather unintentionally, as a side-effect of efforts to enhance economic and political internationalization. Moreover, institutions that gained responsibility for providing these normative goods have often been ones in which states do not play a role, like transnational business corporations or civil society organizations. And finally, it seems to be much more difficult, in these dimensions, to reconcile increasingly internationalized rule making (regulatory responsibility) with the apparent indispensability of state institutions for rule application (operational responsibility).

This problem is even more acute in the democratic than in the constitutional dimension. While states have had some success in exploiting the implementation deficits of transnational legal rules to re-enhance the importance of national courts, the problems of putting international rules for democratic self-determination into practice seem to be much more difficult to alleviate. As a result, there is indeed the danger that the citizens' legal certainty and particularly democratic self-determination will suffer as a result of internationalization processes, and that states will prove unable to live up to their outcome responsibility for the provision of these goods.

Our study hence highlights the increasing internationalization of functions that used to be monopolized by the state in its golden age: especially regulatory and operational responsibilities for the provision of physical security, legal certainty, democratic self-determination and social welfare have increasingly been diffused to institutions beyond the national level, and are now exercised jointly by the state and different international institutions. However, the overall outcome of this internationalization is anything but a *coherent* equilibrium or a *new synergetic* constellation. Rather, we are faced with a pattern of inconsistencies and incongruities. The amount of control that state institutions still exercise over the provision of normative goods varies from one good to the next, and some goods are clearly better protected than others. What is more, the uneven speed and character of internationalization processes with respect to responsibilities for the four normative goods implies an increased risk that activities beneficial to one normative good (e.g., social welfare) might undermine the protection of another (e.g., democracy).

Despite all of these changes, the state itself and its apparatus remain fundamentally intact; it is the array of functions and guarantees it could once provide to its citizens that is becoming unravelled. In the long run, however, this development nevertheless constitutes a threat not only to the state itself but also to international institutions: Unless such institutions become more effective in the operational provision of normative goods, particularly with respect to legal certainty and democratic self-determination, the legitimacy of the international system as a whole might come to be seriously challenged.

Notes

1 Chapters are cited by authors' names, in italics.
2 The 'varieties of internationalism' displayed here may *not* hold evenly across the whole intervention state. Monotony increases as we approach core welfare state institutions like social security. Here, *if* such change happens, former state responsibilities tend not to be shifted but diffused – with the state setting the parameters and exercising tight oversight – combined with a clear institutional preference for intergovernmental and some supranational (EU) modes of

action (Obinger and Starke 2007; on the EU-bent see Obinger *et al.* 2005b: 553–67; on 'intergovernnmental' learning processes about retrenchment see Starke 2007: Part III), with a series of 'national models' serving as moving targets since the 1970s.

3   Again, a look at the welfare state's core reveals a somewhat different picture; here the state, *if* it allows room for such processes at all, mainly plays a *managerial* role in the internationalization of its own transformation (Obinger *et al.* 2005b: 553–68; Rothgang *et al.* 2005, 2008). The nation state is certainly not a bystander, and rarely a promoter, though the judgement on the latter is complicated by different assessments of the 'stateness' of the EU itself, with Commission and ECJ certainly acting as promoters in their spheres.

References

Leibfried, Stephan and Michael Zürn, eds (2005) *Transformations of the State?*, Cambridge: Cambridge University Press.

Levy, Jonah D., ed. (2006) *The State after Statism: New State Activities in the Age of Liberalization*, Cambridge, MA: Harvard University Press.

Obinger, Herbert and Peter Starke (2007) 'Are Welfare States Converging?', in Irene Dingeldey and Heinz Rothgang, eds, *Governance of Welfare State Reform: A Cross National and Cross Sectoral Comparison of Policy and Politics*, Cheltenham: Edward Elgar (forthcoming).

Obinger, Herbert, Stephan Leibfried, Claudia Bogedan, Edith Gindulis, Julia Moser and Peter Starke (2005a) 'Welfare State Transformation in Small Open Economies', in Stephan Leibfried and Michael Zürn, eds, *Transformations of the State?*, Cambridge: Cambridge University Press, 161–85.

Obinger, Herbert, Stephan Leibfried and Francis G. Castles (2005b) 'Bypasses to a Social Europe: Lessons from Federal Experience', *Journal of European Public Policy* 12(3), 545–71.

Rothgang, Heinz, Mirella Cacace, Simone Grimmeisen and Claus Wendt (2005) 'The Changing Role of the State in Healthcare Systems', in Stephan Leibfried and Michael Zürn, eds, *Transformations of the State?*, Cambridge: Cambridge University Press, 187–212.

Rothgang, Heinz, Mirella Cacace, Simone Grimmeisen, Uwe Helmert and Claus Wendt (2008) *The Changing Role ot the OECD Health Care Systems: From Heterogeneity to Homogeneity*, Basingstoke: Palgrave Macmillan (forthcoming).

Starke, Peter (2007) *Radical Welfare State Retrenchment in Comparative Perspective*, Basingstoke: Palgrave Macmillan (forthcoming).

Streeck, Wolfgang and Philippe C. Schmitter (1985) 'Community, Market, State – and Associations? The Prospective Contribution of Interest Governance to Social Order', in Wolfgang Streeck and Philippe C. Schmitter, eds, *Private Interest Government: Beyond Market and State*, London: Sage, 1–29.

Zohlnhöfer, Reimut and Herbert Obinger (2005) 'Selling Off the "Family Silver": The Politics of Privatization', *World Political Science Review* 2(1), 30–52.

Zürn, Michael (2004) 'Global Governance and Legitimacy Problems', *Government and Opposition* 39(2), 260–87.

Index